S0-BYZ-244

CLIENT/
SERVER
COMPUTING

2ND EDITION

PROFESSIONAL REFERENCE SERIES

CLIENT/ SERVER COMPUTING

2ND EDITION

Patrick N. Smith
with Steven L. Guengerich

SAMS PUBLISHING   A Division of Prentice Hall Computer Publishing
201 West 103rd Street, Indianapolis, Indiana 46290

Copyright © 1994 by Sams Publishing

SECOND EDITION

All rights reserved. No part of this book shall be reproduced, stored in a retrieval system, or transmitted by any means, electronic, mechanical, photocopying, recording, or otherwise, without written permission from the publisher. No patent liability is assumed with respect to the use of the information contained herein. Although every precaution has been taken in the preparation of this book, the publisher and author assume no responsibility for errors or omissions. Neither is any liability assumed for damages resulting from the use of the information contained herein. For information, address Sams Publishing, a division of Prentice Hall Computer Publishing, 201 W. 103rd St., Indianapolis, IN 46290.

International Standard Book Number: 0-672-30473-2

Library of Congress Catalog Card Number: 93-87176

97 96 95 94   4 3 2 1

Interpretation of the printing code: the rightmost double-digit number is the year of the book's printing; the rightmost single-digit, the number of the book's printing. For example, a printing code of 94-1 shows that the first printing of the book occurred in 1994.

Composed in Palatino and MCPdigital by Prentice Hall Computer Publishing

Printed in the United States of America

Trademarks

All terms mentioned in this book that are known to be trademarks or service marks have been appropriately capitalized. Sams Publishing cannot attest to the accuracy of this information. Use of a term in this book should not be regarded as affecting the validity of any trademark or service mark.

Publisher
Richard K. Swadley

Associate Publisher
Jordan Gold

Acquisitions Manager
Stacy Hiquet

Managing Editor
Cindy Morrow

Acquisitions Editor
Chris Denny

Development Editor
Dean Miller

Production Editor
Mary Inderstrodt

Editorial and Graphics Coordinator
Bill Whitmer

Editorial Assistants
Sharon Cox
Lynette Quinn

Technical Reviewer
BSG

Marketing Manager
Greg Wiegand

Cover Designer
Tim Amrhein

Book Designer
Michele Laseau

Director of Production and Manufacturing
Jeff Valler

Imprint Manager
Juli Cook

Manufacturing Coordinator
Barry Pruett

Production Analyst
Mary Beth Wakefield

Proofreading Coordinator
Joelynn Gifford

Indexing Coordinator
Johnna VanHoose

Graphics Image Specialists
Dennis Sheehan
Sue VandeWalle

Production
Nick Anderson
Ayrika Bryant
Stephanie Davis
Rich Evers
Dennis Clay Hager
Stephanie J. McComb
Jamie Milazzo
Ryan Rader
Kim Scott
Michelle M. Self
Tonya R. Simpson
Ann Sippel
S A Springer
Marcella Thompson
Suzanne Tully
Alyssa Yesh
Dennis Wesner

Indexer
Jennifer Eberhardt

Overview

Overview

Contents
Contents

**4   Components of Client/Server Applications—
The Server   77**

**5   Components of Client/Server Applications—
Connectivity   121**

About the Series Editor
Steven Guengerich

Steven L. Guengerich is the President of BSG Education, a unit of client/server systems integration specialists, BSG Corporation. He has more than 12 years experience in the strategic planning for emerging information technologies and migration to client/server, network computing systems. He is the author/coauthor for several books, including *Downsizing Information Systems* (Sams, 1992), and was the cofounder of BSG's *NetWare Advisor*.

About the Author
Patrick Smith

Patrick N. Smith is Senior Vice President and Chief Technology Officer of SHL Systemhouse, Inc., and also serves as its senior technologist. He is widely recognized for his ability to communicate complex technological issues in a manner that leads management to understand the potential and opportunity to use technology to improve business effectiveness. During the 25 years he has been involved in the computer industry, Smith also has worked as manager of technical support and as a lecturer in computer science at a major university.

Foreword

A fundamental shift has occurred in the way businesses go about using information systems for their competitive advantage. New techniques, such as business process reengineering, are leading to systems reengineering. And as businesses decentralize and downsize, information systems follow suit. In the years ahead, we believe analysts will look back at this as a time when computing really was invented.

Along with the tremendous potential, however, comes tremendous confusion and chaos in the marketplace. Open systems, object orientation, graphical user interfaces, UNIX, OS/2, CASE, database, and superservers—these are terms that can impact information systems choices in various ways. But in today's rapidly changing business and computing environments, how do you decide which solution is best for your needs? And how do you go about implementing that solution?

This book was written to provide answers to these and similar questions. As one would expect, the information in *Client/Server Computing* comes from years of experience and first-hand implementation of new technologies. Both Patrick Smith, Chief Technology Officer of SHL Systemhouse, Inc. and Steve Guengerich, President of BSG Corporation, are hands-on integrators and established technical authors and series editors. Their knowledge and the knowledge from the professionals in their respective systems integration companies, as well as many other colleagues in the client/server computing industry, is distilled into the pages of *Client/Server Computing*.

We hope you gain a better understanding of and appreciation for the marvelous possibilities of this new computing paradigm as you read *Client/Server Computing*, and that you feel better prepared to ride the fundamental shifts in business and computing throughout the next several years.

Steven G. Papermaster
Chairman and CEO, BSG
January 1994

Preface

The client/server computing model defines the way *successful* organizations will use technology during the next decade. It is the culmination of the trend toward downsizing applications from the mini-computer and mainframe to the desktop. Enabling technologies, such as object-oriented development and graphical user interfaces (GUIs), will liberate the users and owners of information to use technology personally and directly. Users will no longer need continual assistance from professional information systems (IS) personnel to create and store their business data.

The big losers in this change will be traditional vendors and integrators of minicomputer-based solutions. Forrester Research Inc., a reputable computer industry market research firm, routinely surveys the U.S. Fortune 1000 companies. Forrester projects that by 1993 the client/server market will account for $29 billion in sales. The pervasiveness of this technology throughout organizations dictates that all management levels understand the concepts and implications of client/server computing. Information systems (IS) professionals must understand these concepts and implications, as well as the detailed architectural issues involved, in order to be in a position to offer liberating client/server solutions to their users. IS professionals who do not understand these concerns will be relegated forever to a maintenance role on existing systems.

To address both audiences, this book introduces each chapter with an executive summary. In some of the later chapters, this alone may provide the necessary detail for most non-IS professionals. IS professionals will find the additional detail is included in latter parts of each chapter to explain the technology issues more fully.

Extensive use of charts and other graphics enables these materials to be used as part of internal presentations and training.

Patrick N. Smith
SHL Systemhouse, Inc.
January 1994

Acknowledgments

We would like to take this opportunity to thank the many organizations and individuals we have worked with over the past 25 years for the opportunity to experiment and learn on their behalf. The City and County of Los Angeles, in particular, have been the source of much recent experience. Their willingness to look for *world-class* solutions to their business problems has allowed us to gain substantial insight into the role of technology in reengineering the business process. Many members of the Systemhouse Technology Network have contributed directly to this book. Gord Tallas deserves particular credit and thanks for the work he did in pulling together the sample projects in Appendix A. June Ashworth applied her considerable skill and patience in developing the diagrams. Thanks also go to Andy Roehr, Sam Johnson, Eric Reed, Lara Weekes,and Nada Khatib, BSG, who helped with the final manuscript. Finally, we must thank our families for their patience and assistance in getting this book written.

Trademarks

All terms mentioned in this book that are known to be trademarks or service marks have been appropriately capitalized. Sams Publishing cannot attest to the accuracy of this information. Use of a term in this book should not be regarded as affecting the validity of any trademark or service mark.

Introduction

In a competitive world it is necessary for organizations to take advantage of every opportunity to reduce cost, improve quality, and provide service. Most organizations today recognize the need to be market driven, to be competitive, and to demonstrate added value.

A strategy being adopted by many organizations is to flatten the management hierarchy. With the elimination of layers of middle management, the remaining individuals must be empowered to make the strategy successful. Information to support rational decision making must be made available to these individuals. Information technology (IT) is an effective vehicle to support the implementation of this strategy; frequently it is not used effectively. The client/server model provides power to the desktop, with information available to *support* the decision-making process and *enable* decision-making authority.

The Gartner Group, a team of computer industry analysts, noted a widening chasm between user expectations and the ability of information systems (IS) organizations to fulfill them. The gap has been fueled by dramatic increases in end-user comfort with technology (mainly because of prevalent PC literacy); continuous cost declines in pivotal hardware technologies; escalation in highly publicized vendor promises; increasing time delays between vendor promised releases and product delivery (that is, "vaporware"); and emergence of the graphical user interface (GUI) as the perceived solution to all computing problems.

In this book you will see that client/server computing is the technology capable of bridging this chasm. This technology, particularly when integrated into the normal business process, can take advantage of this new literacy, cost-effective technology, and GUI friendliness. In conjunction with a well-architected systems development environment (SDE), it is possible for client/server computing to use the technology of today and be positioned to take advantage of vendor promises as they become real.

The *amount* of change in computer processing-related technology since the introduction of the IBM PC is equivalent to all the change that occurred during the previous history of computer technology. We expect the amount of change in the next few years to be even more geometrically inclined. The increasing rate of change is primarily attributable to the coincidence of four events: a dramatic reduction in the cost of processing hardware, a significant increase in installed and available processing power, the introduction of widely adopted software standards, and the use of object-oriented development techniques. The complexity inherent in the pervasiveness of these changes has prevented most business and government organizations from taking full advantage of the potential to be more competitive through improved quality, increased service, reduced costs, and higher profits. Corporate IS organizations, with an experience based on previous technologies, are often less successful than user groups in putting the new technologies to good use.

Taking advantage of computer technology innovation is one of the most effective ways to achieve a competitive advantage and demonstrate value in the marketplace. Technology can be used to improve service by quickly obtaining the information necessary to make decisions and to act to resolve problems. Technology can also be used to reduce costs of repetitive processes and to improve quality through consistent application of those processes. The use of workstation technology implemented as part of the business process and integrated with an organization's existing assets provides a practical means to achieve competitive advantage and to demonstrate value.

Computer hardware continues its historical trend toward smaller, faster, and lower-cost systems. Competitive pressures force organizations to reengineer their business processes for cost and service efficiencies. Computer technology trends prove to leading organizations that the application of technology is the key to successful reengineering of business processes.

Unfortunately, we are not seeing corresponding improvements in systems development. Applications developed by inhouse computer professionals seem to get larger, run more slowly, and cost more to operate. Existing systems consume all available IS resources for maintenance and enhancements. As personal desktop environments lead users to greater familiarity with a GUI, corporate IS departments continue to ignore this technology. The ease of use and standard look and feel, provided by GUIs in personal productivity applications at the desktop, is creating an expectation in the user community. When this expectation is not met, IS departments are considered irrelevant by their users.

Beyond GUI, multimedia technologies are using workstation power to re-present information through the use of image, video, sound, and graphics. These representations relate directly to the human brain's ability to extract information from images far more effectively than from lists of facts.

Accessing information CAN be as easy as tapping an electrical power utility. What is required is the will among developers to build the skills to take advantage of the opportunity offered by client/server computing.

This book shows how organizations can continue to gain value from their existing technology investments while using the special capabilities that new technologies offer. The book demonstrates how to architect SDEs and create solutions that are solidly based on evolving technologies. New systems can be built to work effectively with today's capabilities and at the same time can be based on a technical architecture that will allow them to evolve and to take advantage of future technologies.

For the near future, client/server solutions will rely on existing minicomputer and mainframe technologies to support applications already in use, and also to provide shared access to enterprise data, connectivity, and security services. To use existing investments and new technologies effectively, we must understand how to integrate these into our new applications. Only the appropriate application of standards based technologies within a designed architecture will enable this to happen.

It will not happen by accident.

The Business
Opportunity

The Business Opportunity

1

Executive Summary

We are in the midst of a fundamental change in both technology and its application. Organizations today expect to get more value from their investments in technology. In the "postscarcity era of computing"[1] the availability of processing power is not a constraint. Cost of platform technology has become a minor factor in selecting among alternatives to build the business solution. The constraining factors are the organizational impact of reengineering the business process and the costs and time required for system development. In addition, the need to re-educate personnel to the required level of expertise can be an extremely expensive proposition.

Open systems enable organizations to buy off-the-shelf solutions to business problems. Open systems standards define the format in which data is exchanged, remote systems are accessed, and services are invoked. The acceptance of open systems standards supports the

[1] *Robert Orfali and Dan Harkey, Client-Server Programming with OS/2 Extended Edition (2: Van Nostrand Reinhold, 1991), p. 95.*

creation of system architectures that can be built from technology components. These standards enable us, for example, to

- Build reusable class libraries to use in object-oriented design and development environments.
- Build niche products that interact with the same data (objects).
- Customize a letter at a personal desktop workstation to include data, addressing and graphics input from a word processor, a personal spreadsheet, a workgroup database, and an existing enterprise host application to be sent by electronic mail to anywhere in the world.

Contrary to the claims of groups ranging from the Open Software Foundation (OSF) to the user/vendor consortium Open User Recommended Solutions (OURS), open systems are not exclusively systems that conform to OSF or OURS committee recommendations, or necessarily to UNIX specifications.

The client/server model makes the enterprise available at the desk. It provides access to data that the previous architectures did not. Standards have been defined for client/server computing. If these standards are understood and used, organizations can reasonably expect to buy solutions today that can grow with their business needs without the constant need to revise the solutions. Architectures based on open systems standards can be implemented throughout the world, as global systems become the norm for large organizations.[2] While a supportable common platform on a global scale is far from standardized, it certainly is becoming much easier to accomplish. From the desktop, enterprise-wide applications are indistinguishable from workgroup and personal applications.

Powerful enabling technologies with built-in conformance to open systems standards are evolving rapidly.

Examples include object-oriented development, relational and object-oriented databases, multimedia, imaging, expert systems, geographic information systems (GIS), voice recognition and voice response, and text management. These technologies provide the opportunity to integrate their generic capabilities—with the particular requirements of an organization—to create a cost-effective and customized business solution. The client/server model provides the ideal platform with

---

[2] *Amdahl Corporation, Globalization, The IT Challenge (Amdahl Corporation, 1950) p. 14.*

which to integrate these enabling technologies. Well-defined interface standards enable integration of products from several vendors to provide the right application solution.

Enterprise systems are those that create and provide a shared information resource for the entire corporation. They do not imply centralized development and control, but they do treat information and technology as corporate resources. Enterprise network management requires all devices and applications in the enterprise computing environment to be visible and managed. This remains a major challenge as organizations move to distributed processing. Standards are defined and are being implemented within the client/server model. Client/server applications give greater viability to worker empowerment in a distributed organization than do today's host-centered environments.

Driving Forces in the 1990s

Opportunities are available to organizations and people who are ready and able to compete in the global market. A competitive global economy will ensure obsolescence and obscurity to those who cannot or are unwilling to compete. All organizations must look for ways to demonstrate value. We are finally seeing a willingness to rethink existing organizational structures and business practices.

Organizations are aggressively downsizing even as they try to aggressively expand their revenue base.

There is more willingness to continue improvement practices and programs to eliminate redundancy and increase effectiveness. Organizations are becoming market-driven while remaining true to their business vision.

To be competitive in a global economy, organizations in developed economies must employ technology to gain the efficiencies necessary to offset their higher labor costs. Reengineering the business process to provide information and decision-making support at points of customer contact reduces the need for layers of decision-making management, improves responsiveness, and enhances customer service.

Empowerment means that knowledge and responsibility are available to the employee at the point of customer contact. Empowerment will ensure that product and service problems and opportunities are identified and finalized. Client/server computing is the most effective source for the tools that empower employees with authority and responsibility.

The following are some key drivers in organizational philosophy, policies, and practices.

Business Process Reengineering

Competitiveness is forcing organizations to find new ways to manage their business, despite fewer personnel, more outsourcing, a market-driven orientation, and rapid product obsolescence. Technology can be the enabler of organizational nimbleness.

Globalization—The World as a Market

To survive and prosper in a world where trade barriers are being eliminated, organizations must look for partnerships and processes that are not restrained by artificial borders. Quality, cost, product differentiation, and service are the new marketing priorities. Our information systems must support these priorities.

Operational Systems—Competition for Investment Dollars

Competition demands that information systems organizations justify their costs. Companies are questioning the return on their existing investments. Centralized IS operations in particular are under the microscope.

Market Driven—Flexible to Meet Needs

Product obsolescence has never been so vital a factor. Buyers have more options and are more demanding.

Technology must enable organizations to anticipate demand and meet it.

Downsized Organizational Structure

Quality and flexibility require decisions to be made by individuals who are in touch with the customer. Many organizations are eliminating layers of middle management. Technology must provide the necessary information and support to this new structure.

Enterprise Network Management

If a business is run from its distributed locations, the technology supporting these units must be as reliable as the existing central systems. Technology for remote management of the distributed technology is essential in order to use scarce expertise appropriately and to reduce costs.

Information and Technology Viewed as a Corporate Asset

Each individual must have access to all information he or she has a "need and right" to access, without regard to where it is collected, determined, or located. We can use technology today to provide this "single-system image" of information at the desk, whatever the technology used to create it.

Cost Competitive—New Offerings

Standardization has introduced many new suppliers and has dramatically reduced costs. Competition is driving innovation. Organizations must use architectures that take advantage of cost-effective offerings as they appear.

Increasing Power and Capacity of Workstations

Desktop workstations now provide the power and mainframe capacity that mainframes did only a few years ago. The challenge is to effectively use this power and capacity to create solutions to real business problems.

Growing Importance of Workgroup Computing

Downsizing and empowerment require that the workgroup have access to information and work collectively. Decisions are being made in the workplace, not in the head office.

Expanded Network Access

Standards and new technologies enable workstation users to access information and systems without regard to location. Remote network management enables experts to provide support and central, system-like reliability to distributed systems. However, distributed systems are not transparent. Data access across a network often has unpredictable result sets; therefore, performance on existing networks is often inadequate, requiring a retooling of the existing network infrastructure to support the new data access environment.

Open Systems—Multivendor Environment

Standards enable many new vendors to enter the market. With a common platform target, every product has the entire marketplace as a potential customer. With the high rate of introduction of products, it is certain that organizations will have to deal with multiple vendors. Only through a commitment to standards-based technology will the heterogeneous multiple vendor environment effectively service the buyer.

Client/Server Computing

Workstation power, workgroup empowerment, preservation of existing investments, remote network management, and market-driven business are the forces creating the need for client/server computing.

The technology is here; what is missing is the expertise to effectively apply it.

Major Issues of the 1990s

Organizational pressures to demonstrate value apply as much to the information systems (IS) functions as to any other element or operating unit of the business. This is a special challenge because most IS organizations have not previously experienced strong financial constraints, nor have they been measured for success using the same business justification "yardstick" as other value-creating units within the business enterprise. IS has not been under the microscope to prove that the role it plays truly adds value to the overall organization. In today's world, organizations that cannot be seen to add value are either eliminated or outsourced.

Complexity and Delivery Cost of IS Services

Fortune 1000 companies, on average, spend 90 percent of IS dollars maintaining existing systems. Major business benefits, however, are available only from "new" systems. Dramatic reductions in the cost of technology help cost justify many systems. Organizations that adapt faster than their competitors demonstrate value and become the leaders in their marketplace. Products and services command a premium price when these organizations are "early to market." As they become commodities, they attract only commodity prices. This is true of both commercial organizations wishing to be competitive in the market with their products and of service organizations wishing to demonstrate value within their department or government sector.

Wise Use of Existing Investments

"It only took God seven days to create the world because he didn't have an existing environment to deal with."[3] Billions of dollars have been invested in corporate computing infrastructure and training. This investment must be fully used. Successful client/server solutions integrate with the existing applications and provide a gradual migration to the new platforms and business models.

Connectivity—Management of Distributed Data Resources

To meet the goals of the 1990s, organizations are downsizing and eliminating middle-management positions. They want to transfer responsibility to empower the person closest to the customer to make decisions. Historically, computer systems have imposed the burden of data collection and maintenance on the front-line work force but have husbanded information in the head office to support decision making by middle management. Information must be made available to the data creators and maintainers by providing the connectivity and distributed management of enterprise databases and applications. The technology of client/server computing will support the movement of information processing to the direct creators and users of information.

---

[3] *Anonymous.*

Online Transaction Processing (OLTP)

OLTP applications traditionally have been used in insurance, financial, government, and sales-related organizations. These applications are characterized by their need for highly reliable platforms that guarantee that transactions will be handled correctly, no data will be lost, response times will be extremely low (less than three seconds is a good rule of thumb), and only authorized users will have access to an application. The IS industry understands OLTP in the traditional mainframe-centered platforms but not in the distributed client/server platforms.

Mission-Critical Applications

Organizations do (and will continue) to rely on technology to drive business. Much of the IS industry does not yet understand how to build mission-critical applications on client/server platforms. As organizations move to employee empowerment and workgroup computing, the desktop becomes the critical technology element running the business. Client/server applications and platforms must provide mainframe levels of reliability.

Executive Information Systems (EIS)

Executive information systems provide a single-screen view of "how well we are doing" by comparing the mass of details contained in their current and historical enterprise databases with information obtained from outside sources about the economy and competition. As organizations enter into partnerships with their customers and suppliers, the need to integrate with external systems becomes essential in order to capture the necessary information for an effective EIS.

Decision Support Systems (DSS)

Organizations want to use the EIS data to make strategic decisions. The DSS should provide "what if" analyses to project the results of these decisions. Managers define expectations, and the local processing capability generates decision alerts when reality does not conform. This is the DSS of the client/server model.

Enterprise Solutions

Information is now recognized as a corporate resource. To be truly effective, organizations must collect data at the source and distribute it, according to the requirements of "need and right to access," throughout the organization. Workgroups will select the platforms that best meet their needs, and these platforms must integrate to support the enterprise solution. Systems built around open systems standards are essential for cost-effective integration.

Single-System Image

Los Angeles county issued a request for information (RFI) stating simply that its goal was "to implement and operate a modern telecommunications network that creates a seamless utility for all County telecommunications applications...from desktop to desktop."[4]

The United States government has initiated a project—the National Information Interchange (NII)—that has the simple objective of "making the intellectual property of the United States available to all with a need and right to access."[5]

"Computers will become a truly useful part of our society only when they are linked by an infrastructure like the highway system and the electric power grid, creating a new kind of free market for information services."[6]

The feature that makes the highway and electric power grids truly useful is their pervasiveness. Every home and office has ready access to these services; thus, they are used—without thought—in the normal course of living and working. This pervasive accessibility has emerged largely because of the adoption of standards for interconnection. If there were no standards for driving, imagine the confusion and danger.

---

[4] *Los Angeles County, RFI for Telecommunications Systems and Services (September 1991).*

---

[5] *Dertouzos, Lester, and Solow, "Made in America," President's Commission on Industrial Productivity, (MIT, 1989), paperback edition VI, p. 163.*

---

[6] *Michael L. Dertouzos, "Building the Information Marketplace," Technology Review, No. 94, (January 1991), pp. 30-31.*

What if every wall plug were a different shape, or the power available on every plug were random? If using a service requires too much thought and attention, that service cannot become a default part of our living and working environment.

"Imagine the United States without its highways. Our millions of cars, buses, and trucks driven in our own backyards and neighborhood parking lots, with occasional forays by the daring few along uncharted, unpredictable, and treacherous dirt roads, full of unspeakable terrors."[7] The parking lot analogy illustrated in Figure 1.1 represents the current information-processing environment in most organizations.

It is easy and transparent to locate and use information on a local area network (LAN), but information located on another LAN is almost inaccessible. End-user access to enterprise data often is unavailable except for predefined information requests. Although computers—from mainframes to PCs—are numerous, powerful, flexible, and widely used, they are still used in relative isolation. When they communicate, they usually do so ineffectively, through arcane and arbitrary procedures.

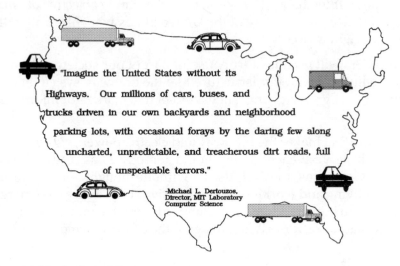

Figure 1.1. Islands of automation.

Information comes with many faces. As shown in Figure 1.2, it can take the form of text, drawings, music, speech, photographs, stock prices,

---

[7] *Ibid.*

invoices, software, live video, and many other entities. Yet once information is computerized, it becomes a deceptively uniform sequence of ones and zeros. The underlying infrastructure must be flexible in the way it transports these ones and zeros. To be truly effective—besides routing these binaries to their destinations—the infrastructure must be able to carry binaries with varying degrees of speed, accuracy, and security to accommodate different computer capabilities and needs.

Because computers are manufactured and sold by vendors with differing views on the most effective technology, they do not share common implementation concepts. Transporting ones and zeros around, however flexibly, isn't enough. Computers based on different technologies cannot comprehend each other's ones and zeros any more than people comprehend foreign languages. We therefore need to endow our IS organizations with a set of widely understood common information interchange conventions. Moreover, these conventions must be based on concepts that make life easier for humans, rather than for computer servants. Finally, the truly useful infrastructure must be equipped with "common servers"—computers that provide a few basic information services of wide interest, such as computerized white and yellow pages.

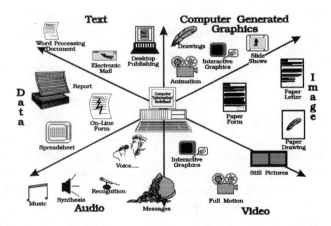

Figure 1.2. Multimedia technologies.

Technological innovation proceeds at a pace that challenges the human mind to understand how to take advantage of its capabilities. Electronic information management, technological innovation in the personal computer, high-speed electronic communication, and digital encoding of information provide new opportunities for enhanced services at lower cost.

Personal computers can provide services directly to people who have minimal computer experience. They provide low-cost, high-performance computing engines at the site that the individual lives, works, or accesses the service—regardless of where the information is physically stored. Standards for user interface, data access, and interprocess communications have been defined for the personal computer and are being adopted by a majority of the vendor community. There is no reason to accept solutions that do not conform to the accepted standards.

Most large organizations today use a heterogeneous collection of hardware, software, and connectivity technologies. There is considerable momentum toward increased use of technology from multiple vendors.

This trend leads to an increasingly heterogeneous environment for users and developers of computer systems. Users are interested in the business functionality, not the technology. Developers rarely are interested in more than a subset of the technology. The concept of the single-system image says that you can build systems that provide transparency of the technology platform to the user and—at the largest extent possible—to the developer.

Developers will need sufficient knowledge of the syntax used to solve the business problem, but will need little or no knowledge of the underlying technology infrastructure. Hardware platforms, operating systems, database engines, and communications protocols are necessary technological components of any computer solution, but they should provide services—not create obstacles to getting the job done. Services should be *masked*; that is, they should be provided in a natural manner without requiring the user to make unnatural gyrations to invoke them. Only by masking these services and by using standard interfaces can we hope to develop systems quickly and economically. At the same time, masking (known as *encapsulation* in object-oriented programming) and standard interfaces preserve the ability to change the underlying technology without affecting the application. There is value in restricting imagination when you build system architectures. Systems development is not an art; it is an engineering discipline that can be learned and used. Systems can be built on the foundations established by previous projects.

Within the single-system image environment, a business system user is totally unaware of where data is stored, how the client and server processors work, and what networking is involved in gaining connectivity. How is this transparency accomplished?

- Every application that the user accesses provides a common "look and feel." Help is provided in the same way by every application. Errors are presented and resolved in the same way by every application. Access is provided through a standard security procedure for every application. Each user has access to all services for which he or she has a need and a right to access.

- The security layer is invisible to the authorized and impenetrable to the unauthorized.

- Navigation from function to function and application to application is provided in the same way in every system. New applications can be added with minimal training, because the standard functions work in the same way, and only the new business functions need be learned. It is not necessary to go to "boot camp for basic training" prior to using each new application. Basic training is a one-time effort because the basics do not change.

Services are provided by the virtual "cloud" server in the sky. Figure 1.3 illustrates the user view of these services. The workstation on the desk appears to provide all services, "the enterprise at the desk."

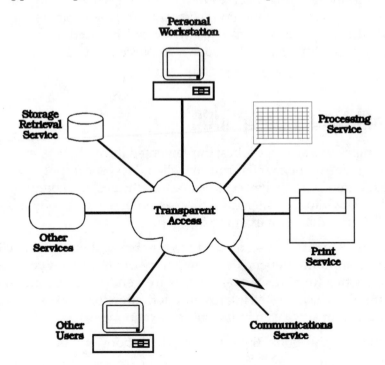

Figure 1.3. Single-system image.

The complexity of a heterogeneous computing platform will result in many interfaces at both the logical and physical level. Organizations evolve from one platform to another as the industry changes, as new technologies evolve that are more cost effective, and as acquisitions and mergers introduce other installed platforms. All these advances must be accommodated. There is complexity and risk when attempting to interoperate among technologies from many vendors. It is necessary to engage in "proof of concept" testing to distinguish the marketing version of products and architectures from the delivered version.

Many organizations use a test lab concept called *technology competency centers* (TCCs) to do this "proof of concept." The TCC concept provides a local, small-scale model of all the technologies involved in a potential single-system, interoperable image.

Installing a proposed solution using a TCC is a low-cost means of ensuring that the solution is viable.

These labs enable rapid installation of the proposed solution into a proven environment. They eliminate the need to set up from scratch all the components that are necessary to support the unique part of a new application. Organizations—Merrill Lynch, Health Canada, SHL Systemhouse, BSG Corporation, Microsoft, and many others—use such labs to do sanity checks on new technologies. The rapid changes in technology capability dictate that such a resource be available to validate new products.

Client/Server Computing

The single-system image is best implemented through the client/server model. Our experience confirms that client/server computing can provide the enterprise to the desktop. Because the desktop computer is the user's view into the enterprise, there is no better way to guarantee a single image than to start at the desktop.

Unfortunately, it often seems as if the number of definitions of client/ server computing depends on how many organizations you survey, whether they're hardware and software vendors, integrators, or IS groups. Each has a vested interest in a definition that makes its particular product or service an indispensable component.

Throughout this book, the following definitions will be used consistently:

- *Client:* A client is a single-user workstation that provides presentation services and the appropriate computing, connectivity, and database services and interfaces relevant to the business need.

- *Server:* A server is one or more multiuser processors with shared memory providing computing, connectivity, and database services and interfaces relevant to the business need.

Client/server computing is an environment that satisfies the business need by appropriately allocating the application processing between the client and the server processors. The client requests services from the server; the server processes the request and returns the result to the client. The communications mechanism is a message passing *interprocess communication* (IPC) that enables (but does not require) distributed placement of the client and server processes. Client/server is a software model of computing, not a hardware definition.

This definition makes client/server a rather generic model and fits what is known in the industry as "cooperative processing" or "peer-to-peer."

Because the client/server environment is typically heterogeneous, the hardware platform and operating system of the client and server are not usually the same. In such cases, the communications mechanism may be further extended through a well-defined set of standard application program interfaces (APIs) and remote procedure calls (RPCs).

The modern diagram representing the client/server model was probably first popularized by Sybase.

Figure 1.4 illustrates the single-system image vision. A client-user relies on the desktop workstation for all computing needs. Whether the application runs totally on the desktop or uses services provided by one or more servers—be they powerful PCs or mainframes—is irrelevant.

Effective client/server computing will be fundamentally platform-independent. The user of an application wants the business functionality it provides; the computing platform provides access to this business functionality. There is no benefit, yet considerable risk, in exposing this platform to its user.

Changes in platform and underlying technology should be transparent to the user. Training costs, business processing delays and errors, staff frustration, and staff turnover result from the confusion generated by changes in environments where the user is sensitive to the technology platform.

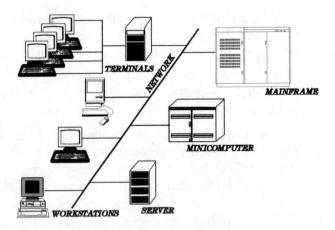

Figure 1.4. A modern client/server architecture.

It is easily demonstrated that systems built with transparency to the technology, for all users, offer the highest probability of solid ongoing return for the technology investment. It is equally demonstrable that if developers become aware of the target platform, development will be bound to that platform. Developers will use special features, tricks, and syntax found only in the specific development platform.

Tools, which isolate developers from the specifics of any single platform, assist developers in writing transparent, portable applications. These tools must be available for each of the three essential components in any application: data access, processing, and interfaces. Data access includes the graphical user interface (GUI) and stored data access. Processing includes the business logic. Interfaces link services with other applications. This simple model, reflected in Figure 1.5, should be kept in mind when following the evolution to client/server computing.

The use of technology layers provides this application development isolation. These layers isolate the characteristics of the technology at each level from the layer above and below. This layering is fundamental to the development of applications in the client/server model. The rapid rate of change in these technologies and the lack of experience with the "best" solutions implies that we must isolate specific technologies from each other. This book will continue to emphasize and expand on the concept of a *systems development environment* (SDE) as a way to achieve this isolation. Figure 1.6 illustrates the degree of visibility to specific technology components required by the developers.

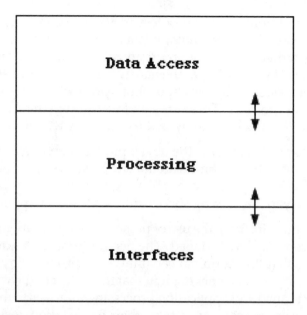

Figure 1.5. *Simplified application model.*

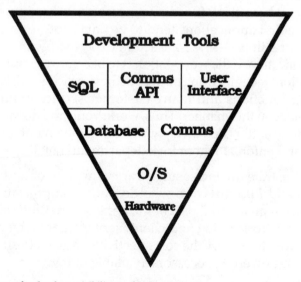

Figure 1.6. *Degree of technology visibility to developer.*

Developer tools are by far the most visible. Most developers need to know only the syntax of these tools to express the business problem in a format acceptable to the technology platform. With the increasing involvement of noncomputer professionals, as technology users and application assemblers, technology isolation is even more important. Very few—perhaps none—of an organization's application development staff needs to be aware of the hardware, system software, specific database engines, specific communications products, or specific presentation services products. These are invoked through the APIs message passing, and RPCs generated by tools or by a few technical specialists.

As you will see in Chapter 6, the development of an application architecture supported by a technical architecture and systems development environment (SDE) is the key to achieving this platform independence and ultimately to developing successful client/server applications.

As organizations increase the use of personal productivity tools, workstations become widely installed. The need to protect desktop real estate requires that host terminal capabilities be provided by the single workstation. It soon becomes evident that the power of the workstation is not being tapped and application processing migrates to the desktop. Once most users are connected from their workstation desktop to the applications and data at the host mainframe or minicomputer, there is significant cost benefit in offloading processing to these powerful workstations. The first applications tend to be data capture and edit. These simplify—but still use—the transaction expected by an already existing host application. If the workstation is to become truly integrated with the application, reengineering of the business process will be necessary. Accounting functions and many customer service applications are easily offloaded in this manner. Thus, workgroup and departmental processing is done at the LAN level, with host involvement for enterprise-wide data and enforcement of interdepartmental business rules.

Figure 1.7 illustrates an increasingly rare viewpoint of tradition-bound developers and MIS directors who do not yet appreciate the role of workstations as an integral part of the application solution. The power of the desktop workstation and client/server technology must be unleashed in order to achieve the cost effectiveness available from the low-cost and high-powered processors available today.

Figure 1.8 illustrates the existing environment in many organizations wherein desktop workstations have replaced the unintelligent terminal to access existing host-based applications.

I'll never let them replace MY host systems with workstations

Figure 1.7. An increasingly rare viewpoint.

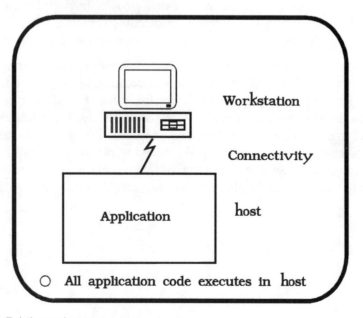

Workstation

Connectivity

host

Application

○ All application code executes in host

Figure 1.8. Existing environment.

In this "dumb" terminal (IBM uses the euphemism *nonprogrammable* to describe its 327x devices) emulation environment, all application logic resides in the minicomputer, mainframe, or workstation. Clearly a $5000 or less desktop workstation is capable of much more than the character display provided by a $500 terminal. In the client/server model, the low-cost processing power of the workstation will replace host processing, and the application logic will be divided appropriately among the platforms. As previously noted, this distribution of function and data is transparent to the user and application developer.

Mainframe-Centric Client/Server Computing

The mainframe-centric model uses the presentation capabilities of the workstation to front-end existing applications. The character mode interface is remapped by products such as Easel and Mozart. The same data is displayed or entered through the use of pull-down lists, scrollable fields, check boxes, and buttons; the user interface is easy to use, and information is presented more clearly. In this mainframe-centric model, mainframe applications continue to run unmodified, because the existing terminal data stream is processed by the workstation-based communications API.

The availability of products such as UniKix and IBM's CICS OS/2 and 6000 can enable the entire mainframe processing application to be moved unmodified to the workstation. This protects the investment in existing applications while improving performance and reducing costs.

Character mode applications, usually driven from a block mode screen, attempt to display as much data as possible in order to reduce the number of transmissions required to complete a function. Dumb terminals impose limitations on the user interface including fixed length fields, fixed length lists, crowded screens, single or limited character fonts, limited or no graphics icons, and limited windowing for multiple application display. In addition, the fixed layout of the screen makes it difficult to support the display of conditionally derived information.

In contrast, the workstation GUI provides facilities to build the screen dynamically. This enables screens to be built with a variable format based conditionally on the data values of specific fields. Variable length fields can be scrollable, and lists of fields can have a scrollable number of rows. This enables a much larger virtual screen to be used with no additional data communicated between the client workstation and server.

Windowing can be used to pull up additional information such as help text, valid value lists, and error messages without losing the original screen contents.

The more robust GUI facilities of the workstation enable the user to navigate easily around the screen.

Additional information can be encapsulated by varying the display's colors, fonts, graphics icons, scrollable lists, pull-down lists, and option boxes. Option lists can be provided to enable users to quickly select input values. Help can be provided, based on the context and the cursor location, using the same pull-down list facilities.

Although it is a limited use of client/server computing capability, a GUI front end to an existing application is frequently the first client/server-like application implemented by organizations familiar with the host mainframe and dumb-terminal approach. The GUI preserves the existing investment while providing the benefits of ease of use associated with a GUI. It is possible to provide dramatic and functionally rich changes to the user interface without host application change.

The next logical step is the provision of some edit and processing logic executing at the desktop workstation. This additional logic can be added without requiring changes in the host application and may reduce the host transaction rate by sending up only valid transactions. With minimal changes to the host application, network traffic can be reduced and performance can be improved by using the workstation's processing power to encode the datastream into a compressed form.

A more interactive user interface can be provided with built-in, context-sensitive help, and extensive prompting and user interfaces that are sensitive to the users' level of expertise. These options can be added through the use of workstation processing power. These capabilities enable users to operate an existing system with less intensive training and may even provide the opportunity for public access to the applications.

Electronic data interchange (EDI) is an example of this front-end processing. EDI enables organizations to communicate electronically with their suppliers or customers. Frequently, these systems provide the workstation front end to deal with the EDI link but continue to work with the existing back-end host system applications. Messages are reformatted and responses are handled by the EDI client, but application processing is done by the existing application server. Productivity may be enhanced significantly by capturing information at the source and making it available to all authorized users. Typically, if users employ a multipart form for data capture, the form data is entered into multiple systems. Capturing this information once to a server in a client/server application, and reusing the data for several client applications can reduce errors, lower data entry costs, and speed up the availability of this information.

Figure 1.9 illustrates how multiple applications can be integrated in this way. The data is available to authorized users as soon as it is captured. There is no delay while the forms are passed around the organization. This is usually a better technique than *forms imaging technology* in which the forms are created and distributed internally in an organization. The use of workflow-management technology and techniques, in conjunction with imaging technology, is an effective way of handling this process when forms are filled out by a person who is physically remote from the organization.

Intelligent Character Recognition (ICR) technology can be an extremely effective way to automate the capture of data from a form, without the need to key. Current experience with this technique shows accuracy rates greater than 99.5 percent for typed forms and greater than 98.5 percent for handwritten forms.

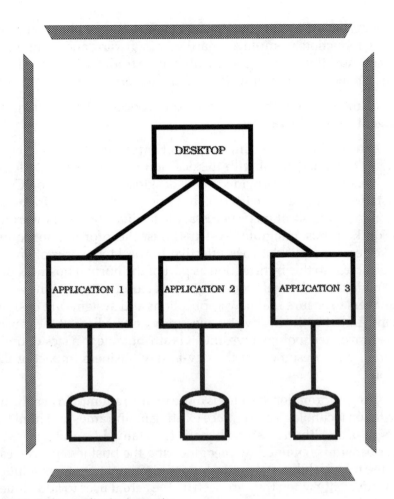

Figure 1.9. *Desktop application integration.*

Downsizing and Client/Server Computing

Rightsizing and downsizing are strategies used with the client/server model to take advantage of the lower cost of workstation technology. Rightsizing and upsizing may involve the addition of more diverse or more powerful computing resources to an enterprise computing environment. The benefits of rightsizing are reduction in cost and/or increased functionality, performance, and flexibility in the applications of the enterprise. Significant cost savings usually are obtained from a resulting reduction in employee, hardware, software, and maintenance expenses. Additional savings typically accrue from the improved effectiveness of the user community using client/server technology.

Downsizing is frequently implemented in concert with a flattening of the organizational hierarchy.

Eliminating middle layers of management implies empowerment to the first level of management with the decision-making authority for the whole job. Information provided at the desktop by networked PCs and workstations integrated with existing host (such as mainframe and minicomputer) applications is necessary to facilitate this empowerment. These desktop-host integrated systems house the information required to make decisions quickly. To be effective, the desktop workstation must provide access to this information as part of the normal business practice. Architects and developers must work closely with business decision makers to ensure that new applications and systems are designed to be integrated with effective business processes. Much of the cause of poor return on technology investment is attributable to a lack of understanding by the designers of the day-to-day business impact of their solutions.

Downsizing information systems is more than an attempt to use cheaper workstation technologies to replace existing mainframes and minicomputers in use. Although some benefit is obtained by this approach, greater benefit is obtained by reengineering the business processes to really use the capabilities of the desktop environment. Systems solutions are effective only when they are seen by the actual user to add value to the business process.

Client/server technology implemented on low-cost standard hardware will drive downsizing. Client/server computing makes the desktop the users' enterprise. As we move from the machine-centered era of computing into the workgroup era, the desktop workstation is empowering the business user to regain ownership of his or her information resource. Client/server computing combines the best of the old with the new—the reliable multiuser access to shared data and resources with the intuitive, powerful desktop workstation.

Object-oriented development concepts are embodied in the use of an SDE created for an organization from an architecturally selected set of tools. The SDE provides more effective development and maintenance than companies have experienced with traditional host-based approaches.

Client/server computing is open computing. Mix and match is the rule. Development tools and development environments must be created with both openness and standards in mind.

Mainframe applications rarely can be downsized—without modifications—to a workstation environment. Modifications can be minor, wherein tools are used to *port* (or rehost) existing mainframe source code—or major, wherein the applications are *rewritten* using completely new tools. In porting, native COBOL compilers, functional file systems, and emulators for DB2, IMS DB/DC, and CICS are available for workstations. In rewriting, there is a broad array of tools ranging from PowerBuilder, Visual Basic, and Access, to larger scale tools such as Forte and Dynasty.

Preserving Your Mainframe Applications Investment Through Porting

Although the percentage of client/server applications development is rapidly moving away from a mainframe-centric model, it is possible to downsize and still preserve a larger amount of the investment in application code. For example, the Micro Focus COBOL/2 Workbench by Micro Focus Company Inc., and XDB Systems Inc., bundles products from Innovative Solutions Inc., Stingray Software Company Inc., and XDB Systems Inc., to provide the capability to develop systems on a PC LAN for production execution on an IBM mainframe. These products, in conjunction with the ProxMVS product from Proximity Software, enable extensive unit and integration testing to be done on a PC LAN before moving the system to the mainframe for final system and performance testing. Used within a properly structured development environment, these products can dramatically reduce mainframe development costs.

Micro Focus COBOL/2 supports GUI development targeted for implementation with OS/2 Presentation Manager and Microsoft Windows 3.x. Another Micro Focus product, the Dialog System, provides support for GUI and character mode applications that are independent of the underlying COBOL applications.

Micro Focus has added an Object Oriented (OO) option to its workbench to facilitate the creation of reusable components. The OO option supports integration with applications developed under Smalltalk/V PM.

IBM's CICS for OS/2, OS400, RS6000, and HP/UX products enable developers to directly port applications using standard CICS call interfaces from the mainframe to the workstation. These applications can then run under OS/2, AIX, OS400, HP/UX, or MVS/VSE without modification. This promises to enable developers to create applications for execution in the CICS MVS environment and later to port them to these other environments without modification. Conversely, applications can be designed and built for such environments and subsequently ported to MVS (if this is a logical move). Organizations envisioning such a migration should ensure that their SDE incorporates standards that are consistent for all of these platforms.

To help ensure success in using these products, the use of a COBOL code generator, such as Computer Associates' (previously Pansophic) Telon PWS, provides the additional advantages of a higher level of syntax for systems development. Telon provides particularly powerful facilities that support the object-oriented development concepts necessary to create a structured development environment and to support code and function reuse. The generated COBOL is input to the Micro Focus Workbench toolkit to support prototyping and rapid application development. Telon applications can be generated to execute in the OS/2, UNIX AIX, OS400, IMS DB/DC, CICS DLI, DB2, IDMS, and Datacom DB environments. This combination—used in conjunction with a structured development environment that includes appropriate standards—provides the capability to build single-system image applications today. In an environment that requires preservation of existing host-based applications, this product suite is among the most complete for client/server computing.

These products, combined with the cheap processing power available on the workstation, make the workstation LAN an ideal development and maintenance environment for existing host processors. When an organization views mainframe or minicomputer resources as real dollars, developers can usually justify offloading the development in only three to six months. Developers can be effective only when a proper systems development environment is put in place and provided with a suite of tools offering the host capabilities plus enhanced connectivity.

Workstation operating systems are still more primitive than the existing host server MVS, VMS, or UNIX operating systems. Therefore, appropriate standards and procedures must be put in place to coordinate shared development. The workstation environment will change. Only projects built with common standards and procedures will be resilient enough to remain viable in the new environment.

The largest savings come from new projects that can establish appropriate standards at the start and do all development using the workstation LAN environment. It is possible to retrofit standards to an existing environment and establish a workstation with a LAN-based maintenance environment. The benefits are less because retrofitting the standards creates some costs. However, these costs are justified when the application is scheduled to undergo significant maintenance or if the application is very critical and there is a desire to reduce the error rate created by changes. The discipline associated with the movement toward client/server-based development, and the transfer of code between the host and client/server will almost certainly result in better testing and fewer errors. The testing facilities and usability of the workstation will make the developer and tester more effective and therefore more accurate.

Business processes use database, communications, and application services. In an ideal world, we pick the best servers available to provide these services, thereby enabling our organizations to enjoy the maximum benefit that current technology provides. Real-world developers make compromises around the existing technology, existing application products, training investments, product support, and a myriad other factors.

Key to the success of full client/server applications is selecting an appropriate application and technical architecture for the organization. Once the technical architecture is defined, the tools are known. The final step is to implement an SDE to define the standards needed to use the tools effectively. This SDE is the collection of hardware, software, standards, standard procedures, interfaces, and training built up to support the organization's particular needs.

The "Real World" of Client/Server Development Tools

Many construction projects fail because their developers assume that a person with a toolbox full of carpenter's tools is a capable builder. To be a successful builder, a person must be trained to build according to standards. The creation of standards to define interfaces to the sewer, water, electrical utilities, road, school, and community systems is essential for successful, cost-effective building. We do not expect a carpenter to design such interfaces individually for every building. Rather, pragmatism discourages imagination in this regard. By reusing the models previously built to accomplish integration, we all benefit from cost and risk reduction.

Computer systems development using an SDE takes advantage of these same concepts: Let's build on what we've learned. Let's reuse as much as possible to save development costs, reduce risk, and provide the users with a common "look and feel."

Selecting a good set of tools affords an opportunity to be successful. Without the implementation of a comprehensive SDE, developers will not achieve such success.

The introduction of a whole new generation of Object Technology based tools for client/server development demands that proper standards be put in place to support shared development, reusable code, interfaces to existing systems, security, error handling, and an organizational standard "look and feel." As with any new technology, there will be changes. Developers can build application systems closely tied to today's technology or use an SDE and develop applications that can evolve along with the technology platform.

Chapter 6 discusses the software development issues and the SDE, in particular, in greater detail.

Advantages of Client/
Server Computing

Advantages of Client/ Server Computing

2

Executive Summary

Organizations want to take advantage of the low-cost and user-friendly environment that existing desktop workstations provide. There is also a strong need and desire to capitalize on existing investment at the desktop and in the portfolio of business applications currently running in the host. Thus, corporate networks are typically put in place to connect user workstations to the host. Immediate benefits are possible by integrating these three technologies: workstations, connectivity, and hosts. Retraining and redevelopment costs are avoided by using the existing applications from an integrated desktop.

Client/server computing provides the capability to use the most cost-effective user interface, data storage, connectivity, and application services. Frequently, client/ server products are deployed within the present organization but are not used effectively. The client/server model provides the technological means to use previous investments in concert with current technology options. There has been a dramatic decline in the cost of the technology components of client/server computing. Organizations see opportunities to use technology to provide business solutions. Service and quality competition in the marketplace further increase the need to take advantage of the benefits available from applications built on the client/server model.

Client/server computing in its best implementations moves the data-capture and information-processing functions directly to the knowledgeable worker—that is, the worker with the ability to respond to errors in the data, and the worker with the ability to use the information made available. Systems used in the front office, directly involved in the process of doing the business, are forced to show value. If they don't, they are discarded under the cost pressures of doing business. Systems that operate in the back room after the business process is complete are frequently designed and implemented to satisfy an administrative need, without regard to their impact on business operations. Client/server applications integrate the front and back office processes because data capture and usage become an integral part of the business rather than an after-the-fact administrative process. In this mode of operation, the processes are continuously evaluated for effectiveness. Client/server computing provides the technology platform to support the vital business practice of continuous improvement.

The Advantages of Client/Server Computing

The client/server computing model provides the means to integrate personal productivity applications for an individual employee or manager with specific business data processing needs to satisfy total information processing requirements for the entire enterprise.

Enhanced Data Sharing

Data that is collected as part of the normal business process and maintained on a server is immediately available to all authorized users. The use of Structured Query Language (SQL) to define and manipulate the data provides support for open access from all client processors and software. SQL grants all authorized users access to the information through a view that is consistent with their business need. Transparent network services ensure that the same data is available with the same currency to all designated users.

Integrated Services

In the client/server model, all information that the client (user) is entitled to use is available at the desktop. There is no need to change into terminal mode or log into another processor to access information. All authorized information and processes are directly available from the desktop interface. The desktop tools—e-mail, spreadsheet, presentation graphics, and word processing—are available and can be used to deal with information provided by application and database servers resident on the network. Desktop users can use their desktop tools in conjunction with information made available from the corporate systems to produce new and useful information.

Figure 2.1 shows a typical example of this integration. A word-processed document that includes input from a drawing package, a spreadsheet, and a custom-developed application can be created. The facilities of Microsoft's Dynamic Data Exchange (DDE) enable graphics and spreadsheet data to be cut and pasted into the word-processed document along with the window of information extracted from a corporate database. The result is displayed by the custom application.

Creation of the customized document is done using only desktop tools and the mouse to select and drag information from either source into the document. The electronic scissors and glue provide powerful extensions to existing applications and take advantage of the capability of the existing desktop processor. The entire new development can be done by individuals who are familiar only with personal productivity desktop tools. Manipulating the spreadsheet object, the graphics object, the application screen object, and the document object using the desktop cut and paste tools provides a powerful new tool to the end user.

Developers use these same object manipulation capabilities under program control to create new applications in a fraction of the time consumed by traditional programming methods. Object-oriented development techniques are dramatically increasing the power available to nonprogrammers and user professionals to build and enhance applications.

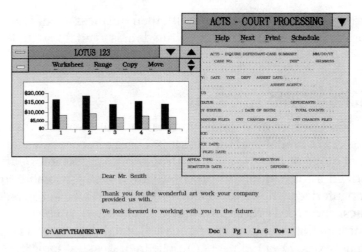

Figure 2.1. *Personal productivity and integrated applications.*

Another excellent and easily visualized example of the integration possible in the client/server model is implemented in the retail automobile service station. Figure 2.2 illustrates the comprehensive business functionality required in a retail gas service station. The service station automation (SSA) project integrates the services of gasoline flow measurement, gas pumps billing, credit card validation, cash registers management, point-of-sale, inventory control, attendance recording, electronic price signs, tank monitors, accounting, marketing, truck dispatch, and a myriad of other business functions. These business functions are all provided within the computer-hostile environment of the familiar service station with the same type of workstations used to create this book. The system uses all of the familiar client/server components, including local and wide-area network services. Most of the system users are transitory employees with minimal training in computer technology. An additional challenge is the need for real-time processing of the flow of gasoline as it moves through the pump. If the processor does not detect and measure the flow of gasoline, the customer is not billed. The service station automation system is a classic example of the capabilities of an integrated client/server application implemented and working today.

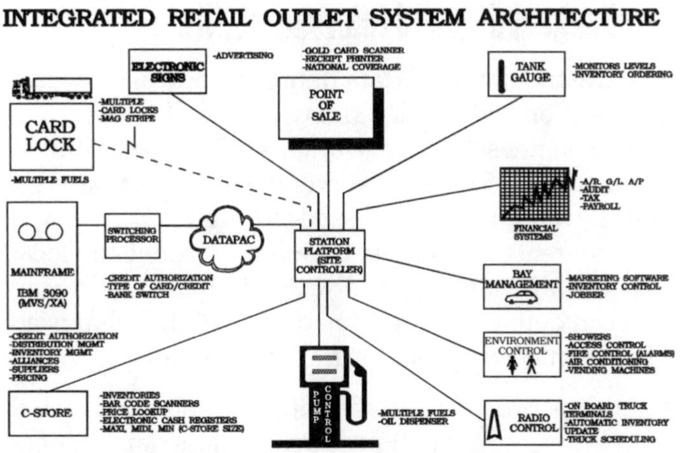

INTEGRATED RETAIL OUTLET SYSTEM ARCHITECTURE

Figure 2.2. Integrated retail outlet system architecture.

Sharing Resources Among Diverse Platforms

The client/server computing model provides opportunities to achieve true open system computing. Applications may be created and implemented without regard to the hardware platforms or the technical characteristics of the software. Thus, users may obtain client services and transparent access to the services provided by database, communications, and applications servers. Operating systems software and platform hardware are independent of the application and masked by the development tools used to build the application.

In this approach, business applications are developed to deal with business processes invoked by the existence of a user-created "event." An event such as the push of a button, selection of a list element, entry in a dialog box, scan of a bar code, or flow of gasoline occurs without the application logic being sensitive to the physical platforms.

Client/server applications operate in one of two ways. They can function as the front end to an existing application—the more limited mainframe-centric model discussed in Chapter 1—or they can provide data entry, storage, and reporting by using a distributed set of clients and servers. In either case, the use—or even the existence—of a mainframe host is totally masked from the workstation developer by the use of standard interfaces such as SQL.

Data Interchangeability and Interoperability

SQL is an industry-standard data definition and access language. This standard definition has enabled many vendors to develop production-class database engines to manage data as SQL tables. Almost all the development tools used for client/server development expect to reference a back-end database server accessed through SQL. Network services provide transparent connectivity between the client and local or remote servers. With some database products, such as Ingres Star, a user or application can define a consolidated view of data that is actually distributed between heterogeneous, multiple platforms.

Systems developers are finally reaching the point at which this heterogeneity will be a feature of all production-class database engine products. Most systems that have been implemented to date use a single target platform for data maintenance. The ability to do high-volume updates at multiple locations and maintain database integrity across all types of errors is just becoming available with production-level quality performance and recovery. Systems developed today that use SQL are inherently transparent to data storage location and the technology of the data storage platform. The SQL syntax does not specify a location or platform. This transparency enables tables to be moved to other platforms and locations without affecting the application code. This feature is especially valuable when adopting proven, new technology or if it makes business sense to move data closer to its owner.

Database services can be provided in response to an SQL request—without regard to the underlying engine. This engine can be provided by vendors such as ASK/Ingres, Oracle, Sybase, or IBM running on Windows NT, OS/2, UNIX, or MVS platform. The system development environment (SDE) and tools must implement the interfaces to the vendor database and operating system products. The developer does not need to know which engine or operating system is running. If the SDE does not remove the developer from direct access to the database server platform, the enthusiasm to be efficient will prevent developers from avoiding the use of "features" available only from a specific vendor. The transparency of platform is essential if the application is to remain portable. Application portability is essential when taking advantage of innovation in technology and cost competitiveness, and in providing protection from the danger of vendor failure.

Database products, such as Sybase used with the Database Gateway product from Micro DecisionWare, provide direct, production-quality, and transparent connectivity between the client and servers. These products may be implemented using DB2, IMS/DB, or VSAM through CICS into DB2, and Sybase running under VMS, Windows NT, OS/2, DOS, and MacOS. Bob Epstein, executive vice president of Sybase, Inc., views Sybase's open server approach to distributed data as incorporating characteristics of the semantic heterogeneity solution.[1] In this solution, the code at the remote server can be used to deal with different database management systems (DBMSs), data models, or processes. The remote procedure call (RPC) mechanism used by Sybase can be interpreted as a message that invokes the appropriate method or procedure on the open server. True, somebody has to write the code that masks the differences. However, certain parts—such as accessing a foreign DBMS (like Sybase SQL Server to IBM DB2)—can be standardized.

ASK's Ingres Star product provides dynamic SQL to support a distributed database between UNIX and MVS. Thus, Ingres Windows 4GL running under DOS or UNIX as a client can request a data view that involves data on the UNIX Ingres and MVS DB2 platform. Ingres is committed to providing static SQL and IMS support in the near future. Ingres' Intelligent Database engine will optimize the query so that SQL requests to distributed databases are handled in a manner that minimizes the number of rows moved from the remote server. This optimization is particularly crucial when dynamic requests are made to distributed databases. With the announcement of the Distributed Relational Database Architecture (DRDA), IBM has recognized the need for open access from other products to DB2. This product provides the application program interfaces (APIs) necessary for other vendors to generate static SQL requests to the DB2 engine running under MVS. Norris van den Berg, manager of Strategy for Programming Systems at IBM's Santa Teresa Laboratory in San Jose, California, points out that IBM's Systems Application Architecture (SAA) DBMSs are different. Even within IBM, they must deal with the issues of data interchange and interoperability in a heterogeneous environment.[2] More importantly,

---

[1] *Edelstein, Herbert A., "Database World Targets Next-Generation Problems," Software Magazine Vol. VII, No. 6 (May 1991), p. 81.*

---

[2] *IBM Santa Teresa laboratory meetings, 1990-1991.*

IBM is encouraging third-party DBMS vendors to comply with its DRDA. This is a set of specifications that will enable all DBMSs to interoperate.

The client/server model provides the capability to make ad hoc requests for information. As a result, optimization of dynamic SQL and support for distributed databases are crucial for the success of the second generation of a client/server application. The first generation implements the operational aspects of the business process. The second generation is the introduction of ad hoc requests generated by the knowledgeable user looking to gain additional insight from the information available.

Masked Physical Data Access

When SQL is used for data access, users can access information from databases anywhere in the network. From the local PC, local server, or wide area network (WAN) server, data access is supported with the developer and user using the same data request. The only noticeable difference may be performance degradation if the network bandwidth is inadequate. Data may be accessed from dynamic random-access memory (D-RAM), from magnetic disk, or from optical disk, with the same SQL statements. Logical tables can be accessed—without any knowledge of the ordering of columns or awareness of extraneous columns—by selecting a subset of the columns in a table. Several tables may be joined into a view that creates a new logical table for application program manipulation, without regard to its physical storage format.

The use of new data types, such as binary large objects (BLOBs), enables other types of information such as images, video, and audio to be stored and accessed using the same SQL statements for data access. RPCs frequently include data conversion facilities to translate the stored data of one processor into an acceptable format for another.

Location Independence of Data and Processing

We are moving from the machine-centered computing era of the 1970s and 1980s to a new era in which PC-familiar users demand systems that are user-centered. Previously, a user logged into a mainframe, mini-, or microapplication. The syntax of access was unique in each platform. Function keys, error messages, navigation methods, security, performance, and editing were all very visible. Today's users expect a standard "look and feel." Users log into an application from the desktop with no concern for the location or technology of the processors involved.

Figure 2.3 illustrates the evolution of a user's view of the computing platform. In the 1970s, users logged into the IBM mainframe, the VAX minicomputer, or one of the early microcomputer applications. It was evident which platform was being used. Each platform required a unique login sequence, security parameters, keyboard options, and custom help, navigation, and error recovery. In the current user-centered world, the desktop provides the point of access to the workgroup and enterprise services without regard to the platform of application execution. Standard services such as login, security, navigation, help, and error recovery are provided consistently among all applications.

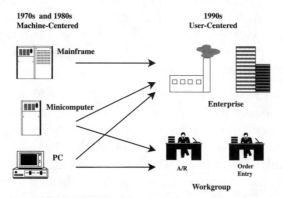

Figure 2.3. The computing transformation.

Developers today are provided with considerable independence. Data is accessed through SQL without regard to the hardware, operating system, or location providing the data. Consistent network access methods envelop the application and SQL requests within an RPC. The network may be based in Open Systems Interconnect (OSI), Transmission Control Protocol/Internet Protocol (TCP/IP), or Systems Network Architecture (SNA), but no changes are required in the business logic coding. The developer of business logic deals with a standard process logic syntax without considering the physical platform. Development languages such as COBOL, C, and Natural, and development tools such as Telon, Ingres 4GL, PowerBuilder, CSP, as well as some evolving CASE tools such as Bachman, Oracle CASE, and Texas Instruments' IEF all execute on multiple platforms and generate applications for execution on multiple platforms.

The application developer deals with the development language and uses a version of SDE customized for the organization to provide standard services. The specific platform characteristics are transparent and subject to change without affecting the application syntax.

Centralized Management

As processing steers away from the central data center to the remote office and plant, workstation server, and local area network (LAN) reliability must approach that provided today by the centrally located mini- and mainframe computers. The most effective way to ensure this is through the provision of monitoring and support from these same central locations. A combination of technologies that can "see" the operation of hardware and software on the LAN—monitored by experienced support personnel—provides the best opportunity to achieve the level of reliability required.

The first step in effectively providing remote LAN management is to establish standards for hardware, software, networking, installation, development, and naming. These standards, used in concert with products such as IBM's Systemview, Hewlett-Packard's Openview, Elegant's ESRA, Digital's EMA, and AT&T's UNMA products, provide the remote view of the LAN. Other tools, such as PC Connect for remote connect, PCAssure from Centel for security, products for hardware and software inventory, and local monitoring tools such as Network General's Sniffer, are necessary for completing the management process.

Technology Revolution

The changes in computer technology that have taken place during the past five years are significantly greater than those of the preceding 35 years of computer history. There is no doubt that we will continue to experience an even greater rate of change during the coming five-year period.

Future Technologies

Consulting a crystal ball, projecting the future, and making decisions based on the projections is a common failure of the computer industry. Predicting the future is a risky business. Industry leaders, technicians, and investors have been equally unsuccessful on occasion. Figures 2.4, 2.5, and 2.6 repeat some of the more familiar quotes from past fortune tellers projecting the future.

It is important, however, to achieve an educated view of where technology is headed during the life of a new system. The architecture on which a new system is built must be capable of supporting all users throughout its life. Large organizations traditionally have assumed that their applications will provide useful service for 5 to 10 years. Many systems are built with a view of only what is available and provable today, and they are ready to fall apart like a deck of cards when the operating environment changes and the architecture cannot adapt to the new realities. Properly architected systems consider not only the reality of today but also an assessment of the likely reality five years after the date of implementation.

Figure 2.4. Workstation market potential. (Source: J. Opel, IBM, 1982.)

Figure 2.5. Technology pessimism. (Source: UNIVAC, 1950, on opportunity for UNIVAC1.)

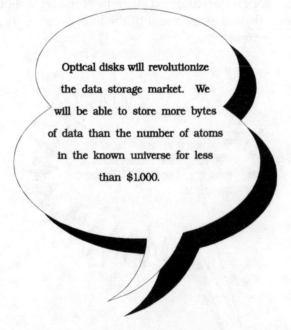

Figure 2.6. Technology optimism. (Source: Anonymous bankrupt investor, 1986.)

Despite predictions that the scope of change in computer technology in the next five years will exceed that seen in the entire computer era (1950 through 1994), a view of history still provides the only mirror we have into the future.

Computing Power Compared

A 1990 survey of U.S. Fortune 1000 companies, completed by a well-known computer industry research firm, found that on an MIPS (millions of instructions per second) basis, more than 90 percent of the processing power available to organizations exists at the desktop. This cheap computing power is typically underused today. It is a sunk cost available to be used as clients in the implementation of client/server applications.

Figure 2.7 illustrates the portion of processor capacity allocated to the central site and the desktop. In most organizations, the 9 percent of processor capacity residing in the "glass house" central computer center provides 90 percent or more of enterprise computing. The 90 percent of processor capacity on the desktop and installed throughout the organization provides less than 10 percent of the processing power to run the business. Most workstation systems are used for personal productivity applications, such as word processing, presentation graphics, and spreadsheet work. The personal productivity functions performed on these machines typically occupy the processor for a maximum of two to three hours per day.

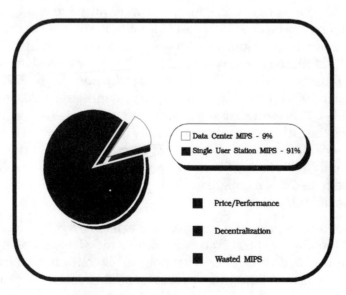

Figure 2.7. Managing the shift to distributed processing.

Input/Output (I/O) Compared

Most applications require information that is manipulated also to be read and saved. In the next example, added to the CPU processing is the requirement to perform 1000 physical data read or write operations per second. Figure 2.8 shows the costs of performing these operations.

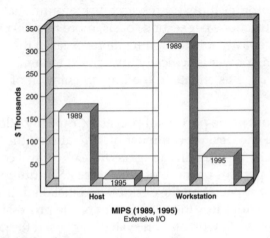

Figure 2.8. The I/O bottleneck.

The same portion of the mainframe configuration required to provide one MIPS execution capability can simultaneously handle this I/O requirement. The workstation configuration required to simultaneously handle these two tasks in 1989 cost at least twice that of the mainframe configuration. In addition, the configuration involved multiple processors without shared memory access. In order to preserve data integrity, the I/O must be read only. The dramatic reduction in workstation cost projected in 1995 is predicated on the use of symmetric multiprocessors to provide CPUs with shared memory and on the use of coprocessors providing the cached controllers necessary to support parallel I/O. (Parallel I/O enables multiple I/O requests to several devices to be serviced concurrently with host CPU processing.) However, the costs are still projected to be 75 percent greater than costs on the mainframe for this high rate of I/O.

The difference in price and functionality is primarily explained by the fact that the IBM 3090-600 is an example of a massively parallel processor optimized to do I/O. Every channel, DASD controller, tape controller, and console contains other processors. The processing capacity of these other processors is three to eight times the processing capacity of the main processor. These processors have direct memory access (DMA) to the shared memory of the configuration, with minimal impact on the processing capacity of the main processor. These processors enable I/O operations to proceed in parallel with little or no main processor involvement.

For the immediate future, forecasts show little slackening in demand for large host processors to provide enterprise database engine services for large companies, especially Fortune 500 firms. Ad hoc processing demands generated by the availability of workplace requestors will further increase the I/O demand. The RISC and Intel processors, as configured today and envisioned over the next five years, continue to use the main processor to perform much of the processing involved in I/O functions. This is an economical strategy for most client applications and many server applications where the I/O demands do not approach those found in large host mainframe configurations. Distributed database technology reduces the demands for I/O against a single database configuration and distributes the I/O with the data to the remote server processors. Despite the dramatic increase in CPU power, there hasn't been a corresponding increase in the capability to do "real" I/O. Some mechanical limitations are not solved by increased CPU power. In fact, the extra CPU merely enables I/O requests to be generated more rapidly.

Figure 2.9 illustrates that CPU to I/O ratios became significantly unbalanced between 1980 and 1990. Between 1980 and 1990, for the same dollar expenditure, processor capacity increased by 100 times while I/O capacity increased by only 18 times. There is no indication that this rate of change will decline in the future. In fact, it is likely that with increased use of symmetric multiprocessors, CPU power availability will increase more rapidly. This in turn will generate even greater I/O demands and further widen the gap.

Only through the effective use of real storage (D-RAM) can we hope to use the available CPU power. Data can be accessed from D-RAM without the need to do physical I/O except to log the update. Database technology uses a sequential log to record changes. These sequential writes can be buffered and done very rapidly. The random updates to the database are done when the system has nothing better to do or when the shared D-RAM containing the updated data is required for other data. The log is used to recover the database after any failure that terminates the application.

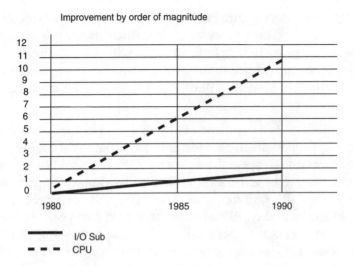

Figure 2.9. *Processor power versus I/O capacity. (Source: International Data Corporation.)*

Another complication in the I/O factor is the steadily decreasing cost of permanent data storage devices. As the cost of traditional data storage devices—disk and tape—decreases, new technologies with massively greater capacity have evolved. Optical storage devices provide greater storage for less cost but with a somewhat slower rate of access than magnetic disk technologies. Most industry experience demonstrates that the amount of data an organization wants to store depends on the cost of storage, not on any finite limit to the amount of data available. If the cost of storage is halved, twice as much data will be available to store for the same budget. This additional data may come from longer histories, external sources, or totally new forms of data, such as image, audio, video, and graphics. New applications may be justified by the reduction in cost of data stores.

Workstation technologies can deal with personal data, data extracted from central systems for analysis by the end user, data from integrated external sources for comparison, and integrated new types of data such as voice annotation to documents. All these data forms provide additional uses for lower-cost, permanent data storage. Decision-support systems can use workstation technologies and massive amounts of additional data to provide useful, market-driven recommendations.

Relational database technologies also can limit the amount of real I/O required to respond to information requests. The use of descriptor indexes that contain data values extracted from columns of the database tables enables search criteria to be evaluated by accessing only the indexes. Access to the physical database itself is required only when the index search results in the identification of rows from the relational table that satisfy the search criteria. Large relational tables, which are accessed through complex searches, can demonstrate dramatically different performance and cost of access depending on the effectiveness of the database search engine. Products such as DB2 and Ingres, which do extensive query optimization, often demonstrate significantly better performance than other products in complex searches. Products that were developed to deal with a small memory model often exhibit dramatic CPU overhead when the size of resident indexes gets very large. DB2 achieves linear improvement in performance as indexes are allocated more D-RAM. Oracle, on the other hand, does not perform well in the IBM System 370 MVS implementation because of its overhead in managing very large main storage buffer pools.

Main Storage

Arguably, the most dramatic technological revolution affecting the computer industry today is caused by the increase in the amount of main storage (D-RAM) available to an application. D-RAM is used for the execution of programs and the temporary storage of permanent data.

Computer users have entered the era of very large and inexpensive D-RAM. Figure 2.10 represents the manner in which this technology has evolved and continues to evolve. Every three years, a new generation of D-RAM technology is released. Each new generation is released with four times the capacity of the previous generation for the same chip price. At the point of introduction and at any given time during its life cycle, the cost of these chips is reduced to a price equal to the price of chips from the previous generation. As the capacity of individual D-RAM chips has increased, the quantity of D-RAM available to the client (and server) has increased massively. Laboratory and manufacturing evidence reveals that this trend will continue at least through 1996.

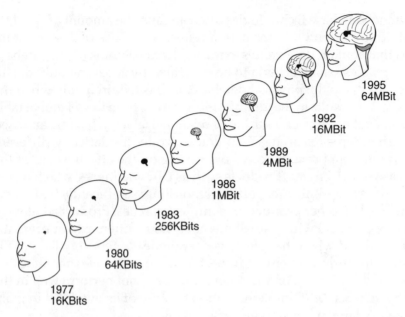

Figure 2.10. *D-RAM chip evolution.*

Desktop workstations purchased in 1988 with 1 megabit (Mbit) D-RAM chips were available in 1992 with 4Mbit DRAM chips for the same or lower cost. In 1988, typical desktop workstations contained 1 to 4 megabytes (Mbytes) of D-RAM. In 1992, these same configurations contain from 4 to 16Mbytes. In 1995, these configurations will use 16Mbit chips and be available with 16 to 64Mbytes for the same price. By 1998—within the life span of many applications being developed today—these configurations will use 64Mbit chips and contain from 64 to 256Mbytes of D-RAM for the same price.

A revolutionary change is occurring in our capability to provide functionality at the desktop. Most developers cannot generate anywhere near the amount of code necessary to fill a 64Mbyte processor on the desk. Yet applications being built today will be used on desktop processors with this amount of D-RAM. As Chapter 3 discusses more fully, the client workstation can now contain in D-RAM all the software that the user will want to use. This eliminates the delay that was previously inherent in program switching—that is, program loading and startup. It is now practical to use a multitasking client workstation with several active tasks and to switch regularly among them. Virtual storage is a reality. Workstation D-RAM costs were less than $50 per megabyte in 1992. The cost difference for an additional 4 megabytes is only $200. Only one year earlier, short-sighted application designers may have made system design decisions based on a cost of $1000 for 4Mbytes.

The same chip densities used for desktop processors are used in host servers. The typical mainframe computer in 1988 contained from 64 to 256Mbytes of D-RAM. In 1992, 256 to 1,024Mbytes were typical. By 1995, these same host servers will contain 1,024 to 4,096Mbytes of D-RAM. After 1998, host servers will contain 4,096 to 16,192Mbytes of D-RAM. These quantities are large enough to mandate that we take a completely different view of the way in which software will be built and information will be managed. During the useful life of systems being conceived today, the I/O bottleneck will be eliminated by the capability to access permanent information from D-RAM.

We are on the verge of the postscarcity era of processor power. In this era, essentially unlimited computing power will become available. With the client/server model, this processing power is available in every workplace—a fundamental paradigm shift to the information-processing industry and to its customers. We expect to see a significant shakeout in the industry as hardware-only vendors respond to these changes. What will this mean for developers and consumers?

- Only manufacturers who offer the lowest prices and who diversify into the software industry will be successful.
- Computer technology consumers are now on the verge of a related paradigm shift in the way computer technology affects their business. Only the most effective users can hope to demonstrate real value in a competitive marketplace.

Software Trends

To achieve the benefit of this advance in technology, organizations must choose software that can use it. Traditional development tools, operating systems, character mode user interfaces, and non-SQL-based database technology cannot take advantage of this quantity of D-RAM and the power available from workstation technology.

Graphical Screen Designs

Graphical user interfaces (GUIs) require large amounts of D-RAM to hold the screen image, pull-down lists, help text, navigation paths, and logic associated with all possible selectable events. Because a GUI enables processing to be selected randomly rather than in the traditional sequential, top-to-bottom order, all possible process logic and GUI management code associated with the image must be available in D-RAM to provide appropriate responses.

GUI functions require subsecond response time. Industry analysis has determined, and our experience confirms, that pull-down lists, button selects, and event invocation should take place within 0.1 second to provide a *suitable* user interface. Suitable means that the user is unaware of the GUI operations but is focused on the business function being performed. This performance is feasibly provided with today's workstations configured with reasonable amounts of $50 per megabyte D-RAM (in 1992) and properly architected applications.

CICS developers do not good GUI developers make.[3] GUI application development requires a special mindset. Education, experience, and imagination are prerequisites for moving from the character mode world to the GUI world. Laying out a character mode screen requires that fields are lined up row to row and the screen is not cluttered with too many fields. GUI layout is more difficult, because there are so many options. Colors, pull-down lists, option buttons, text boxes, scrollbars, check boxes, and multiple windows are all layout capabilities. The skills that a layout artist commonly possesses are more appropriate to the task than those which a programmer usually demonstrates.

Relational Databases

Another dramatic change in software is in the area of database management. Traditional file system and database technologies rely on locality of reference for good performance in accessing data. Locality of reference implies that all data needed to satisfy a request is stored physically close together. However, today's business environment requires multikeyed access to rows of information derived from multiple tables. Performance is only possible in these environments when database searches are performed in main storage using extracted keys organized into searchable lists. Physical access to the database is restricted to the selection of rows that satisfy all search criteria.

Relational database technology, using SQL, best meets these criteria. Despite the protestations symbolized in Figure 2.11, this commonly held

---

[3] *Gary Pollreis of Systemhouse, in frustration after a day spent with first-time GUI designers and developers.*

view of relational technology is no longer valid. This incorrect view is frequently promulgated by those who have invested their careers in becoming experts in nonrelational technology. Experience indicates that in concert with good development standards and current technology, relational systems perform as well or better than previous technologies. In addition to providing independence of the physical storage from the logical view, SQL processors extract the row descriptors (column values) to separate indexes that are managed in main storage. The search request can be evaluated against the indexes to identify the rows that satisfy all search criteria. Only these identified rows are physically retrieved from external storage.

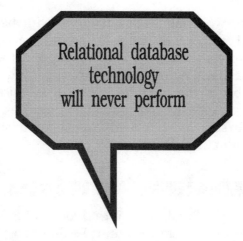

Figure 2.11. Doubting database administrators.

Standards for use are an important part of a successful implementation of any tool. For example, developers can defeat the effectiveness of SQL in the client/server implementation by coding boolean selection criteria with program logic rather than embedded SQL. Boolean selection criteria retrieves all rows that satisfy the first SELECT condition so that the program logic can be executed to filter unwanted rows. When all the application logic and database processing reside on the same processor, this is a manageable overhead. In a client/server implementation, this causes database selection to operate at the LAN or WAN communication rates rather than at the I/O subsystem rates. Frequently, developers—hoping to reduce the overhead of query optimization—use the boolean technique for dynamic SQL, with the unfortunate result that performance is dramatically reduced as the additional physical data access time is incurred. It is important to select tools in the client/server world that generate fully qualified SQL SELECT statements.

Relational systems can and do perform, but poor standards of use can defeat them. An example of successful performance, this book has implemented an application, described in Appendix A, that processes more than 400 update transactions per second into a five-table relational database view. This specific example is implemented under DB2 on a midsize ES9000 processor.

Connectivity

The era of desktop workstations began in 1981 with the introduction of the IBM personal computer (PC). The PC provided early users with the capability to do spreadsheets, word processing, and basic database services for personal data. Within three years, it became clear that high-quality printers, backup tapes, high-capacity disk devices, and software products were too expensive to put on everyone's desktop. LAN technology evolved to solve this problem. Novell is and has been the most successful vendor in the LAN market.

Step 1—Workstations Emulate Corporate Systems

Figure 2.12 shows the trend in the introduction of PCs into organizations during the period from 1980 until 1995. In most large organizations, desktop workstations provide personal productivity and some workgroup functions, but host services still provide most other business functions. The lack of desktop real estate encourages the addition of terminal emulation services to the workstation. This emulation capability connects the workstation directly to the corporate systems. The connection was and generally still is provided by a direct connection from the workstation to the host server or its controller. It is possible to use a sub-$5,000 workstation as a $500 dumb terminal.

Connectivity provides the opportunity to move beyond terminal emulation to use the full potential of the workstation. Often the first client/server applications in a large organization use existing mainframe applications. These are usually presentation services-only applications.

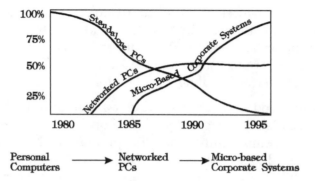

Figure 2.12. Trends in PC-micro expenditures.

Step 2—Adding Servers for Database and Communications

The next step in connectivity is the implementation of specialized servers to provide database and communications services. These servers provide LAN users with a common database for shared applications and with a shared node to connect into the corporate network. The communications servers eliminate the need for extra cabling and workstation hardware to enable terminal emulation. The LAN cabling provides the necessary physical connection, and the communications server provides the necessary controller services.

Step 3—Full-Fledged Client/Server Applications

With its implementation of communications and database servers in place, an organization is ready for the next step up from presentation services-only client/server applications to full-fledged client/server applications. These new applications are built on the architecture defined as part of the system development environment (SDE).

User Productivity

Personal computer users are accustomed to being in control of their environment. Recently, users have been acclimated to the GUI provided by products such as Windows 3.x, OPEN LOOK, MacOS, and NeXtStep.

Productivity is enhanced by the standard look and feel that most applications running in these environments provide. A user is trained both to get into applications and to move from function to function in a standard way. Users are accustomed to the availability of context-sensitive help, "friendly" error handling, rapid performance, and flexibility.

Compare the productivity achieved by a financial or budget analyst using a spreadsheet program such as Lotus 1-2-3 or Excel to that achieved when similar functionality is programmed in COBOL on a mainframe. Adding a new variable to an analysis or budget is a trivial task compared to the effort of making functions perform a similar change in the mainframe-based COBOL package. In the first instance, the change is made directly by the user who is familiar with the requirement into a visible model of the problem. In the instance of the mainframe, the change must be made by a programmer, who discusses the requirement with the analyst, attempts to understand the issues, and then tries to make the change using an abstraction of the problem.

The personal computer user makes the change and sees the result. The mainframe programmer must make the change, compile the program, invoke the program, and run the test. If the user understands the request, the implications, and the syntactical requirements, he or she may get it right the first time. Usually, it takes several iterations to actually get it right, often in concert with a frustrated user who tries to explain the real requirement.

We aren't suggesting that all applications can be developed by nonprogrammers using desktop-only tools. However, now that it has become rather easy to build these types of applications on the desktop, it is important for professional IS people to understand the expectations raised in the minds of the end-user community.

Ways to Improve Performance

Client/server-developed applications may achieve substantially greater performance when compared with traditional workstations or host-only applications.

Offload Work to Server

Database and communications processing are frequently offloaded to a faster server processor. Some applications processing also may be offloaded, particularly for a complex process, which is required by many users. The advantage of offloading is realized when the processing power of the server is significantly greater than that of the client workstation. Shared databases or specialized communications interfaces are best supported by separate processors. Thus, the client workstation is available to handle other client tasks. These advantages are best realized when the client workstation supports multitasking or at least easy and rapid task switching.

Reduce Total Execution Time

Database searches, extensive calculations, and stored procedure execution can be performed in parallel by the server while the client workstation deals directly with the current user needs. Several servers can be used together, each performing a specific function. Servers may be multiprocessors with shared memory, which enables programs to overlap the LAN functions and database search functions. In general, the increased power of the server enables it to perform its functions faster than the client workstation. In order for this approach to reduce the total elapsed time, the additional time required to transmit the request over the network to the server must be less than the saving. High-speed local area network topologies operating at 4, 10, 16, or 100Mbs (megabits per second) provide high-speed communications to manage the extra traffic in less time than the savings realized from the server. The time to transmit the request to the server, execute the request, and transmit the result to the requestor, must be less than the time to perform the entire transaction on the client workstation.

Use a Multitasking Client

As workstation users become more sophisticated, the capability to be simultaneously involved in multiple processes becomes attractive. Independent tasks can be activated to manage communications processes, such as electronic mail, electronic feeds from news media and the stock exchange, and remote data collection (downloading from remote servers). Personal productivity applications, such as word processors, spreadsheets, and presentation graphics, can be active. Several of these applications can be dynamically linked together to provide the desktop information processing environment. Functions such as Dynamic Data Exchange (DDE) and Object Linking and Embedding (OLE) permit including spreadsheets dynamically into word-processed documents. These links can be *hot* so that changes in the spreadsheet cause the word-processed document to be updated, or they can be *cut and paste* so that the current status of the spreadsheet is copied into the word-processed document.

Systems developers appreciate the capability to create, compile, link, and test programs in parallel. The complexity introduced by the integrated CASE environment requires multiple processes to be simultaneously active so the workstation need not be dedicated to a single long-running function. Effective use of modern CASE tools and workstation development products requires a client workstation that supports multitasking.

How to Reduce Network Traffic

Excessive network traffic is one of the most common causes of poor system performance. Designers must take special care to avoid this potential calamity.

Minimize Network Requests

In the centralized host model, network traffic is reduced to the input and output of presentation screens. In the client/server model, it is possible to introduce significantly more network traffic if detailed consideration is not given to the requestor-server interface.

In the file server model, as implemented by many database products, such as dBASE IV, FoxPro, Access, and Paradox, a search is processed in the client workstation. Record-level requests are transmitted to the server, and all filtering is performed on the workstation. This has the effect of causing all rows that cannot be explicitly filtered by primary key selection to be sent to the client workstation for rejection. In a large database, this action can be dramatic. Records that are owned by a client cannot be updated by another client without integrity conflicts. An in-flight transaction might lock records for hours if the client user leaves the workstation without completing the transaction. For this reason, the file server model breaks down when there are many users, or when the database is large and multikey access is required.

However, with the introduction of specific database server products in the client/server implementation, the search request is packaged and sent to the database server for execution. The SQL syntax is very powerful and—when combined with server trigger logic—enables all selection and rejection logic to execute on the server. This approach ensures that the answer set returns only the selected rows and has the effect of reducing the amount of traffic between the server and client on the LAN. (To support the client/server model, dBASE IV, FoxPro, and Paradox products have been retrofitted to be SQL development tools for database servers.)

The performance advantages available from the client/server model of SQL services can be overcome. For example, if by using an unqualified SQL SELECT, all rows satisfying the request are returned to the client for further analysis. Minimally qualified requests that rely on the programmer's logic at the workstation for further selection can be exceedingly dangerous. Quite possibly, 1 million rows from the server can be returned to the client only to be reduced by the client to 10 useful rows. The JOIN function in SQL that causes multiple tables to be logically combined into a single table can be dangerous if users don't understand the operation of the database engine.

A classic problem with dynamic SQL is illustrated by a request to Oracle to JOIN a 10-row table at the client with a 1-million-row table at the server. Depending on the format of the request, either 10 useful rows may be transferred to the client or 1 million rows may be transferred so that the useless 999,990 can be discarded. You might argue that a competent programmer should know better; however, this argument breaks down when the requestor is a business analyst. Business analysts should not be expected to work out the intricacies of SQL syntax. Their tools must protect them from this complexity. (Some DBMSs are now making their optimizers more intelligent to deal with just these cases. So, it is important to look beyond transaction volumes when looking at DBMS engines.) If your business requirement necessitates using these types of dynamic SQL requests, it is important, when creating an SDE, that the architecture definition step selects products that have strong support for query optimization. Products such as Ingres are optimized for this type of request.

Online Transaction Processing (OLTP) in the client/server model requires products that use views, triggers, and stored procedures. Products such as Sybase, Ellipse, and Ingres use these facilities at the host server to perform the join, apply edit logic prior to updates, calculate virtual columns, or perform complex calculations. Wise use of OLTP can significantly reduce the traffic between client and server and use the powerful CPU capabilities of the server. Multiprocessor servers with shared memory are available from vendors such as Compaq, Hewlett Packard, and Sun. These enable execution to be divided between processors. CPU-intensive tasks such as query optimization and stored procedures can be separated from the database management processes.

Ease Strain on Network Resources

The use of application and database servers to produce the answer set required for client manipulation will dramatically reduce network traffic. There is no value in moving data to the client when it will be rejected there. The maximum reduction in network overhead is achieved when the only data returned to the client is that necessary to populate the presentation screen. Centralized operation, as implemented in minicomputer and mainframe environments, requires every computer interaction with a user to transfer screen images between the host and the workstation. When the minicomputer or mainframe is located geographically distant from the client workstation, WAN services are invoked to move the screen image. Client/server applications can reduce expensive WAN overhead by using the LAN to provide local communications services between the client workstation and the server. Many client/server applications use mixed LAN and WAN services: some information is managed on the LAN and some on the WAN. Application design must evaluate the requirements of each application to determine the most effective location for application and database servers.

How to Reduce Costs

Cost of operation is always a major design factor. Appropriate choice of technology and allocation of the work to be done can result in dramatic cost reduction.

Each mainframe user requires a certain amount of the expensive mainframe CPU to execute the client portion of the application. Each CICS user uses CPU cycles, disk queues, and D-RAM. These same resources are orders of magnitude cheaper on the workstation. If the same or better functionality can be provided by using the workstation as a client, significant savings can be realized. Frequently existing workstations currently used for personal productivity applications, such as terminal emulation, e-mail, word processing, and spreadsheet work may be used for mission-critical applications. The additional functionality of the client portion of a new application can thus be added without buying a new workstation. In this case, the cost savings of offloading mainframe processing can be substantial.

When you use a communications server on a LAN, each client workstation does not need to contain the hardware and software necessary to connect to the WAN. Communications servers can handle up to 128 clients for the cost of approximately six client communications cards and software. Despite the dramatic reductions in the price of D-RAM, companies will continue to need their existing client workstations. These devices may not be capable of further D-RAM upgrades, or it may not be feasible from a maintenance perspective to upgrade each device. The use of server technology to provide some of the functionality currently provided within a client workstation frees up valuable D-RAM for use by the client applications. This is particularly valuable for DOS-based clients.

The WAN communications functions and LAN services may each be offloaded in certain implementations. The use of WAN communications servers has the additional advantage of providing greater functionality from the dedicated communications server.

Vendor Independence

If client and server functionality is clearly split and standards-based access is used, there can be considerable vendor independence among application components. Most organizations use more expensive and more reliable workstations from a mainstream vendor such as Compaq, IBM, Apple, Sun, or Hewlett-Packard for their servers. Other organizations view client workstation technology as a commodity and select lower-priced and possibly less-reliable vendor equipment. The mainstream vendors have realized this trend and are providing competitively priced client workstations. Each of the mainstream vendors reduced its prices by at least 65 percent between 1991-93, primarily in response to an erosion of market share for client workstations.

The controversy over whether to move from offering a high-priced but best-quality product line to offering a more competitive commodity traumatized the industry in 1991, forcing Compaq to choose between retaining its founder as CEO or replacing him with a more fiscally aware upstart.

The resulting shakeout in the industry has significantly reduced the number of vendors and makes the use of traditionally low priced clones very risky. Hardware can generally be supported by third-party engineers, but software compatibility is a serious concern as organizations find they are unable to install and run new products.

The careful use of SQL and RPC requests enable database servers and application services to be used without regard to the vendor of the database engine or the application services platform. As noted previously, the operating system and hardware platform of the server can be kept totally independent of the client platform through the proper use of an SDE. However, use of these types of technologies can vastly complicate the development process.

An excellent example of this independence is the movement of products such as FoxPro and Paradox to use client services to invoke, through SQL, the server functions provided by Sybase SQL Server. A recent survey of client development products that support the Sybase SQL Server product identified 129 products. This is a result of the openness of the API provided by Sybase. Oracle also has provided access to its API, and several vendors—notably Concentric Data Systems, SQL Solutions, and DataEase—have developed front-end products for use with Oracle. ASK also has realized the importance of open access to buyers and is working with vendors such as Fox and PowerBuilder to port their front ends in support of the Ingres database engine.

An application developed to run in a single PC or file server mode can be migrated without modification to a client/server implementation using a database server. Sybase, Oracle, and Ingres execute transparently under Windows NT, OS/2, or UNIX on many hardware platforms. With some design care, the server platform identity can be transparent to the client user or developer. Despite this exciting opportunity, programmers or manufacturers often eliminate this transparency by incorporating UNIX-, Windows NT-, or OS/2-specific features into the implementation. Although FoxPro can work with SQL and Sybase, the default Xbase format for database access does not use SQL and therefore does not offer this independence. To take advantage of this platform transparency, organizations must institute standards into their development practices.

Faster Delivery of Systems

Some software development and systems integration vendors have had considerable success using client/server platforms for the development of systems targeted completely for mainframe execution. These developer workstations are often the first true client/server applications implemented by many organizations. The workstation environment, powerful multitasking CPU availability, single-user databases, and integrated testing tools all combine to provide the developer with considerable productivity improvements in a lower-cost environment. Our analysis shows that organizations that measure the "real" cost of mainframe computing will cost justify workstation development environments in 3 to 12 months.

Client/server application development shows considerable productivity improvement when the software is implemented within an SDE. As previously noted, organizational standards-based development provides the basis for object-oriented development techniques and considerable code reuse. This is particularly relevant in the client/server model, because some natural structuring takes place with the division of functionality between the client and server environments. Reuse of the server application functionality, database, and network services is transparent and almost automatic. Because the applications are built with little regard to standard front-end functionality, many features are part of the standard GUI and are automatically reused.

Smaller and Simpler Problems

Client/server applications frequently are involved with data creation or data analysis. In such applications, the functionality is personal to a single user or a few users. These applications frequently can be created using standard desktop products with minimal functionality. For example, data may be captured directly into a form built with a forms development tool, edited by a word processor, and sent on through the e-mail system to a records management application. In the back end, data may be downloaded to a workstation for spreadsheet analysis.

Less Bureaucratic Inertia

Mainframes provide the stable, reliable environment that is desirable and necessary for production execution. This same stability is the bane of developers who require rapid changes to their test environments. The workstation environment is preferable because it is personal and responds to the user's priorities. Developers can make changes at their own pace and then deal with the mainframe bureaucracy if and when the application goes into production in the mainframe environment.

Many users typically run applications on the mainframe. Changes made to such applications affect all their users. In some instances, the entire mainframe may be unavailable during the implementation of a new application. Network reconfiguration, database utilities, application definition, and system software maintenance all can impact users beyond those specifically involved in a change. It is awkward to migrate only a portion of the users from the previous implementation to the new one. Typically, it is all or none of the users who must upgrade. This change process requires thorough and all-encompassing tests and careful control over the move to production.

The client/server environment provides more flexibility for phased implementation of the new production environment. The application is replicated at many different locations so the users may implement the new software individually rather than all at once. This environment adds the additional and significant complication of multiple updates. New products are now available from vendors such as Synchrony, Hewlett-Packard, and IBM that automate and control this function.

Workgroup client/server applications frequently are used by fewer users. These users can be directly supported by the developer immediately after implementation. Corrections can be made and reimplemented more readily. This is not to suggest that in the client/server world change and production control procedures are not necessary, only that they can be less onerous for workgroup applications. Remote LAN management will be required for enterprise applications implemented throughout the corporation. Only in this way will support equivalent to that available today for host-based applications be available to remote client/server users.

Components of Client/
Server Applications
The Client

Components of Client/ Server Applications— The Client

3

Executive Summary

The client in the client/server model is the desktop workstation. Any workstation that is used by a single user is a client. The same workstation, when shared simultaneously by multiple users, is a server. An Apple Macintosh SE, an IBM PS/2 Model 30, an ALR 386/220, a Compaq SystemPro, an NCD X-Terminal, a Sun Sparcstation, a DECstation 5000—all are used somewhere as a client workstation. There is no specific technological characteristic of a client.

During the past 10 years, workstation performance improved dramatically. For the same cost, workstation CPU performance increased by 50 times, main memory has increased by 25 times, and permanent disk storage has increased by 30 times. This growth in power allows much more sophisticated applications to be run from the desktop.

Communications and network speeds have improved equally in the last 10 years. In 1984, the performance and reliability of remote file, database, and print services were inadequate to support business applications. With the advent of high-speed local and wide area networks (LANs and WANs), networking protocols, digital switches, and fiber-optic cabling, both performance and reliability improved substantially. It is now practical to use these remote services as part of a critical business application.

The client workstation may use the DOS, Windows, Windows NT, OS/2, MacOS (also referred to as System 7), or UNIX operating system. The client workstation frequently provides personal productivity functions, such as word processing, which use only the hardware and software resident right on the workstation. When the client workstation is connected to a LAN, it has access to the services provided by the network operating system (NOS) in addition to those provided by the client workstation. The workstation may load software and save word-processed documents from a server and therefore use the file server functions provided through the NOS. It also can print to a remote printer through the NOS. The client workstation may be used as a terminal to access applications resident on a host minicomputer or mainframe processor. This enables the single workstation to replace the terminal, as well as provide client workstation functionality.

In a client/server application, functions are provided by a combination of resources using both the client workstation processor and the server processor. For example, a database server provides data in response to an SQL request issued by the client application. Local processing by the client might calculate the invoice amount and format the response to the workstation screen.

Client workstations can provide business functions using a mixture of personal productivity products in conjunction with a custom application. For example, a document created by a word processor can include input from a spreadsheet program and the invoice data created by the client/server application. The capability to cut and paste input from several different sources is one of the most powerful aspects of a client workstation. It provides the end user with tools to create new applications—without the need to go to professional programmers for assistance.

The Role of the Client

In the client/server model, the client is primarily a consumer of services provided by one or more server processors. The model provides a clear separation of functions based on the idea of servers acting as service providers responding to requests from clients. It is important to understand that a workstation can operate as a client in some instances while acting as a server in other instances. For example, in a LAN Manager environment, a workstation might act as a client for one user while simultaneously acting as a print server for many users. This chapter discusses the client functions.

The client almost always provides presentation services. User input and final output, if any, are presented at the client workstation. Current technology provides cost effective support for a graphical user interface (GUI). This book recommends that all new applications, with direct interaction by a human, be developed using a GUI. The windowing environment enables the client user to be involved in several simultaneous sessions. Such functions as word processing, spreadsheet, e-mail, and presentation graphics—in addition to the custom applications built by the organization—can be active simultaneously. Windows 3.x and Mac System 7 do not support true multitasking; thus, only one task at a time can safely be engaged in a communications session. Windows NT, OS/2, and UNIX are preemptive multitasking operating systems and thus will support any number of active communications sessions.

Facilities such as Dynamic Data Exchange (DDE), Object Level Embedding (OLE), and Communicating Object Request Broker Architecture (CORBA), which are discussed later in this chapter, provide support for cut-and-paste operations between word processors, databases, spreadsheets, and graphics in a windowing environment. Beyond this, a selectable set of tasks may be performed at the client. In fact, the client workstation can be both client and server when all information and logic pertinent to a request is resident and operates within the client workstation.

Software to support specific functions—for example, field edits, context-sensitive help, navigation, training, personal data storage, and manipulation—frequently executes on the client workstation. All these functions use the GUI and windowing functionality. Additional business logic for calculations, selection, and analysis can reside on the client workstation.

A client workstation uses a local operating system to host both basic services and the network operating system interfaces. This operating system may be the same or different from that of the server. Most personal computer users today use DOS or Windows 3.x as their client operating system, because current uses are primarily personal productivity applications—not ones requiring a client/server.

Those users running client/server applications from DOS or Windows typically run only a single business process at a time. However, the demand to use these familiar operating systems is driving the development of client/server tools such as PowerBuilder for Windows, and new multitasking versions of Windows (such as Windows NT, Windows 4—expected to be available in late 1994—and Cairo, expected in late 1995). Fortunately, the advent of products such as Digitalk's Parts and Parc Place's Visual Works provide development tools that are equally happy running in the Windows 3.x or OS/2, UNIX, and Windows NT worlds.

Because UNIX and OS/2 have lacked the familiar personal productivity tools such as word processors, e-mail, spreadsheets, presentation graphics, and database management systems, DOS and Windows have become the client operating systems of choice. Until recently, few personal productivity applications for OS/2 and UNIX were in place, and client/server requirements that dictate OS/2 and UNIX were not evident. Now, improvements in the capability of these operating systems to run personal productivity applications, and increased user needs for high reliability or for multitasking has increased the popularity of OS/2, X-Terminals, and UNIX. Native execution of Windows 3.1 applications under Windows NT, OS/2, and many UNIX implementations offers the best of all worlds for the desktop user: reliability and functionality.

The current availability of OS/2 Version 2.1, UNIX, and Windows NT with integrated support for DOS, Windows 3.x, and X-Windows—as well as support for multitasking in a reliable environment—is a continuing reason for making these the client operating systems the choice for developing business critical client/server applications. As noted, the dramatic reduction in processor and D-RAM costs make the extra resources required for OS/2, UNIX, and Windows NT minimal. Finally, the software licensing costs for OS/2 2.x, UNIX from Sun and USL are comparable to that for DOS and Windows 3.x.

UNIX supports many of the most familiar personal computer applications, such as Lotus 1-2-3, WordPerfect, and dBASE IV. This fact—

coupled with the availability of low-cost, high-performance RISC processors—is making UNIX a strong contender as a client for client/server applications. During 1994-1995, it is expected that multitasking desktops provided by Windows NT, Windows 4.x, UNIX, and OS/2 will become the operating systems of choice for clients in a client/server environment. Selection between Windows versions, UNIX, and OS/2 will be made on the basis of cost performance rather than functionality. Previously purchased PC limitations will encourage many organizations to remain with Windows 4 and OS/2 rather than Windows NT or UNIX, which might require new hardware acquisitions. OSF/1 (a commercial-grade UNIX) is now available for the Intel platform and is causing organizations to reexamine the use of UNIX on the PC. The current licensing costs for OS/2 may give OS/2 the edge unless OSF/1 costs are much less than current UNIX licenses.

The Common Open Software Environment (COSE) group of UNIX kernel vendors has agreed on a common set of API's for most UNIX services. This allows application developers to build one application for all platforms. This will serve to expand the number of applications that will run across the various UNIX platforms. In turn, this will increase the use of UNIX on the desktop and subsequently reduce the per-seat cost.

Windows 3.x is by far the dominant GUI and even with its single tasking limitations, it is a leading client operating system candidate for client/server applications. Microsoft's Windows 4, the planned upgrade for Windows 3.x, is discussed more fully in Appendix B. It will provide a client platform that can better use the capabilities of the new generation of Intel processors while continuing to provide the GUI and API's of Windows 3.x. This operating system is likely to gain a significant share of the client user base in 1995. The complexity and resource requirements of Windows NT suggest it will not displace many Windows desktops prior to the availability of Windows 4.

In terms of known "wild cards" for the client OS, IBM and Apple have formed an alliance with Motorola to develop a new client operating system in a venture known now as Taligent. This new OS is based on AIX, OS/2, and Mac System 7. The result should be a client platform with the ease of use interface of Mac System 7, and the functionality and connectivity of AIX and OS/2. (This subject is discussed more fully in Chapter 10.) This initiative will bear fruit during 1994 and will compete during 1995 for the role of preferred client platform. Microsoft's competitor in this market, currently code named Cairo, will reach the market in late 1995 and will compete during 1996 for the multitasking desktop market.

With the uncertainty surrounding the operating system alternatives, it is important that all development be done with an SDE that isolates the operating system from the application. Then, if operating system changes are warranted the applications should be able to port without any impact beyond recompilation.

Client Services

The ideal client/server platform operates in an open systems environment using a requester-server discipline that is based on well-defined standards. This enables multiple hardware and software platforms to interact. When the standard requester-server discipline is adhered to, servers may grow and change their operating system and hardware platforms without changing the client applications. Clients can be entry-level Intel 386SX machines or very powerful RISC-based workstations, and run the same application issuing the same requests for service as long as the standard requester-server discipline is adhered to. Traditional host applications that use the client for presentation services operate only by sending and receiving a character data stream to and from a server. All application logic resides on the server. This is the manner in which many organizations use workstation technology today. The expensive mainframe CPU is being used to handle functions that are much more economically provided by the workstation.

First-generation client/server applications using software such as Easel enable the input and output data streams to be reformatted at the client without changes to the host applications. They use an API that defines the data stream format. Easel uses the IBM-defined Extended High Level Language Application Program Interface (EHLLAPI). GUI front ends may add additional functionality, such as the capability to select items for input from a list, selectively use color, or merge other data into the presentation without changing the host application.

An example of this form of client is an application developed for the emergency command and control services required by E911 dispatch applications. This computer application supports calls to the 911 emergency telephone number and dispatches fire, police, ambulance, or emergency vehicles to an incident. This application traditionally has been implemented on a fault-tolerant minicomputer with access provided from a character mode dumb terminal. The information is displayed in list form, and the operator can move the cursor to an item on the list for selection or rekey the data for input. Prior implementations of this application handled the address of the caller by displaying it on the screen as a text field.

In the client/server implementation of this system, the workstation user deals only with a GUI. The workstation plots this address onto a map that in turn displays the location of the fire. In addition, the locations of all fire stations and vehicles are plotted on the map. The dispatch operator can see at a glance the entire status of fire support close to the fire. Previous implementations of this application displayed lists of optional fire vehicles. From this list, the operator keyed in a selected vehicle. The GUI front end, however, enables the vehicles to be shown in a window and selected by using a mouse pointer. This not only reduces the cost of execution but can significantly reduce errors, increase productivity, and reduce stress experienced by the dispatch operator.

GUIs enable users to be more productive with less training, because the interface is more intuitive. Several studies comparing the productivity and learning curve for users of GUI applications versus traditional character mode applications have demonstrated improvements of greater than 200 percent.

The functionality of the client process can be further extended at the client by adding logic that is not implemented in the host server application. Local editing, automatic data entry, help capabilities, and other logic processes can be added in front of the existing host server application. If many errors are detected at the client, or functions such as online help are completely off loaded, the workload of the host server decreases. There is an opportunity to provide extensive interactive help and training integrated into a client/server application using only the services of the client workstation and NOS.

One example of this functionality is shown by an application developed for the state of Hawaii. To determine welfare eligibility, state employees conduct an extensive analysis of each applicant's personal situation. The process of capturing this information is time-consuming and stressful for the case worker and the applicant. Hawaii addressed this requirement by using an "unattended" kiosk for the interview—an interactive video unit provides the questions and displays a set of possible responses. Users enter responses on a touch screen and can respond to the questions at their own rate. The case worker is not tied up with the mechanics of filling out the questionnaire, and the state has the opportunity through the interactive video to ensure that applicants are aware of all their rights and responsibilities. The case worker and applicant review the application after it is completed. The existing computer system captures and edits the data and performs the final eligibility determination. A dramatically different and more effective user interface is provided while preserving much of the investment in existing computer systems.

Completion of multipart forms often involves redundant data entry into multiple computer systems or applications. Collecting this data at the source or into a common data entry function and distributing it to the other data entry functions can reduce costs and errors. Ideally, the information is entered by the individual or process responsible for the data creation. This enables the individual with the knowledge to make corrections and to do so immediately. The workgroup LAN server captures the data and stores it. When a business process defined to capture data from one copy of the form is invoked, the stored data is automatically merged into the form. This is updated, by the user, with additional data that is now available. In this manner, data is keyed only once and every business process uses the same data. Information is made available immediately after capture and can be distributed electronically to all authorized users.

It is possible to make fundamental changes in the business process, using a Business Process Reengineering (BPR) methodology and client/server computing. One such example uses electronic imaging. Many firms have found that it pays to put a series of steps that formerly involved different people handling each step, onto the shoulders of a single "case worker." One insurance company, for example, estimated that it took 22 days to approve a policy, during which time the papers were worked on for only 17 minutes. The remainder of the time was spent shuffling papers between specialists—from credit-checkers to actuaries to salespeople and back. By enabling everyone in an organization to share information more or less instantly, new technology highlights the fact that most insurance policies never need be seen by most of these specialists. As long as specialists can be consulted quickly when needed, the vast majority of policies can be handled by a single person. Mutual Benefit Life used such a procedure to boost productivity among clerical staff by 60 percent.[1]

---

[1]"*Reinventing Companies,*" The Economist *321, NO. 7728 (October 12, 1991), pp. 67-68.*

Another commonly used technique to leverage the power and ease of use of the workstation is provided by tools, such as Trinzic's Forest & Trees. These tools provide easy-to-use facilities to manipulate data either stored on the existing host databases or downloaded to local servers. This technique of "data mining" through the use of powerful developer tools to provide rapid development of new management decision support functions, portends the future for systems development. Future developers will be *knowledge workers* —technologists with an equally strong business understanding using tools that are intuitive and powerful. Data will be provided to the workstation user in a form consistent with his or her business understanding.

Why is workstation technology so effective? It supports the new business paradigm of employee empowerment. It provides the windowing capabilities to simultaneously access and display all information necessary to complete the business process. The capability of powerful workstation technology to recommend and make decisions based on historical precedent can dramatically reduce cost and improve service by shortening the decision-making cycle.

Request for Service

Client workstations request services from the attached server. Whether this server is in fact the same processor or a network processor, the application format of the request is the same. NOS software translates or adds the specifics required by the targeted requester to the application request.

Interprocess communication (IPC) is the generic term used to describe communication between running processes. In the client/server model, these processes might be on the same computer, across the LAN, or across the WAN.

The most basic service provided by the NOS is *redirection*. This service intercepts client workstation operating system calls and redirects them to the server operating system. In this way, requests for disk directories, disk files, printers, printer queues, serial devices, application programs, and named pipes are trapped by the redirection software and redirected (over the LAN) to the correct server location. It is still possible for some of these services to be provided by the client workstation. The local disk drives may be labeled A: and C: and the remote drives labeled D:, E:, and F:.

How does redirection work?

1. Any request for drive A: or C: is passed through to the local file system by the redirection software. Requests for other drives are passed to the server operating system. Printers are accessed through virtual serial and parallel ports defined by the NOS redirector software.
2. The NOS requester software constructs the remote procedure call (RPC) to include the API call to the NOS server.
3. The NOS server then processes the request as if it were executed locally and ships the response back to the application.

Novell commercialized this redirector concept for the Intel and MS-DOS platforms, and it has been adopted by all NOS and UNIX network file system (NFS) vendors. The simplicity of executing standard calls to a virtual network of services is its main advantage.

Remote Procedure Call (RPC)

Over the years, good programmers have developed modular code using structured techniques and subroutine logic. Today, developers want subroutines to be stored as a named objects "somewhere" and made available to everyone with the right to use them. Remote procedure calls (RPCs) provide this capability. RPCs standardize the way programmers must write calls, so that remote procedures can recognize and respond correctly.

If an application issues a functional request and this request is embedded in an RPC, the requested function can be located anywhere in the enterprise that the caller is authorized to access. The RPC facility provides for the invocation and execution of requests from processors running different operating systems and using hardware platforms different from that of the caller. Many RPCs also provide data translation services. The call causes dynamic translation of data between processors with different physical data storage formats. These standards are evolving and being adopted by the industry.

Fax/Print Services

The NOS enables the client to generate print requests even when the printer is busy. These are redirected by the NOS redirector software and managed by the print server queue manager. The client workstation can view the status of the print queues at any time. Many print servers notify the client workstation when the print request is completed. Fax services are made available in exactly the same manner as print servers, with the same requester server interface and notification made available.

Window Services

A client workstation may have several windows open on-screen at any time. The capability to activate, view, move, size, or hide a particular window is provided by the window services of the client operating system. These services are essential in a client/server implementation, because they interact with message services provided to notify the user of events that occur on a server. Application programs are written with no sensitivity to the windowing. Each application is written with the assumption that it has a virtual screen. This virtual screen can be an arbitrary size and can even be larger than the physical screen.

The application, using GUI software, places data into the virtual screen, and the windowing services handle placement and manipulation of the application window. This greatly simplifies application development, because there is no need for the developer to build or manage the windowing services. The client user is totally in control of his or her desktop and can give priority to the most important tasks at hand simply by positioning the window of interest to the "front and center." The NOS provides software on the client workstation to manage the creation of pop-up windows that display alerts generated from remote servers. E-mail receipt, print complete, Fax available, and application termination are examples of alerts that might generate a pop-up window to notify the client user.

Remote Boot Services

Some applications operate well on workstations without any local disk storage; X-terminals and workstations used in secure locations are examples. The client workstation must provide sufficient software burned into erasable programmable read-only memory (E-PROM) to start the initial program load (IPL)—that is, boot—process. E-PROM is included in all workstations to hold the Basic Input/Output System (BIOS) services. This mini-operating system is powerful enough to load the remote software that provides the remaining services and applications functions to the client workstation or X-terminal.

Other Remote Services

Applications can be invoked from the client to execute remotely on a server. Backup services are an example of services that might be remotely invoked from a client workstation. Business functions such as downloading data from a host or checking a list of stock prices might also be invoked locally to run remotely. Software is provided by the NOS to run on the client workstation to initiate these remote applications.

Mobile computing is increasingly being used to remain functional while out of the office. With appropriate architectural forethought, applications can be built to operate effectively from the office LAN or the remote laptop. Current technology supports full-powered workstations with the capability for GUI applications consistent with the desktop implementation. The IPC protocol of choice for mobile access is TCP/IP based.

Utility Services

The operating system provides local functions such as copy, move, edit, compare, and help that execute on the client workstation.

Message Services

Messages can be sent and received synchronously to or from the network. The message services provide the buffering, scheduling, and arbitration services to support this function.

Network Services

The client workstation communicates with the network through a set of services and APIs that create, send, receive, and format network messages. These services provide support for communications protocols, such as NetBIOS, IPX, TCP/IP, APPC, Ethernet, Token Ring, FDDI, X.25, and SNA. These are more fully described in Chapter 5, "Components of Client/Server Applications—Connectivity."

Application Services

In addition to the remote execution services that the NOS provides, custom applications will use their own APIs embedded in an RPC to invoke specialized services from a remote server.

Database Services

Database requests are made using the SQL syntax. SQL is an industry standard language supported by many vendors. Because the language uses a standard form, the same application may be run on multiple platforms. There are syntactical differences and product extensions available from most vendors. These are provided to improve developer productivity and system performance and should be carefully evaluated to determine whether their uses are worth the incompatibility implied by using proprietary components. Using unique features may prevent the use of another vendor's products in a larger or smaller site. Certain extensions, such as stored procedures, are evolving into *de facto* standards.

The use of stored procedures is often a way of avoiding programmer use of proprietary extensions needed for performance. A clear understanding, by the technical architects on the project, of where the standards are going is an important component of the SDE standards for the project.

Network Management Services-Alerts

Most network interface cards (NICs) can generate alerts to signify detected errors and perhaps to signify messages sent and received. These alerts are valuable in remote LAN management to enable early detection of failures. Because many errors are transient at first, simple remote detection may allow problems to be resolved before they become critical. Applications may also generate alerts to signify real or potential problems. Certain error conditions indicate that important procedures are not being followed. Application program failure may occur because current versions of software are not being used.

Support for a remote client workstation may be greatly simplified if alerts are generated by the applications. This should be part of every standard SDE. Many alert situations can be generated automatically from standard code without the involvement of the application developer. A more complete discussion of network management issues is included in the communications section of Chapter 5.

Dynamic Data Exchange (DDE)

DDE is a feature of Windows 3.x and OS/2 Presentation Manager that enables users to pass data between applications from different vendors through support for common APIs. For example, a charting package can be linked to a database to provide the latest chart data whenever the chart is referenced.

Object Linking and Embedding (OLE)

OLE is an extension to DDE that enables objects to be created with the object components software *aware*. Aware means that a reference to the object or one of its components automatically launches the appropriate software to manipulate the data. For example, a document created with a word processor may include an image created by a graphics package. The image can be converted to the internal graphics form of the word processor, such as WPG form for WordPerfect. With OLE, the image can be included in its original form within the document object; whenever the image is selected or highlighted, the graphics package will take control to manipulate the image. Activation of the software is totally transparent to the users as they navigate through the document.

Currently with OLE, one software package accesses data created from another through the use of a *viewer* or *launcher*. These viewers and launchers must be custom built for every application. With the viewer, users can see data from one software package while they are running another package. Launchers invoke the software package that created the data and thus provide the full functionality of the launched software.

Both these techniques require the user to be aware of the difference between data sources. DDE and OLE provide a substantial advantage: any DDE- or OLE-enabled application can use any software that supports these data interchange APIs. An e-mail application will be able to attach any number of components into the mail object without the need to provide custom viewers or launchers.

Not all Windows applications support OLE, but Microsoft has released its OLE 2.0 software development kit (SDK). The toolkit greatly simplifies OLE integration into third-party, developed applications. Organizations wanting to create a consistent desktop are beginning to use the OLE SDK as part of custom applications.

OLE 2.0 extends OLE capabilities to enable a group of data to be defined as an object and saved into a database. This object can then be dragged and dropped into other applications and edited without the need to switch back to the application which created it. This provides a more seamless interface for the user. In OLE 1.x, double-clicking a Lotus 1-2-3 for Windows spreadsheet embedded in a Microsoft Word for Windows document launches 1-2-3 and opens the document in a 1-2-3 window. Under OLE 2.0, the active window (Word's) menu and toolbar change to that of 1-2-3. The user deals only with the object, with no need to be aware of the multiple software being loaded.

Common Object Request Broker Architecture (CORBA)

CORBA is a specification from the Object Management Group (OMG), a UNIX vendor consortium. OLE focuses on data sharing between applications on a single desktop, and CORBA addresses cross-platform data transfer and the process of moving objects over networks. CORBA support enables Windows and UNIX clients to share objects. A word processor operating on a Windows desktop can include graphics generated from a UNIX workstation.

Enterprise View

It is important for application designers and developers to understand and remember that the user view of the system is through the client workstation. Whatever technological miracles are performed at the server, a poor design or implementation at the client on the desktop still result in unfavorable user perception of the entire application!

Components of Client/
Server Applications—
The Server

Components of Client/
Server Applications—
The Server

4

Executive Summary

The server is a multiuser computer. There is no special hardware requirement that turns a computer into a server. The hardware platform should be selected based on application demands and economics. Servers for client/server applications work best when they are configured with an operating system that supports shared memory, application isolation, and preemptive multitasking. An operating system with preemptive multitasking enables a higher priority task to preempt or take control of the processor from a currently executing, lower priority task.

The server provides and controls shared access to server resources. Applications on a server must be isolated from each other so that an error in one cannot damage another. Preemptive multitasking ensures that no single task can take over all the resources of the server and prevent other tasks from providing service. There must be a means of defining the relative priority of the tasks on the server. These requirements are specific to the client/server implementation and not to the file server implementation. Because file servers execute only the single task of file service, they can operate in a more limited operating environment without the need for application isolation and preemptive multitasking.

The traditional minicomputer and mainframe hosts have acted as de facto enterprise servers for the network of terminals they support. Because the only functionality available to the terminal user is through the host, personal productivity data as well as corporate systems information is stored on this host server. Network services, application services, and database services are provided centrally from the host server.

Many organizations download data from legacy enterprise servers for local manipulation at workstations. In the client/server model, the definition of server will continue to include these functions, perhaps still implemented on the same or similar platforms. Moreover, the advent of open systems based servers is facilitating the placement of services on many different platforms. Client/server computing is a phenomenon that developed from the ground up. Remote workgroups have needed to share expensive resources and have connected their desktop workstations into local area networks (LANs). LANs have grown until they are pervasive in the organization. However, frequently (similar to parking lots) they are isolated one from the other.

Many organizations have integrated the functionality of their dumb terminals into their desktop workstations to support character mode, host-based applications from the single workstation. The next wave of client/server computing is occurring now, as organizations of the mid-1990s begin to use the cheaper and more available processing power of the workstation as part of their enterprise systems.

The Novell Network Operating System (NOS), NetWare, is the most widely installed LAN NOS. It provides the premier file and print server support. However, a limitation of NetWare for the needs of reliable client/server applications has been the requirement for an additional separate processor running as a database server. The availability of database server software—from companies such as Sybase and Oracle—to run on the NetWare server, is helping to diffuse this limitation. With the release of Novell 4.x, Netware supports an enterprise LAN (that is, a thousand internetworked devices) with better support for Directory Services and TCP/IP internetworking.

DEC demonstrated the Alpha AXP processor running Processor-Independent NetWare in native mode at the PC Expo exhibit in June 1993. HP, Sun, and other vendors developing NetWare on RISC-based systems announced shipment of developer kits for availability in early 1994. Native NetWare for RISC is scheduled for availability in late 1994. This will provide scalability for existing Netware users who run out of capacity on their Intel platforms.

Banyan VINES provides the competitive product to Novell 4.x for enterprise LANs. Directory services are provided in VINES through a feature called StreetTalk. VINES 5.5 provides excellent WAN connectivity and is very popular among customers with a heterogeneous mainframe and minicomputer enterprise. However, it suffers from a weak support for file and printer sharing and a general lack of application package support. Banyan's Enterprise Network Services (ENS) with StreetTalk provides the best Directory Services implementation today. StreetTalk enables users to log into the network rather than to a server. This single logon ID enables access to all authorized servers anywhere in the network. Banyan made ENS available for Netware 3.11 and plans to make it available for Netware 4.x and Microsoft's Windows NT Advanced Server.

Microsoft's LAN Manager NOS and its several derivatives—including IBM Lan Server, HP LAN Manager/UX and DEC Pathworks—provide file and printer services but with less functionality, and more user complexity, than Novell's NetWare. The operating systems that support LAN Manager provide the necessary shared memory, protected memory, and preemptive multitasking services necessary for reliable client/server computing. They provide this support by operating natively with the OS/2, UNIX, VMS, and MVS operating systems. These operating systems all provide these services as part of their base functionality. The scalability of the platforms provides a real advantage for organizations building client/server, and not just file server, applications.

The lack of reasonable directory services restricts LAN Manager from the enterprise LAN role today. Microsoft has just released Advanced Server, the Windows NT version of LAN Manager. This provides a much stronger Intel platform than LAN Manager. In conjunction with the Banyan ENS, Advanced Server is a strong competitor to Novell's NetWare as the preferred NOS.

Network File System (NFS) is the standard UNIX support for shared files and printers. NFS provides another option for file and print services to client workstations with access to a UNIX server. PC NFS is the PC product that runs on the client and provides connectivity to the NFS file services under UNIX. NFS with TCP/IP provides the additional advantage of easy-to-use support for remote files and printers.

Novell and NFS can interoperate effectively because of the increasing support for TCP/IP as a LAN and WAN protocol. Recent announcements by IBM and Microsoft of alliances with Novell and Banyan promise a future in which all of the features of each NOS will be selectively available to everyone. Until these products improve their capability to work together, organizations still have the challenge of determining which NOS to select. Most will choose to use NetWare plus Windows clients with OS/2, UNIX, VMS, or MVS servers for their client/server applications. There will be a significant increase during 1994-95 in the use of NFS based servers with support now available on all major UNIX platforms as well as OS/2, MVS, and VMS.

There is no preeminent hardware technology for the server. The primary characteristic of the server is its support for multiple simultaneous client requests for service. Therefore, the server must provide multitasking support and shared memory services. High-end Intel, RISC (including Sun SPARC, IBM/Motorola PowerPC, HP PA RISC, SGI MIPS, and DEC Alpha), IBM System/370, and DEC VAX processors are all candidates for the server platform. The server is responsible for managing the server-requester interface so that an individual client request response is synchronized and directed back only to the client requester. This implies both security when authorizing access to a service and integrity of the response to the request.

With object-oriented technology (OOT) increasingly used to build operating systems and development environments, servers are becoming ubiquitous (anything, anywhere, and anytime) and transparent in technology and location to the user and developer. NeXtStep provides the only production ready model of what will be the dominant developer model in 1995 and beyond. Sun's DOE implementation of the OMG defined CORBA standards provides a view of the future role of the object server. This is the first implementation of the vision of the original OOT scientists. The future promises applications assembled from object repositories containing the intellectual property of a business combined with commercial objects made available by OOT developers executing on servers somewhere.

The Role of the Server

Servers provide application, file, database, print, fax, image, communications, security, systems, and network management services. These are each described in some detail in the following sections.

It is important to understand that a server is an architectural concept, not a physical implementation description. Client and server functions can be provided by the same physical device. With the movement toward peer computing, every device will potentially operate as a client and server in response to requests for service.

Application servers provide business functionality to support the operation of the client workstation. In the client/server model these services can be provided for an entire or partial business function invoked through an InterProcess Communication (IPC) request for service. Either message-based requests (*à la* OLTP) or RPCs can be used. A collection of application servers may work in concert to provide an entire business function. For example, in a payroll system the employee information may be managed by one application server, earnings calculated by another application server, and deductions calculated by a third application server. These servers may run different operating systems on various hardware platforms and may use different database servers. The client application invokes these services without consideration of the technology or geographic location of the various servers. Object technology provides the technical basis for the application server, and widespread acceptance of the CORBA standards is ensuring the viability of this trend. File servers provide record level data services to nondatabase applications.

Space for storage is allocated, and free space is managed by the file server. Catalog functions are provided by the file server to support file naming and directory structure. Filename maximum length ranges from 8 to 256 characters, depending on the particular server operating system support. Stored programs are typically loaded from a file server for execution on a client or host server platform.

Database servers are managed by a database engine such as Sybase, IBM, Ingres, Informix, or Oracle. The file server provides the initial space, and the database engine allocates space for tables within the space provided by the file server. These host services are responsible for providing the specialized data services required of a database product—automatic backout and recovery after power, hardware, or software failure, space management within the file, database reorganization, record locking, deadlock detection, and management. Print servers provide support to receive client documents, queue them for printing, prioritize them, and execute the specific print driver logic required for the selected printer. The print server software must have the necessary logic to support the unique characteristics of each printer. Effective print server support will include error recovery for jams and operator notification of errors with instructions for restart.

Fax servers provide support similar to that provided by print servers. In addition, fax servers queue up outgoing faxes for later distribution when communications charges are lower. Because fax documents are distributed in compressed form using either Group III or Group IV compression, the fax server must be capable of dynamically compressing and decompressing documents for distribution, printing, and display. This operation is usually done through the addition of a fax card to the server. If faxing is rare, the software support for the compression and decompression options can be used. Image servers operate in a manner similar to fax servers.

Communications servers provide support for wide area network (WAN) communications. This support typically includes support for a subset of IBM System Network Architecture (SNA), asynchronous protocols, X.25, ISDN, TCP/IP, OSI, and LAN-to-LAN NetBIOS communication protocols. In the Novell NetWare implementation, Gateway Communications provides a leading communications product. In the LAN Server and LAN Manager environments, OS/2 communications server products are available from IBM and DCA. In the Banyan VINES environment, the addition of DCA products to VINES provides support for SNA connectivity. UNIX servers provide a range of product add-ons from various vendors to support the entire range of communications requirements. VMS servers support DECnet, TCP/IP, and SNA as well as various asynchronous and serial communications protocols. MVS servers provide support for SNA, TCP/IP, and some support for other asynchronous communications.

Security at the server restricts access to software and data accessed from the server. Communications access is controlled from the communications server. In most implementations, the use of a user login ID is the primary means of security. Using LAN Server, some organizations have implemented integrated Response Access/Control Facility (RACF) security by creating profiles in the MVS environment and downloading those to the LAN server for domain control. Systems and network management services for the local LAN are managed by a LAN administrator, but WAN services must be provided from some central location. Typically, remote LAN management is done from the central data center site by trained MIS personnel. This issue is discussed in more detail in Chapter 8.

Server Functionality in Detail

The discussion in the following sections more specifically describes the functions provided by the server in a NOS environment.

Request Processing

Requests are issued by a client to the NOS services software resident on the client machine. These services format the request into an appropriate RPC and issue the request to the application layer of the client protocol stack. This request is received by the application layer of the protocol stack on the server.

File Services

File services handle access to the virtual directories and files located on the client workstation and to the server's permanent storage. These services are provided through the redirection software implemented as part of the client workstation operating environment. As Chapter 3 described, all requests are mapped into the virtual pool of resources and redirected as necessary to the appropriate local or remote server. The file services provide this support at the remote server processor. In the typical implementation, software, shared data, databases, and backups are stored on disk, tape, and optical storage devices that are managed by the file server.

To minimize the effort and effect of installation and maintenance of software, software should be loaded from the server for execution on the client. New versions can be updated on the server and made immediately available to all users. In addition, installation in a central location reduces the effort required for each workstation user to handle the installation process. Because each client workstation user uses the same installation of the software, optional parameters are consistent, and remote help desk operators are aware of them. This simplifies the analysis that must occur to provide support. Sharing information, such as word processing documents, is easier when everyone is at the same release level and uses the same default setup within the software. Central productivity services such as style sheets and macros can be set up for general use. Most personal productivity products do permit local parameters such as colors, default printers, and so forth to be set locally as well.

Backups of the server can be scheduled and monitored by a trained support person. Backups of client workstations can be scheduled from the server, and data can be stored at the server to facilitate recovery. Tape or optical backup units are typically used for backup; these devices can readily provide support for many users. Placing the server and its backups in a secure location helps prevent theft or accidental destruction of backups. A central location is readily monitored by a support person who ensures that the backup functions are completed. With more organizations looking at multimedia and image technology, large optical storage devices are most appropriately implemented as shared servers.

Fax/Print/Image Services

High-quality printers, workstation-generated faxes, and plotters are natural candidates for support from a shared server. The server can accept input from many clients, queue it according to the priority of the request and handle it when the device is available. Many organizations realize substantial savings by enabling users to generate fax output from their workstations and queue it at a fax server for transmission when the communication costs are lower. Incoming faxes can be queued at the server and transmitted to the appropriate client either on receipt or on request. In concert with workflow management techniques, images can be captured and distributed to the appropriate client workstation from the image server. In the client/server model, work queues are maintained at the server by a supervisor in concert with default algorithms that determine how to distribute the queued work.

Incoming paper mail can be converted to image form in the mail room and sent to the appropriate client through the LAN rather than through interoffice mail. Centralized capture and distribution enable images to be centrally indexed. This index can be maintained by the database services for all authorized users to query. In this way, images are captured once and are available for distribution immediately to all authorized users. Well-defined standards for electronic document management will allow this technology to become fully integrated into the desktop work environment. There are dramatic opportunities for cost savings and improvements in efficiency if this technology is properly implemented and used. Chapter 10 discusses in more detail the issues of electronic document management.

Database Services

Early database servers were actually file servers with a different interface. Products such as dBASE, Clipper, FoxPro, and Paradox execute the database engine primarily on the client machine and use the file services provided by the file server for record access and free space management. These are new and more powerful implementations of the original flat-file models with extracted indexes for direct record access. Currency control is managed by the application program, which issues lock requests and lock checks, and by the database server, which creates a lock table that is interrogated whenever a record access lock check is generated. Because access is at the record level, all records satisfying the primary key must be returned to the client workstation for filtering. There are no facilities to execute procedural code at the server, to execute joins, or to filter rows prior to returning them to the workstation. This lack of capability dramatically increases the likelihood of records being locked when several clients are accessing the same database and increases network traffic when many unnecessary rows are returned to the workstation only to be rejected.

The lack of server execution logic prevents these products from providing automatic partial update backout and recovery after an application, system, or hardware failure. For this reason, systems that operate in this environment require an experienced system support programmer to assist in the recovery after a failure. When the applications are very straightforward and require only a single row to be updated in each interaction, this recovery issue does not arise. However, many client/server applications are required to update more than a single row as part of one logical unit of work.

Client/server database engines such as Sybase, IBM's Database Manager, Ingres, Oracle, and Informix provide support at the server to execute SQL requests issued from the client workstation. The file services are still used for space allocation and basic directory services, but all other services are provided directly by the database server. Relational database management systems are the current technology for data management. Figure 4.1 charts the evolution of database technology from the first computers in the late 1950s to the object-oriented database technologies that are becoming prevalent in the mid-1990s.

Database Trends

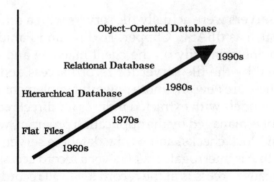

Figure 4.1. Database trends.

Flat Files: Sorting Physical Records

Database technology has evolved from the early 1960s' flat-file view when data was provided through punch cards or disk files simulating punch cards. These original implementations physically stored data columns and records according to the user view. The next column in the user view was the next column in the physical record, and the next record in the user view was the next physically stored record. Sorting the physical records provided the means by which a user was presented with a different view of related records. Columns were eliminated from view by copying the records from one location to another without the unnecessary columns. Many organizations today still use the flat-file approach to data management for reporting and batch update input. Data is extracted and sorted for efficient input to a batch report. Data is captured for update and sorted for more efficient input to a batch update program.

Hierarchical Databases: Adjacent Storage of Related Record Types

The second generation of database technology, the hierarchical database, could store related record types physically or logically next to each other. In the hierarchical model implementation, when a user accesses a physical record type, other application-related data is usually stored physically close and will be moved from disk to DRAM all together. Internally stored pointers are used to navigate from one record to the next if there is insufficient space close by at data creation time to insert the related data. Products such as IMS and IDMS implemented this technique very successfully in the early 1970s. Many organizations continue to use database applications built to use this technology.

The major disadvantage with the hierarchical technique is that only applications that access data according to its physical storage sequence benefit from locality of reference. Changes to application requirements that necessitate a different access approach require the data to be reorganized. This process, which involves reading, sorting, and rewriting the database into a new sequence, is not transparent to applications that rely on the original physical sequence. Indexes that provide direct access into the database provide the capability to view and access the information in a sequence other than the physical sequence. However, these indexes must be known to the user at the time the application is developed. The developer explicitly references the index to get to the data of interest. Thus, indexes cannot be added later without changing all programs that need this access to use the index directly. Indexes cannot be removed without changing programs that currently access the index. Most implementations force the application developer to be sensitive to the ordering and occurrence of columns within the record. Thus, columns cannot be added or removed without changing all programs that are sensitive to these records.

Application sensitivity to physical implementation is the main problem with hierarchical database systems. Application sensitivity to physical storage introduced considerable complexity into the navigation as application programmers traverse the hierarchy in search of their desired data. Attempts by database vendors to improve performance have usually increased the complexity of access. If life is too easy today, try to create a bidirectionally virtually paired IMS logical relationship; that is why organizations using products such as IMS and IDMS usually have highly paid database technical support staff.

Relational Databases: Extracted Indexes and SQL

As hardware technology evolves, it is important for the data management capabilities to evolve to use the new capabilities. Figure 4.2 summarizes the current essential characteristics of the database world. The relational database is the de facto standard today; therefore, investment by vendors will be in products that target and support fully compliant SQL databases.

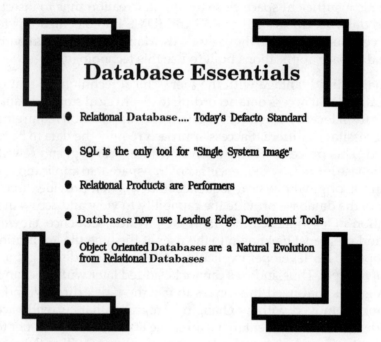

Database Essentials

- Relational Database.... Today's Defacto Standard

- SQL is the only tool for "Single System Image"

- Relational Products are Performers

- Databases now use Leading Edge Development Tools

- Object Oriented Databases are a Natural Evolution from Relational Databases

Figure 4.2. Database essentials.

Relational database technology provides the current data management solution to many of the problems inherent in the flat-file and hierarchical technologies. In the late 1970s and early 1980s, products such as Software AG's ADABAS and System 2000 were introduced in an attempt to provide the application flexibility demanded by the systems of the day. IBM with IMS and Cullinet with IDMS attempted to add features to their products to increase this flexibility. The first relational products were introduced by ADR with Datacom DB and Computer Corporation of America with Model 204.

Each of these implementations used extracted indexes to provide direct access to stored data without navigating the database or sorting flat files. All the products attempted to maintain some of the performance advantages afforded by locality of reference (storage of related columns and records as close as possible to the primary column and record).

Datacom and Model 204 introduced—for the first time—the Structured Query Language (SQL). SQL was invented in the early 1970s by E. F. (Ted) Codd of IBM Labs in Santa Teresa, California. The primary design objective behind SQL was to provide a data access language that could be shown mathematically to manipulate the desired data correctly. The secondary objective was to remove any sense of the physical storage of data from the view of the user. SQL is another flat-file implementation; there are no embedded pointers. SQL uses extracted indexes to provide direct access to the rows (records) of the tables (files) of interest. Each column (field) may be used as part of the search criteria.

SQL provides (especially with SQL2 extensions) a very powerful data access language. Its algebra provides all the necessary syntax to define, secure, and access information in an SQL database. The elegance of the language intrigued the user and vendor community to the extent that standards committees picked up the language and defined a set of standards around the language syntax. SQL1 and SQL2 define an exact syntax and a set of results for each operation. As a consequence, many software vendors have developed products that implement SQL. This standardization will eventually enable users to treat these products as commodities in the same way that PC hardware running DOS has become a commodity. Each engine will soon be capable of executing the same set of SQL requests and producing the same result. The products will then be differentiated based on their performance, cost, support, platform availability, and recovery-restart capabilities.

Dr. Codd has published a list of 13 rules that every SQL database engine should adhere to in order to be truly compliant. No products today can meet all of these criteria. The criteria, however, provide a useful objective set for the standards committees and vendors to strive for. We have defined another set of product standards that we are using to evaluate SQL database engines for the development of client/server applications. In particular, products should be implemented with support for the following products and standards:

- ANSI SQL and IBM DB2 standards
- A variety of front-end query products
- C and COBOL SQL precompilers
- Support for and compatibility with server NOS: NetWare, OS/2 (LAN Manager, LAN Server), Windows NT, Mac System 7, and/or UNIX (VINES, SCO, Sun, HP/UX USL, SVR4…), and MVS
- Support for client Operating Systems: DOS, Windows, OS/2, Windows NT, Mac System 7, or UNIX (Solaris, USL, SCO, HP/UX, SVR4…)

Production-capable client/server database engines must be able to provide a similar operational environment to that found in the database engines present in minicomputer and mainframe computers today. Capabilities for comparison include performance, auditability, and recovery techniques. In particular, the following DBMS features must be included in the database engine:

- Performance optimization tools
- Dynamic transaction backout
- Roll back from, roll forward to last backup
- Audit file recovery
- Automatic error detection and recovery
- File reclamation and repair tools
- Support for mirrored databases
- Capability to split database between physical disk drives
- Remote distributed database management features
- Maintenance of accurate and duplicate audit files on any LAN node

In the client/server implementation, you should offload database processing to the server. Therefore, the database engine should accept SQL requests from the client and execute them totally on the server, returning only the answer set to the client requestor. The database engine should provide support for stored procedures or triggers that run on the server.

The client/server model implies that there will be multiple concurrent user access. The database engine must be able to manage this access without requiring every developer to write well-behaved applications.

The following features must be part of the database engine:

- Locking mechanisms to guarantee data integrity
- Deadlock detection and prevention
- Multithreaded application processing
- User access to multiple databases on multiple servers

Object-Oriented—A Bright Future

With the increasing maturity and popularity of OOTs for development, there has been a significant increase in maturity and acceptance of object-oriented database management systems (OODBMS). Object-oriented database management systems provide support for complex data structures: such as compound documents, CASE entity relationship models, financial models, and CAD/CAM drawings. OODBMS proponents claim that relational database management systems (RDBMS) can handle only simple data structures (such as tables) and simple transaction-processing applications that only need to create views combining a small number of tables. OODBMS proponents argue that there is a large class of problems that need to be and will be more simply implemented if more complex data structures can be viewed directly. RDBMS vendors agree with the need to support these data structures but argue that the issue is one of implementation, not architecture.

Relational databases are characterized by a simple data structure. All access to data and relationships between tables are based on values. A data value occurrence is uniquely determined by the concatenation of the table name, column name, and the value of the unique identifier of the row (the primary key). Relationships between tables are determined by a common occurrence of the primary key values. Applications build a view of information from tables by doing a join based on the common values. The result of the join is another table that contains a combination of column values from the tables involved in the join.

The development of a relational algebra defining the operations that can be performed between tables has enabled efficient implementations of RDBMSs. The establishment of industry standards for the definition of and access to relational tables has speeded the acceptance of RDBMSs as the de facto standard for all client/server applications today. Similar standards do not yet exist for OODBMSs. There is a place for both models. To be widely used, OODBMSs need to integrate transparently with RDBMS technology. Table 4.1 compares the terminology used by RDBMS and OODBMS proponents.

Table 4.1. Comparison of object-oriented and relational database management system features.

OODBMS	RDBMS
Class	Collection of rows in table
Object	Row
Type	Table definition (user type extension)
Method	Stored procedure (extension)
Index	Index
Object Identify	No match
Collection	Array (extension)
Inheritance	No match
Encapsulation	No match
Computationally	Transact SQL, PL/SQL, and stored complete procedures
No match	SQL portability
No match	Mathematically provable

There remain some applications for which RDBMSs have not achieved acceptable performance. Primarily, these are applications that require very complex data structures. Thousands of tables may be defined with many relationships among them. Frequently, the rows are sparsely populated, and the applications typically require many rows to be linked, often recursively, to produce the necessary view.

The major vendors in this market are Objectivity Inc., Object Design, Ontos, and Versant. Other vendors such as HP, Borland, and Ingres have incorporated object features into their products.

The application characteristics that lead to an OODBMS choice are shown in Figure 4.3. OODBMS will become production capable for these types of applications with the introduction of 16Mbps D-RAM and the creation of *persistent* (permanent) databases in D-RAM. Only the logging functions will use real I/O. Periodically, D-RAM databases will be backed up to real magnetic or optical disk storage. During 1993, a significant number of production OODBMS applications were implemented. With the confidence and experience gained from these applications, the momentum is building, and 1994 and 1995 will see a significant increase in the use of OODBMSs for business critical applications. OODBMSs have reached a maturity level coincident with the demand for multimedia enabled applications. The complexities of dealing with multimedia demands the features of OODBMS for effective storage and manipulation.

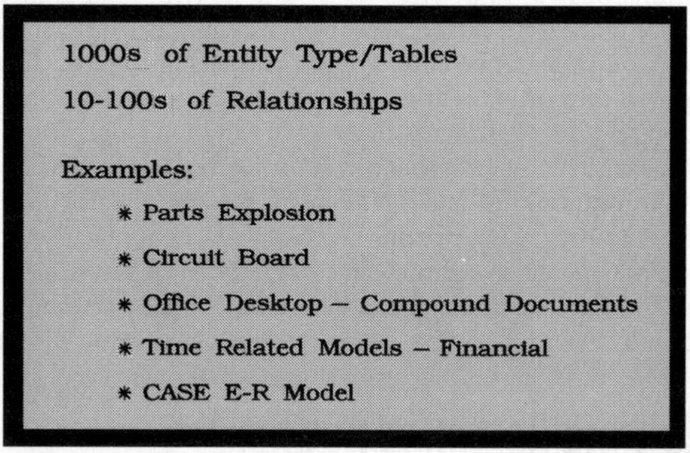

```
1000s  of  Entity  Type/Tables
10-100s  of  Relationships

Examples:
    * Parts  Explosion
    * Circuit  Board
    * Office  Desktop — Compound  Documents
    * Time  Related  Models — Financial
    * CASE  E-R  Model
```

Figure 4.3. Object-oriented database.

To enable more complex data types to be manipulated by a single command, OODBMSs provide encapsulated processing logic with the object definition.

Communications Services

Client/server applications require LAN and WAN communication services. Basic LAN services are integral to the NOS. WAN services are provided by various communications server products. Chapter 5 provides a complete discussion of connectivity issues in the client/server model.

Security Services

Client/server applications require similar security services to those provided by host environments. Every user should be required to log in with a user ID and password. If passwords might become visible to unauthorized users, the security server should insist that passwords be changed regularly. The enterprise on the desk implies that a single logon ID and logon sequence is used to gain the authority once to access all information and process for the user has a need and right of access. Because data may be stored in a less physically secure area, the option should exist to store data in an encrypted form. A combination of the user ID and password should be required to decrypt the data.

New options, such as floppyless workstations with integrated data encryption standard (DES) coprocessors, are available from vendors such as Beaver Computer Company. These products automatically encrypt or decrypt data written or read to disk or a communication line. The encryption and decryption are done using the DES algorithm and the user password. This ensures that no unauthorized user can access stored data or communications data. This type of security is particularly useful for laptop computers participating in client/server applications, because laptops do not operate in surroundings with the same physical security of an office. To be able to access the system from a laptop without properly utilizing an ID number and password would be courting disaster.

The Network Operating System

The network operating system (NOS) provides the services not available from the client OS.

Novell NetWare

NetWare is a family of LAN products with support for IBM PC-compatible and Apple Macintosh clients, and IBM PC-compatible servers. NetWare is a proprietary NOS in the strict sense that it does not require another OS, such as DOS, Windows, Windows NT, OS/2, Mac System 7, or UNIX to run on a server. A separate Novell product—Portable NetWare for UNIX—provides server support for leading RISC-based UNIX implementations, IBM PC-compatible systems running Windows NT, OS/2, high-end Apple Macs running Mac System 7, and Digital Equipment Corporation VAXs running VMS.

NetWare provides the premier LAN environment for file and printer resource sharing. It had 62 percent of the market share in 1993. It is widely installed as the standard product in many organizations. NetWare is the original LAN NOS for the PC world. As such, it incorporates many of the ease-of-use features required for sharing printers, data, software, and communications lines. Agreements between Novell and IBM to remarket the product and provide links between NetWare and the LAN Server product confirm the commitment to Novell NetWare's use within large organizations. Figure 4.4 shows the major components of the NetWare architecture, illustrating client and server functions.

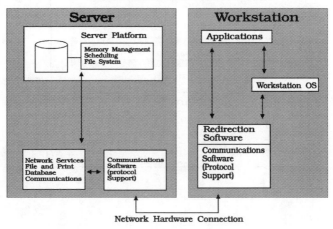

Figure 4.4. NetWare architecture.

Novell has committed to move NetWare to an open architecture. Through the use of open protocol technology (OPT), Novell makes NetWare fully network protocol independent. Two standardized interfaces—open datalink interface (ODI) and NetWare Streams—enable other vendors to develop products for the NetWare environment. This facilitates its integration into other platforms. Figure 4.5 outlines the NetWare open architecture. The diagram also illustrates the wide range of connectivity supported by NetWare. Client workstations can use Mac System 7, OS/2, DOS, Windows, Windows NT, NetWare, or UNIX NFS operating environments. OS/2, Windows NT, and UNIX servers may be installed on the same LAN as NetWare servers to provide support for products that require these platforms. Novell's purchase of USL from AT&T has increased its commitment to early support for native UNIX servers. HP, Sun, DEC, and Novell have announced an agreement to port NetWare to their respective UNIX platforms. Novell has won the battle to be *the* standard for the file/print server in the LAN environment.

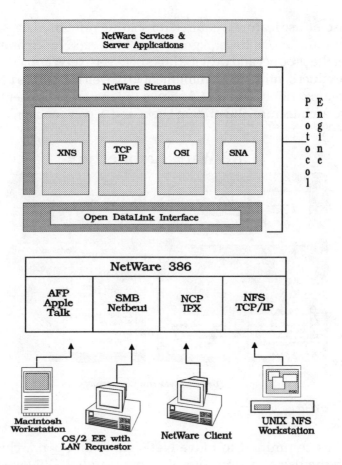

Figure 4.5. *NetWare open services.*

Novell's published goal is to provide NetWare services totally independent of network media, network transport protocols, client/server protocols, and server and client operating systems, at each layer of network design.

NetWare has benefitted from its high performance and low resource requirements as much as it has from its relative ease of use. This performance has been provided through the use of a proprietary operating system and network protocols. Even though this has given Novell an advantage in performance, it has caused difficulties in the implementation of application and database servers in the Novell LAN. Standard applications cannot run on the server processor, because NetWare does not provide compatible APIs. Instead, NetWare provides a high performance capability called a NetWare Loadable Module (NLM) that enables database servers such as Sybase and Oracle, and communications servers such as Gateway Communications provides, to be linked into the NetWare NOS. In addition, the tailored operating environment does not provide some system features, such as storage protection and multitasking, in the same fundamental way that OS/2 and UNIX do. However, Novell is committed to address these issues by supporting the use of UNIX, OPENVMS, OS/2, and Windows NT as native operating environments.

With the release of NetWare 4.0, Novell addressed the serious issue of enterprise computing with improved network directory services (NDS), one thousand node domains, and LAN/WAN support for TCP/IP. Native NetWare 4.x will be available to developers in early 1994 and production ready by the end of 1994. For the other end of the product range, Novell released NetWare Lite in 1993 to address the small business and simple workgroup requirements of LANs with five or fewer workstations. This enables organizations to remain with NetWare as the single LAN technology everywhere. Clearly, Novell's pitch is that systems management and administration are greatly simplified with the single standard of "NetWare Everywhere."

LAN Manager

LAN Manager and its IBM derivative, LAN Server, are the standard products for use in client/server implementations using OS/2 as the server operating system. LAN Manager/X is the standard product for client/server implementations using UNIX System V as the server operating system. Microsoft released its Advanced Server product with Windows NT in the third quarter of 1993. During 1994, it will be enhanced with support for the Microsoft network management services, currently referred to as "Hermes," and Banyan's Enterprise Network Services (ENS). Advanced Server is the natural migration path for existing Microsoft LAN Manager and IBM LAN Server customers. Existing LAN Manager/X customers probably won't find Advanced Server an answer to their dreams before 1995.

AT&T has taken over responsibility for the LAN Manager/X version. Vendors such as Hewlett-Packard (HP) have relicensed the product from AT&T. AT&T and Microsoft have an agreement to maintain compatible APIs for all base functionality.

LAN Manager and Advanced Server provide client support for DOS, Windows, Windows NT, OS/2, and Mac System 7. Server support extends to NetWare, AppleTalk, UNIX, Windows NT, and OS/2. Client workstations can access data from both NetWare and LAN Manager servers at the same time. LAN Manager supports NetBIOS and Named Pipes LAN communications between clients and OS/2 servers. Redirection services are provided to map files and printers from remote workstations for client use.

Advanced Server also supports TCP/IP communication. In early 1994, Advanced Server still will be a young product with many missing pieces. Even more troublesome, competitiveness between Microsoft and Novell is delaying the release of client requestor software and NetWare Core Protocol (NCP) support. Microsoft has added TCP/IP support to LAN Manager 2.1 and Advanced Server along with NetView and Simple Network Management Protocol (SNMP) agents. Thus, the tools are in place to provide remote LAN management for LAN Manager LANs. Microsoft has announced support for IBM NetView 6000 for Advanced Server management.

Advanced Server provides integrated support for peer-to-peer processing and client/server applications. Existing support for Windows NT, OS/2, UNIX, and Mac System 7 clients lets application, database, and communication servers run on the same machine as the file and print server. This feature is attractive in small LANs. The native operating system support for preemptive multitasking and storage protection ensures that these server applications do not reduce the reliability of other services. Even as Windows NT is rolled out to provide the database, application, and communications services to client/server applications, the use of Novell as the LAN NOS of choice will continue for peripheral resource sharing applications.

Microsoft has attempted to preempt the small LAN market with its Windows for Workgroups (WfW) product. This attacks the same market as NetWare Lite with a low-cost product that is tightly integrated with Windows. It is an attractive option for small organizations without a requirement for larger LANs. The complexities of systems management make it less attractive in an enterprise environment already using Novell. WfW can be used in conjunction with Novell for a workgroup wishing to use some WfW services, such as group scheduling.

IBM LAN Server

IBM has entered into an agreement to resell and integrate the Novell NetWare product into environments where both IBM LAN Server and Novell NetWare are required. NetWare provides more functional, easier-to-use, and higher-performance file and print services. In environments where these are the only LAN functions, NetWare is preferable to LAN Manager derivatives. The capability to interconnect to the SNA world makes the IBM product LAN Server attractive to organizations that prefer to run both products. Most large organizations have department workgroups that require only the services that Novell provides well but may use LAN Server for client/server applications using SNA services such as APPN.

IBM and Microsoft had an agreement to make the APIs for the two products equivalent. However, the dispute between the two companies over Windows 3.x and OS/2 has ended this cooperation. The most recent releases of LAN Manager NT 3 and LAN Server 3 are closer to the agreed equivalency, but there is no guarantee that this will continue. In fact, there is every indication that the products will diverge with the differing server operating system focuses for the two companies. IBM has priced LAN Server very attractively so that if OS/2 clients are being used, LAN Server is a low-cost option for small LANs. LAN Server supports DOS, Windows, and OS/2 clients. No support has been announced for Mac System 7, although it is possible to interconnect AppleTalk and LAN Server LANs to share data files and communication services.

Banyan VINES

Banyan VINES provides basic file and print services similar to those of Novell and Lan Manager.

VINES incorporates a facility called StreetTalk that enables every resource in a Banyan enterprise LAN to be addressed by name. VINES also provides intelligent WAN routing within the communications server component. These two features are similar to the OSI Directory Services X.500 protocol.

StreetTalk enables resources to be uniquely identified on the network, making them easier to access and manage. All resources, including file services, users, and printers, are defined as objects. Each object has a StreetTalk name associated with it.

StreetTalk names follow a three-level hierarchical format: Item@Group@Organization. For example, a user can be identified as

Psmith@Cerritos@Tnet. All network objects are stored in a distributed database that can be accessed globally. Novell's NDS is similar to StreetTalk in functionality. However, there are key differences. NDS can partition and replicate the database, which will generally improve performance and reliability. NDS is X.500-compliant and enables multiple levels of hierarchy.

StreetTalk supports a fixed three-level hierarchy. The NDS architecture offers more flexibility but with corresponding complexity, and StreetTalk is less flexible but less complex to manage.

One advantage the current version of StreetTalk has over NDS is that StreetTalk objects can have unlimited attributes available for selection. To locate a printer with certain attributes, the command: "Locate a color laser printer with A4 forms on the 7th floor of Cerritos" finds and uses the printer with the desired characteristics.

VINES V5.5 offers ISDN and TI support for server-to-server communications over a WAN, as well as integration of DOS, Windows, OS/2, and Mac clients. VINES does not support NFS clients.

Novell and Microsoft have announced support for Banyan ENS within their products to be available in Q2 1994. Banyan and DCA provide SNA services to the VINES environment. VINES supports UNIX, DOS, Windows, OS/2, and Mac System 7 clients.

PC Network File Services (NFS)

NFS is the standard file system support for UNIX. PC NFS is available from SunSelect and FTP to provide file services support from a UNIX server to Windows, OS/2, Mac, and UNIX clients.

NFS lets a client mount an NFS host's filing system (or a part of it) as an extension of its own resources. NFS's resource-sharing mechanisms encompass interhost printing. The transactions among NFS systems traditionally ride across TCP/IP and Ethernet, but NFS works with any network that supports 802.3 frames.

SunSelect includes instructions for adding PC-NFS to an existing LAN Manager or Windows for Workgroups network using Network Driver Interface Specification (NDIS) drivers.

With the increasing use of UNIX servers for application and database services, there is an increasing realization that PC NFS may be all that is required for NOS support for many workgroups. This can be a low-cost and low-maintenance option because the UNIX server is easily visible from a remote location.

What Are the Available Platforms?

Client/server computing requires that LAN and WAN topologies be in place to provide the necessary internetworking for shared applications and data. Gartner Group[1] surveyed and estimated the Microsystems' integration topologies for the period 1986-1996; the results appear in Figure 4.6. Of special interest is the projection that most workstations will be within LANs by 1996, but only 14 percent will be involved in an enterprise LAN by that date. These figures represent a fairly pessimistic outlook for interconnected LAN-to-LAN and enterprise-wide connectivity. These figures probably will prove to be substantially understated if organizations adopt an architectural perspective for the selection of their platforms and tools and use these tools within an organizationally optimized systems development environment (SDE).

MicroSystems Integration Configuration
1986 - 1996

PC/WS Configuration	1986	1991	1996
Stand-Alones	85.4%	43%	15%
LANs	3.3%	14%	16%
LAN to LAN/WAN	1.1%	11%	20%
LAN to HOST	6.1%	26%	35%
Enterprise-Wide	4.1%	6%	14%

Figure 4.6. *Microsystems integration configuration 1986-1996. (Source: The Gartner Group.)*

---

[1]*Gartner Group, presentation notes, MicroSystems Integration, September 1991.*

Workstations in LAN Configuration

This model is the most basic implementation providing the standard LAN services for file and printer sharing.

LAN-to-LAN/WAN Configuration

Routers and communication servers will be used to provide communication services between LANs and into the WAN. In the client/server model, these connections will be provided transparently by the SDE tools. There are significant performance implications if the traffic volumes are large. IBM's LU6.2 implementation in APPC and TCP/IP provides the best support for high-volume, LAN-to-LAN/WAN communications. DEC's implementation of DECnet always has provided excellent LAN-to-WAN connectivity. Integrated support for TCP/IP, LU6.2, and IPX provides a solid platform for client/server LAN-to-WAN implementation within DECnet. Novell 4.x provides support for TCP/IP as both the LAN and WAN protocol. Internetworking also is supported between IPX and TCP/IP.

LAN-to-Host Configuration

The lack of real estate on the desktop encouraged most organizations to move to a single device—using terminal emulation from the workstation—to access existing mainframe applications. It will take considerable time and effort before all existing host-based applications in an organization are replaced by client/server applications. In the long term, the host will continue to be the location of choice for enterprise database storage and for the provision of security and network management services.

Mainframes are expensive to buy and maintain, hard to use, inflexible, and large, but they provide the stability and capacity required by many organizations to run their businesses. As Figure 4.7 notes, in the view of International Data Corporation, they will not go away soon. Their roles will change, but they will be around as part of the enterprise infrastructure for many more years. Only organizations who create an enterprise architecture strategy and transformational plans will accomplish the migration to client/server in less than a few years. Without a well-architected strategy, gradual evolution will produce failure.

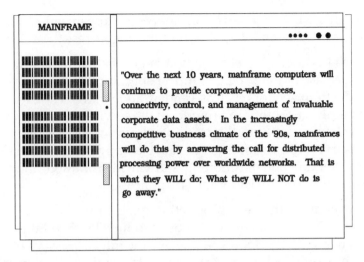

Figure 4.7. The role of the mainframe. (Source: International Data Corporation, conference handout notes, 1991.)

Enterprise-Wide

Information that is of value or interest to the entire business must be managed by a central data administration function and appear to be stored on each user's desk. These applications are traditionally implemented as Online Transaction Processing (OLTP) to the mainframe or minicomputer. With the client/server model, it is feasible to use database technology to replicate or migrate data to distributed servers. Wherever data resides or is used, the location must be transparent to the user and the developer. Data should be stored where it best meets the business need.

OLTP on a LAN

Online Transaction Processing applications are found in such industries as insurance, finance, government, and sales—all of which process large numbers of transactions. Each of these transactions requires a minimal amount of user think time to process. In these industries, data is frequently collected at the source by the knowledgeable worker. As such, the systems have high requirements for availability, data integrity, performance, concurrent access, growth potential, security, and manageability. Systems implemented in these environments must prove their worth or they will be rejected by an empowered organization. They must be implemented as an integral part of the job process.

OLTP has traditionally been the domain of the large mainframe vendors—such as IBM and DEC—and of special-purpose, fault-tolerant processors from vendors such as Tandem and Stratus. The client/server model has the capability to provide all the services required for OLTP at much lower cost than the traditional platforms. All the standard client/server requirements for a GUI—application portability, client/server function partitioning, software distribution, and effective development tools—exist for OLTP applications.

The first vendor to deliver a production-quality product in this arena is Cooperative Solutions with its Ellipse product. Prior to Ellipse, OLTP systems required developers to manage the integrity issues of unit-of-work processing, including currency control and transaction rollback. Ellipse provides all the necessary components to build systems with these features. Ellipse currently operates with Windows 3.x, OS/2 clients, and OS/2 servers using the Sybase database engine. Novell is working with Cooperative Solutions to port Ellipse as a Novell NetWare Loadable Module (NLM). It provides a powerful GUI development environment using a template language as a shorthand for development. This language provides a solid basis for building an organizational SDE and lends itself well to the incorporation of standard components.

OLTP with UNIX

As UNIX has matured, it has added many of the features found in other commercial operating systems such as VMS and MVS. There are now several offerings for OLTP with UNIX. IBM is promoting CICS 6000 as a downsizing strategy for CICS MVS. Database services will be provided by a combination of AIX and MVS servers.

Novell purchased the Tuxedo product from AT&T with its acquisition of USL. OSF selected the Transarc Ensina product as the basis for OLTP with DCE. The DCE recognition quickly placed Ensina in the lead in terms of supported UNIX platforms. IBM has released a version of DCE for AIX that includes the Ensina technology. NCR provides a product called TopEnd as part of its Cooperation series.

Client/server TP monitor software is becoming increasingly necessary now that client/server systems are growing to include several database servers supporting different vendors' databases and servicing tens, hundreds, and even thousands of users that need to access and update the same data. UNIX-based OTLP products are maturing to provide the same level of functionality and reliability as traditional mainframe-based IBM Customer Information Control Systems (CICS), yet at less cost and with graphical front ends.

The Server Operating System

Servers provide the platform for application, database, and communication services. There are six operating system platforms that have the greatest potential and/or are prevalent today: NetWare, OS/2, Windows NT, MVS, VMS, and UNIX.

NetWare

NetWare is used by many organizations, large and small, for the provision of file, printer, and network services. NetWare is a self-contained operating system. It does not require a separate OS (as do Windows NT, OS/2, and UNIX) to run. Novell is taking steps to allow NetWare to run on servers with UNIX. Novell purchased USL and will develop shrink-wrapped products to run under both NetWare and UNIX System V, Release 4.2. The products will enable UNIX to simultaneously access information from both a NetWare and a UNIX server.

OS/2

OS/2 is the server platform for Intel products provided by IBM in the System Application Architecture (SAA) model. OS/2 provides the storage protection and preemptive multitasking services needed for the server platform. Several database and many application products have been ported to OS/2. The only network operating systems directly supported with OS/2 are LAN Manager and LAN Server. Novell supports the use of OS/2 servers running on separate processors from the NetWare server. The combination of Novell with an OS/2 database and application servers can provide the necessary environment for a production-quality client/server implementation. Appendix A describes such an implementation.

Windows NT

With the release of Windows NT (New Technology) in September of 1993, Microsoft staked its unique position with a server operating system. Microsoft's previous development of OS/2 with IBM did not create the single standard UNIX alternative that was hoped for. NT provides the preemptive multitasking services required for a functional server. It provides excellent support for Windows clients and incorporates the necessary storage protection services required for a reliable server operating system. Its implementation of C2 level security goes well beyond that provided by OS/2 and most UNIX implementations. It will take most of 1994 to get the applications and ruggedizing necessary to provide an industrial strength platform for business critical applications. With Microsoft's prestige and marketing muscle, NT will be installed by many organizations as their server of choice.

MVS

IBM provides MVS as a platform for large applications. Many of the existing application services that organizations have purchased operate on System 370-compatible hardware running MVS. The standard networking environment for many large organizations—SNA—is a component of MVS. IBM prefers to label proprietary systems today under the umbrella of SAA. The objective of SAA is to provide all services on all IBM platforms in a compatible way—the IBM version of the single-system image.

There is a commitment by IBM to provide support for the LAN Server running natively under MVS. This is an attractive option for organizations with large existing investments in MVS applications. The very large data storage capabilities provided by System 370-compatible platforms with MVS make the use of MVS for LAN services attractive to large organizations. MVS provides a powerful database server using DB2 and LU6.2. With broad industry support for LU6.2, requests that include DB2 databases as part of their view can be issued from a client/server application. Products such as Sybase provide high-performance static SQL support, making this implementation viable for high-performance production applications.

OPENVMS

Digital Equipment Corporation provides OPENVMS as its server platform of choice. VMS has a long history in the distributed computing arena and includes many of the features necessary to act as a server in the client/server model. DEC was slow to realize the importance of this technology, and only recently did the company enter the arena as a serious vendor. NetWare supports the use of OPENVMS servers for file services. DEC provides its own server interface using a LAN Manager derivative product called Pathworks.

Pathworks runs native on the VAX and RISC Alpha RXP. This is a particularly attractive configuration because it provides access on the same processor to the application, database, and file services provided by a combination of OPENVMS, NetWare, and LAN Manager. Digital and Microsoft have announced joint agreements to work together to provide a smooth integration of Windows, Windows NT, Pathworks, and OPENVMS. This will greatly facilitate the migration by OPENVMS customers to the client/server model.

VAX OPENVMS support for database products such as RDB, Sybase, Ingres, and Oracle enables this platform to execute effectively as a database server for client/server applications. Many organizations have large investments in VAX hardware and DECnet networking. The option to use these as part of client/server applications is attractive as a way to maximize the value of this investment. DECnet provides ideal support for the single-system image model. LAN technology is fundamental to the architecture of DECnet. Many large organizations moving into the client/server world of computing have standardized on DECnet for WAN processing. For example, Kodak selected Digital as its networking company even after selecting IBM as its mainframe outsourcing company.

UNIX

UNIX is a primary player as a server system in the client/server model. Certainly, the history of UNIX in the distributed computing arena and its open interfaces provide an excellent opportunity for it to be a server of choice. To understand what makes it an open operating system, look at the system's components. UNIX was conceived in the early 1970s by AT&T employees as an operating environment to provide services to software developers who were discouraged by the incompatibility of new computers and the lack of development tools for application development. The original intention of the UNIX architecture was to define a standard set of services to be provided by the UNIX kernel. These services are used by a shell that provides the command-line interface. Functionality is enhanced through the provision of a library of programs. Applications are built up from the program library and custom code. The power and appeal of UNIX lie in the common definition of the kernel and shell and in the large amount of software that has been built and is available. Applications built around these standards can be ported to many different hardware platforms.

The objectives of the original UNIX were very comprehensive and might have been achieved except that the original operating system was developed under the auspices of AT&T. Legal ramifications of the consent decree governing the breakup of the Regional Bell Operating Companies (RBOCs) prevented AT&T from getting into the computer business. As a result, the company had little motivation early on to promote UNIX as a product.

To overcome this, and in an attempt to achieve an implementation of UNIX better suited to the needs of developers, the University of California at Berkeley and other institutions developed better varieties of UNIX. As a result, the original objective of a portable platform was compromised. The new products were surely better, but they were not compatible with each other or the original implementation. Through the mid-1980s, many versions of UNIX that had increasing functionality were released. IBM, of course, entered the fray in 1986 with its own UNIX derivative, AIX. Finally, in 1989, an agreement was reached on the basic UNIX kernel, shell functions, and APIs.

The computing community is close to consensus on what the UNIX kernel and shell will look like and on the definition of the specific APIs. Figure 4.8 shows the components of the future standard UNIX operating system architecture.

During all of these gyrations, one major UNIX problem has persisted that differentiates it from DOS, Windows NT, and OS/2 in the client/ server world. Because the hardware platforms on which UNIX resides come from many manufacturers and are based on many different chip sets, the "off-the-shelf" software that is sold for PCs is not yet available for UNIX. Software is sold and distributed in its executable form, so it must be compiled and linked by the developer for the target platform.

This means that organizations wishing to buy UNIX software must buy it for the specific target platform they are using. This also means that when they use many platforms in a distributed client/server application, companies must buy different software versions for each platform.

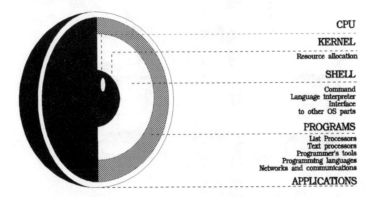

CPU
KERNEL
Resource allocation
SHELL
Command
Language interpreter
Interface
to other OS parts
PROGRAMS
List Processors
Text processors
Programmer's tools
Programming languages
Networks and communications
APPLICATIONS

Figure 4.8. UNIX architecture.

In addition to the complexity this entails, a more serious problem exists with software versioning. Software vendors update their software on a regular basis, adding functionality and fixing problems. Because the UNIX kernel is implemented on each platform and the software must be compiled for the target platform, there are differences in the low-level operation of each platform. This requires that software vendors port their applications to each platform they support. This porting function can take from several days to several months. In fact, if the platform is no longer popular, the port may never occur. Thus, users who acquire a UNIX processor may find that their software vendor is no longer committed to upgrading their software for this platform.

The major UNIX developer groups—UNIX International, Open Systems Foundation (OSF), and X/Open—have worked on plans to develop a binary compatible UNIX. If and when this happens, every new processor will execute the same metamachine language. Despite the fact that at the machine level there will be differences, the executable code will be in this metalanguage. Software developers then will be able to develop off-the-shelf UNIX applications. When we achieve this level of compatibility, the true promise of UNIX will be reached, and its popularity should take off. Figure 4.9 reflects the evolution of UNIX versions from the early 1970s to the 1995 objective of a unified UNIX. A unified UNIX will support off-the-shelf applications running on every platform.

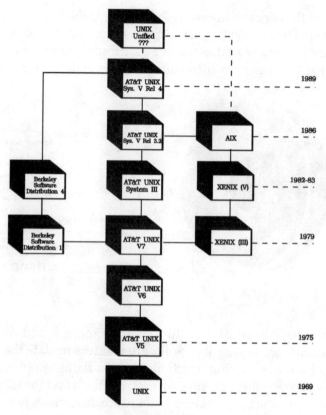

Figure 4.9. UNIX history.

The Open Software Foundation (OSF), a nonprofit consortium founded in 1988, now encompasses 74 companies, including Computer Associates, DEC, Groupe Bull, HP, IBM, Microsoft, Novell, Nippon Telegraph and Telephone Corp., Siemens Nixdorf, and even UNIX International Inc. (which was the standards-setting group for AT&T's, then X/Open's, UNIX System V). The OSF has set a goal to build distributed computing environment (DCE) compatibility into its distributed computing architecture. The OSF aims to provide an X/Open and POSIX compliant UNIX-like operating system using the Motif graphical user interface. The OSF has developed the Architecture Neutral Distribution Format (ANDF) with the intention of providing the capability to create and distribute shrink-wrapped software that can run on a variety of vendor platforms. The first operating system version OSF/1 was delivered by OSF in 1992 and implemented by DEC in 1993.

The important technologies defined for OSF include

- Remote procedure call (RPC) services
- Data-sharing services
- E-mail naming
- Security software
- Time services
- Parallel programming support
- Data-sharing and print services
- DOS file and printer clients

UNIX is particularly desirable as a server platform for client/server computing because of the large range of platform sizes available and the huge base of application and development software available. Universities are contributing to the UNIX momentum by graduating students who see only UNIX during their student years. Government agencies are insisting on UNIX as the platform for all government projects. The combination of these pressures and technology changes should ensure that UNIX compatibility will be mandatory for server platforms in the last half of this decade.

OSF initially developed Motif, a graphical user interface for UNIX, that has become the de facto UNIX GUI standard. The Distributed Computing Environment (DCE) is gaining acceptance as the standard for distributed application development although its Distributed Management Environment has yet to achieve such widespread support. OSF/1, the OSF defined UNIX kernel, has been adopted only by DEC, although most other vendors have made promises to support it. OSF/1 brings the promise of a UNIX micro kernel more suitable to the desktop environment than existing products.

The desire for a standard UNIX encourages other organizations. For example, the IEEE tackled the unified UNIX issue by establishing a group to develop a standard portable operating system called POSIX. The objective is to develop an ANSI standard operating system. POSIX isn't UNIX, but it is UNIX-like. POSIX standards (to which most vendors pledge compliance) exist today. DEC's OPENVMS operating system, for example, supports published POSIX standards. POSIX at this point, however, does little to promote interoperability and portability because so little of the total standard has been finalized. Simple applications that will run across different POSIX-compliant platforms will be written. However, they will be limited applications because developers will be unable to use any of the rich, non-POSIX features and functions that the vendors offer beyond the basic POSIX-compliant core.

X/Open started in Europe and has spread to include most major U.S. computer makers. X/Open is having significant impact in the market because its goal is to establish a standard set of Application Programming Interfaces (APIs) that will enable interoperability. These interfaces are published in the X/Open Portability Guide. Applications running on operating systems that comply with these interfaces will communicate with each other and interoperate, even if the underlying operating systems are different. This is the key objective of the client/server model.

The COSE announcement by HP, IBM, SCO, Sun, and Univel (Novell/USL) in March 1993 at the Uniforum Conference is the latest attempt to create a common ground between UNIX operating systems. The initial COSE announcement addresses only the user's desktop environment and graphical user interface, although in time it is expected to go further. COSE is a more pragmatic group attempting to actually "get it done."

Another major difference from previous attempts to create universal UNIX standards is the involvement of SCO and Sun. These two organizations own a substantial share of the UNIX market and have tended to promote proprietary approaches to the desktop interface. SCO provides its Open Desktop environment, and Sun offers Open Look. The commitment to Motif is a significant concession on their part and offers the first real opportunity for complete vendor interoperability and user transparency to platform.

In October of 1993, Novell agreed to give the rights to the UNIX name to X/Open so that all vendors can develop to the UNIX standards and use the UNIX name for their products. This largely symbolic gesture will eliminate some of the confusion in the marketplace over what software is really UNIX. COSE is looking beyond the desktop to graphics, multimedia, object technology, and systems management. Networking support includes Novell's NetWare UNIX client networking products, OSF's DCE, and SunSoft's Open Network Computing. Novell has agreed to submit the NetWare UNIX client to X/Open for publication as a standard. In the area of graphics, COSE participants plan to support a core set of graphics facilities from the X Consortium, the developer of X Windows.

Addressing multimedia, the COSE participants plan to submit two joint specifications in response to the Interactive Multimedia Association's request for technology. One of those specifications, called Distributed Media Services (DMS), defines a network-independent infrastructure supporting an integrated API and data stream protocol. The other—the Desktop Integrated Media Environment—will define multimedia access and collaboration tools, including at least one basic tool for each data type supported by the DMS infrastructure. The resulting standard will provide users with consistent access to multimedia tools in multivendor environments.

COSE also addresses object technology, an area targeted by IBM and Sun. The group will support the efforts of the Object Management Group (OMG) and its Common Object Request Broker (CORBA) standard for deploying and using distributed objects. IBM already has a CORBA-compliant object system in beta test for AIX. Sun built an operating system code named Spring as a proof of concept in 1992. Sun has a major project underway, called Distributed Objects Everywhere (DOE), that is producing very exciting productivity results. Finally, COSE will focus on the management of distributed file systems, distribution, groups and users, print spooling, software installation licensing, and storage.

It is not a coincidence that these vendors are coming together to define a standard UNIX at this time. The COSE effort is a defensive reaction to the release of Microsoft's Windows NT. With this commitment to a 32-bit desktop and server operating system, Microsoft has taken the wind out of many of the UNIX claims to technical superiority. Despite its numerous advantages as a desktop and server operating system, UNIX never has been widely accepted in the general corporate world that favors DOS/Windows and Novell's NetWare. A key drawback to UNIX in the corporate arena has been the lack of a single UNIX standard. UNIX has a well established position as the operating system of choice for distributed relational databases from vendors like Informix, Ingres, Oracle, and Sybase. Most of these vendors, however, will port their products to Windows NT as well. Any effort to reduce the problems associated with the multiple UNIX variants will do much to bolster the stature of UNIX as a worthwhile alternative to Windows NT.

Distributed Computing Environment (DCE)

Spin this fantasy around in your mind. All the major hardware and software vendors get together and agree to install a black box in their systems that will, in effect, wipe away their technological barriers. This black box will connect a variety of small operating systems, dissimilar hardware platforms, incompatible communications protocols, all sorts of applications and database systems, and even unlike security systems. And the black box will do all this transparently, not only for end users but also for systems managers and applications developers.[2] OSF proposes the distributed computing environment (DCE) as this black box. DCE is the most important architecture defined for the client/server model. It provides the bridge between existing investments in applications and new applications based on current technology. Figure 4.10 shows this architecture defined by the OSF.

The first product components of DCE were released in the third quarter of 1991. DCE competes directly with Sun's open network computing (ONC) environment and indirectly with many other network standards. OSF/1 and DCE are almost certain to win this battle because of the massive market presence of the OSF sponsors. IBM has now committed to making its AIX product OSF/1 compatible by early 1994. It will be 1995 before the product is mature and complete enough to be widely used as part of business applications. In the interim, product vendors and systems integrators will use it to build portable products and applications. The general availability of code developed for previous, similar product components will speed the process and enable new development to be modelled on the previous releases.

DCE has been described as another layer grouping in the OSI model.[3] DCE provides the link between pure communications on the lower layers and end-user applications. Figure 4.11 shows "where DCE fits in" between the operating system kernel and the user application services.

---

[2]*J.W. Semich, "The Distributed Connection:DEC," Datamation 37, No. 15 (August 1, 1991), p. 28.*

[3]*Jerry Cashin, "OSI DEC Attempt to Add OSI Service," Software Magazine 11, No. 3 (March 1991), p. 87.*

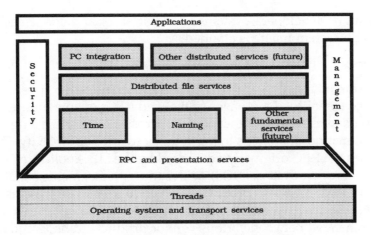

Figure 4.10. Distributed computing environment (DCE) architecture.

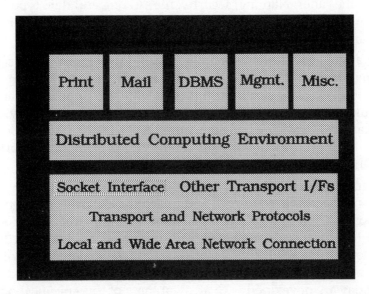

Figure 4.11. DCE on OS Layer 6.5.

DCE is a prepackaged group of integrated interoperability applications that connect diverse hardware and software systems, applications, and databases. To provide these services, DCE components must be present on every platform in a system. These components become active whenever a local application requests data, services, or processes from somewhere. The OSF says that DCE will make a network of systems from multiple vendors appear as a single stand-alone computer to applications developers, systems administrators, and end users. Thus, the single-system image is attained.

The various elements of DCE are as follows:

■ Remote Procedure Call (RPC) and Presentation Services: Interface Definition Languages (IDLs) and RPCs enable programmers to transfer control and data across a network in a transparent manner that helps to mask the network's complexity. DCE uses the RPC originally developed by the HP Apollo Network Computing System (NCS), with some enhancements by DEC and IBM. NCS also provides the Network Data Representation (NDR), a virtual data representation. NDR enables data to be exchanged between various vendor products transparently. Conversions (as necessary) will take place with no intervention by the caller. Naming, security, file system, and data type conversions may take place as data is transported between various platforms.

■ Naming: User-oriented names, specifying computers, files, and people should be easily accessible in a distributed environment. These directory services must offer standard appearance and rules for all clients. DCE supports the X.500 directory services standard, adding extensions from DEC's Domain Name Service (DECdns). The standardized X.500 code is Siemens Nixdorf's DIR-X X.500 service.

■ Security: Distributed applications and services must identify users, control access to resources, and guard the integrity of all applications. DCE uses the Kerberos authentication service, developed by MIT as part of its Athena networking project and enhanced by Hewlett-Packard. This service is one of the major challenges to making products available quickly, because very few products today are developed with an awareness of this specification.

■ Threads: This terminology represents a method of supporting parallel execution by managing multiple threads of control within a process operating in a distributed environment. Threads enable systems to start up multiple processes and forget about them until they are completed. This is especially important for network servers that may have to handle many requests from many clients at the same time. They must be able to do this without waiting for the previous request to complete. DCE is using DEC's Concert Multithread Architecture (CMA) implementation.

- Time Service: A time service synchronizes all system clocks of a distributed environment so that executing applications can depend on equivalent clocking among processes. Consider that many machines operating in many time zones may provide processes as part of a single application solution. It is essential that they agree on the time in order to manage scheduled events and time-sequenced events. DCE is using a modification of DEC's Distributed Time Synchronization Service (DECdts).

- Distributed File Services: By extending the local file system throughout the network, users gain full access to files on remote configurations. DCE uses Sun's Network File System (NFS) Version 2 and provides next-generation capabilities with the Andrew File System (AFS), developed at Carnegie-Mellon University and commercialized by Transarc Corp. Diskless operations under AFS are supported by development work done by Hewlett-Packard.

- PC Integration: Integration enables PCs using MS-DOS, Windows NT, and OS/2 to access file and print services outside the MS-DOS environment. DCE uses Microsoft's LAN Manager/X.

- Management: Although partly addressed by the previous components, management is so complex in a distributed, heterogeneous configuration that OSF has defined a new architecture: distributed management environment (DME). DME provides a common framework for the management of stand-alone and distributed systems. This framework provides consistent tools and techniques for managing different types of systems and enables vendors to build system management applications that work on a variety of platforms. OSF will base DME on technology from Hewlett-Packard's OpenView product.

- Communications: DCE is committed to support the OSI protocol stack.

System Application Architecture (SAA)

SAA is IBM's distributed environment. SAA was defined by IBM in 1986 as an architecture to integrate all IBM computers and operating systems, including MVS, VM/CMS, OS/400, and OS/2-EE. SAA defines standards for a common user access (CUA) method, common programming interfaces (CPI), and a common communication link (APPC).

To support the development of SAA-compliant applications, IBM described SAA frameworks (that somewhat resemble APIs). The first SAA framework is AD/Cycle, the SAA strategy for CASE application development. AD/Cycle is designed to use third-party tools within the IBM SAA hardware and mainframe Repository Manager/MVS data storage facility. Several vendors have been selected by IBM as AD/Cycle partners, namely: Intersolv, KnowledgeWare, Bachman, Synon, Systematica, and Easel Corp. Several products are already available, including the Easel WorkBench toolkit, Bachman DB2, CSP tools, and the KnowledgeWare Repository and MVS tools.

Unfortunately, the most important component, the Repository Manager, has not yet reached production quality in its MVS implementation and as yet there are no plans for a client/server implementation. Many original IBM customers involved in evaluating the Repository Manager have returned the product in frustration. Recently, there has been much discussion about the need for a production-quality, object-oriented database management system (OODBMS) to support the entity relationship (ER) model underlying the repository. Only this, say some sources, will make implementation and performance practical. A further failing in the SAA strategy is the lack of open systems support. Although certain standards, such as Motif, SQL, and LU6.2, are identified as part of SAA; the lack of support for AIX has prevented many organizations from adopting SAA. IBM has published all the SAA standards and has licensed various protocols, such as LU6.2. The company has attempted to open up the SAA software development world. IBM's director of open systems strategy, George Siegle, says that IBM believes in openness through interfaces. Thus, the complete definition of APIs enables other vendors to develop products that interface with IBM products and with each other. Recent announcements, such as support for CICS AIX, point to a gradual movement to include AIX in the SAA platforms. The first SAA application that IBM released, OfficeVision, was a disaster. The product consistently missed shipping dates and lacked much of the promised functionality. IBM has largely abandoned the product now and is working closely with Lotus and its workgroup computing initiatives.

IBM has consistently defined common database, user interface, and communications standards across all platforms. This certainly provides the opportunity to build SAA-compliant client/server applications. The recent introduction of CICS for OS/2, AIX, and OS/400 and the announcement of support for AIX mean that a single transaction-processing platform is defined across the entire range of products. Applications developed under OS/2 can be ported to interoperate between OS/2, OS/400, MVS, and eventually AIX, without modification. COBOL and C are common programming languages for each platform. SQL is the common data access language in all platforms.

The failure of SAA is attributable to the complexity of IBM's heterogenous product lines and the desire of many organizations to move away from proprietary to open systems solutions. This recognition led IBM to announce its new Open Enterprise plan to replace the old System Application Architecture (SAA) plan with an open network strategy. SystemView is a key IBM network product linking OS/2, UNIX, and AS/400 operating systems. Traditional Systems Network Architecture (SNA) networking will be replaced by new technologies, such as Advanced Peer-to-Peer Communications (APPC) and Advanced Peer-to-Peer Networking (APPN).

IBM has defined SystemView as its DME product. SystemView defines APIs to enable interoperability between various vendor products. It is expected to be the vehicle for linking AIX into centralized mainframe sites. IBM has stated that SystemView is an open structure for integrating OSI, SNA, and TCP/IP networks. At this time, SystemView is a set of guidelines to help third-party software developers and customers integrate systems and storage management applications, data definitions, and access methods. The guidelines are intended to further support single-system image concepts.

5

Components of Client/ Server Applications— Connectivity

Executive Summary

The network is the computer is the most appropriate description of client/server computing. Users want to feel that somewhere on the network the services they need are available and are accessible based on a need and right of access, without regard to the technologies involved. When ready to move beyond personal productivity stand-alone applications and into client/server applications, organ-izations must address the issues of connectivity. Initially, most users discover their need to access a printer that is not physically connected to their client workstation. Sharing data files among non-networked individuals in the same office can be handled by "sneakernet" (hand-carrying diskettes), but printing is more awkward. The first LANs installed are usually basic networking services to support this printer-sharing requirement. Now a printer anywhere in the local area can be authorized for shared use.

The physical medium to accomplish this connection is the LAN cabling. Each workstation is connected to a cable that routes the transmission either directly to the next workstation on the LAN or to a hub point that routes the transmission to the appropriate destination. There are two primary LAN topologies that use Ethernet (bus) and Token Ring (ring).

Ethernet and Token Ring are implemented on well-defined Institute of Electrical and Electronic Engineers (IEEE) industry standards. These standards define the product specification detail and provide a commitment to a fixed specification. This standardization has encouraged hundreds of vendors to develop competitive products and in turn has caused the functionality, performance, and cost of these LAN connectivity products to improve dramatically over the last five years. Older LAN installations that use nonstandard topologies (such as ARCnet) will eventually require replacement.

There is a basic functional difference in the way Ethernet and Token Ring topologies place data on the cable. With the Ethernet protocol, the processor attempts to dump data onto the cable whenever it requires service. Workstations contend for the bandwidth with these attempts, and the Ethernet protocol includes the appropriate logic to resolve collisions when they occur. On the other hand, with the Token Ring protocol, the processor only attempts to put data onto the cable when there is capacity on the cable to accept the transmission. Workstations pass along a *token* that sequentially gives each workstation the right to put data on the network.

Recent enhancements in the capabilities of intelligent hubs have changed the way we design LANs. Hubs owe their success to the efficiency and robustness of the 10BaseT protocol, which enables the implementation of Ethernet in a star fashion over Unshielded Twisted Pair (UTP) wiring. Now commonly used, hubs provide integrated support for the different standard topologies such as Ethernet, Token Ring, and Fiber (specifically, the FDDI protocol) over different types of cabling. By repeating or amplifying signals where necessary, they enable the use of high quality UTP cabling in virtually every situation.

Hubs have evolved to provide tremendous flexibility for the design of the physical LAN topologies in large office buildings or plants.

Various design strategies are now available. They are also an effective vehicle to put management intelligence throughout the LANs in a corporation, allowing control and monitoring capabilities from a network management center.

Newer token-passing protocols, such as Fiber Distributed Data Interface (FDDI) and Copper Distributed Data Interface (CDDI), will increase in use as higher performance LANs (particularly backbone LANs) are required. CDDI can be implemented on the same LAN cable as Ethernet and Token Ring if the original selection and installation are done carefully according to industry recommendations. FDDI usually appears first as the LAN-to-LAN bridge between floors in large buildings.

Wireless LANs offer an alternative to cabling. Instead of cabling, these LANs use the airwaves as the communications medium. Motorola provides a system—Altair—that supports standard Ethernet transmission protocols and cards. The Motorola implementation cables workstations together into microcells using standard Ethernet cabling. These microcells communicate over the airwaves to similarly configured servers. Communications on this frequency do not pass through outside walls, so there is little problem with interference from other users.

Wireless LANs are attractive when the cost of installing cabling is high. Costs tend to be high for cabling in old buildings, in temporary installations, or where workstations move frequently. NCR provides another implementation of wireless LAN technology using publicly accessible frequencies in the 902-MHz to 928-MHz band. NCR provides proprietary cards to provide the communications protocol. This supports lower-speed communications that are subject to some interference, because so many other devices, such as remote control electronic controllers (like a VCR controller) and antitheft devices, use this same frequency.

It is now a well-accepted fact that LANs are the preferred vehicle to provide overall connectivity to all local and distant servers. WAN connectivity should be provided through the interconnection of the LANs. Router and bridges are devices that perform that task. Routers are the preferred technology for complex network topologies, generating efficient routing of data packets between two systems by locating and using the optimal path. They also limit the amount of traffic on the WAN by efficiently filtering and by providing support for multiple protocols across the single network.

WAN bandwidth for data communications is a critical issue. In terminal-to-host networks, traffic generated by applications could be modeled, and the network would then be sized accordingly, allowing for effective use of the bandwidth. With LAN interconnections, and applications that enable users to transfer large files (such as through e-mail attachments) and images, this modeling is much harder to perform. WAN services that have recently emerged, such as Frame Relay, SMDS (Switched Multimegabit Data Service), and imminent ATM (Asynchronous Transfer Mode) services, enable the appropriate flexibility inherently required for these applications.

Frame Relay uses efficient statistical multiplexing to provide shared network resources to users. Each access line is shared by traffic destined for multiple locations. The access line speed is typically sized much higher than the average throughput each user is paying for. This enables peak transmissions (such as when a user transmits a large file) that are much faster because they use all available bandwidth.

SMDS is a high-speed service that uses cell relay technology, which enables data, voice, and video to share the same network fabric. Available from selected RBOCs as a wide-area service, it supports high speeds well over 1.5 Mbps.

ATM is an emerging standard and set of communication technologies that span both the LAN and the WAN to create a seamless network. It provides the appropriate capabilities to support all types of voice, data, and video traffic. Its speed is defined to be 155 Mbps, with variations and technologies that may enable it to run on lower speed circuits when economically appropriate. It will operate both as a LAN and a WAN technology, providing full and transparent integration of both environments.

ATM will be the most significant connectivity technology after 1995. ATM provides the set of services and capabilities that will truly enable the "computing anywhere" concept, in which the physical location of systems and data is made irrelevant to the user. It also provides the network managers with the required flexibility to respond promptly to business change and new applications.

Interoperability between distributed systems is not guaranteed by just providing network-based connectivity. Systems need to agree on the end-to-end handshakes that take place while exchanging data, on session management to set up and break conversations, and on resource access strategies. These are provided by a combination of network protocols such as Novell's IPX/SPX, NetBIOS, TCP/IP, and remote process interoperability technologies, such as RPC technology from Sun, Netwise, Sybase, Oracle, IBM's APPC, CPIC, and Named Pipes.

Network Management is an integral part of every network. The Simple Network Management Protocol (SNMP) is a well-accepted standard used to manage LANs and WANs through the management capabilities of hubs, routers, and bridges. It can be extended to provide basic monitoring performance measurements of servers and workstations. Full systems management needs much more functionality than SNMP can offer. The OSI management protocol, the Common Management Information Protocol (CMIP), which has the flexibility and capability to fully support such management requirements, will likely compete with an improved version of SNMP, SNMP V2.

Open Systems Interconnect

The OSI reference model shown in Figure 5.1 provides an industry standard framework for network and system interoperability. The existence of heterogeneous LAN environments in large organizations makes interoperability a practical reality. Organizations need and expect to view their various workgroup LANs as an integrated corporate-wide network. Citicorp, for example, is working to integrate its 100 independent networks into a single global net.[1] The OSI model provides the framework definition for developers attempting to create interoperable products.[2] Because many products are not yet OSI-compliant, there often is no direct correspondence between the OSI model and reality.

The OSI model defines seven protocol layers and specifies that each layer be insulated from the other by a well-defined interface.

---

[1]*Diane Medina, "Citicorp pulls it together; bank plans integration of 100 networks into one global net,"* Information Week, *No. 347 (November 18, 1991), p. 50.*

---

[2]*William Stallings,* Handbook of Computer-Communications Standards OSI Model and OSI Standards, *vol. 1 (Howard W. Sams), 1990.*

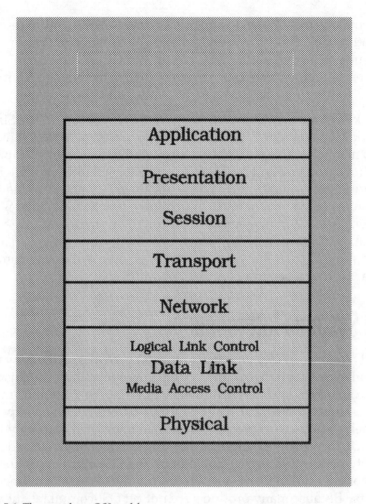

Figure 5.1. *The seven-layer OSI model.*

Physical Layer

The physical layer is the lowest level of the OSI model and defines the physical and electrical characteristics of the connections that make up the network. It includes such things as interface specifications as well as detailed specifications for the use of twisted-pair, fiber-optic, and coaxial cables. Standards of interest at this layer for client/server applications are IEEE 802.3 (Ethernet), and IEEE 802.5 (Token Ring) that define the requirements for the network interface card (NIC) and the software requirements for the media access control (MAC) layer. Other standards here include the serial interfaces EIA232 and X.21.

Data Link Layer

The data link layer defines the basic packets of data expected to enter or leave the physical network. Bit patterns, encoding methods, and tokens are known to this layer. The data link layer detects errors and corrects them by requesting retransmission of corrupted packets or messages. This layer is actually divided into two sublayers: the media access control (MAC) and the logical link control (LLC). The MAC sublayer has network access responsibility for token passing, collision sensing, and network control. The LLC sublayer operates above the MAC and sends and receives data packets and messages.

Ethernet, Token Ring, and FDDI define the record format of the packets (frames) being communicated between the MAC layer and Network layer. The internal formats are different and without conversion workstations cannot interoperate with workstations that operate with another definition.

Network Layer

The network layer is responsible for switching and routing messages to their proper destinations. It coordinates the means for addressing and delivering messages. It provides for each system a unique network address, determines a route to transmit data to its destination, segments large blocks of data into smaller packets of data, and performs flow control.

Transport Layer

When a message contains more than one packet, the transport layer sequences the message packets and regulates inbound traffic flow. The transport layer is responsible for ensuring end-to-end error-free transmission of data. The transport layer maintains its own addresses that get mapped onto network addresses. Because the transport layer services process on systems, multiple transport addresses (origins or destination) can share a single network address.

Session Layer

The session layer provides the services that enable applications running at two processors to coordinate their communication into a single session. A session is an exchange of messages—a dialog between two processors. This layer helps create the session, inform one workstation if the other drops out of the session, and terminate the session on request.

Presentation Layer

The presentation layer is responsible for translating data from the internal machine form of one processor in the session to that of the other.

Application Layer

The application layer is the layer to which the application on the processor directly talks. The programmer codes to an API defined at this layer. Messages enter the OSI protocol stack at this level, travel through the layers to the physical layer, across the network to the physical layer of the other processor, and up through the layers into the other processor application layer and program.

Communications Interface Technology

Connectivity and interoperability between the client workstation and the server are achieved through a combination of physical cables and devices, and software that implements communication protocols.

LAN Cabling

One of the most important and most overlooked parts of LAN implementation today is the physical cabling plant. A corporation's investment in cabling is significant. For most though, it is viewed strictly as a tactical operation, a necessary expense. Implementation costs are too high, and maintenance is a nonbudgeted, nonexistent process. The results of this shortsightedness will be seen in real dollars through the life of the technology. Studies have shown that over 65 percent of all LAN downtime occurs at the physical layer.

It is important to provide a platform to support robust LAN implementation, as well as a system flexible enough to incorporate rapid changes in technology. The trend is to standardize LAN cabling design by implementing distributed star topologies around wiring closets, with fiber between wiring closets. Desktop bandwidth requirements can be handled by copper (including CDDI) for several years to come; however, fiber between wiring closets will handle the additional bandwidth requirements of a backbone or switch-to-switch configuration.

Obviously, fiber to the desktop will provide extensive long-term capabilities; however, because of the electronics required to support various access methods in use today, the initial cost is significant. As recommended, the design will provide support for Ethernet, 4M and 16M Token Ring, FDDI, and future ATM LANs.

Cabling standards include RG-58 A/U coaxial cable (thin-wire 10Base2 Ethernet), IBM Type 1 (shielded, twisted pair for Token Ring), unshielded twisted pair (UTP for 10BaseT Ethernet or Token Ring) and Fiber Distributed Data Interface (FDDI for 10BaseT or Token Ring). Motorola has developed a wireless Ethernet LAN product—Altair—that uses 18-GHz frequencies. NCR's WaveLAN provides low-speed wireless LAN support.

Wireless LAN technology is useful and cost-effective when the cost of cable installation is high. In old buildings or locations where equipment is frequently moved, the cost of running cables may be excessive. In these instances wireless technology can provide an attractive alternative. Motorola provides an implementation that uses standard Ethernet NICs connecting a group of closely located workstations together with a transmitter. The transmitter communicates with a receiver across the room to provide the workstation server connection. Recent reductions in the cost of this technology make it attractive for those applications where the cost of cabling is more than $250 per workstation.

Wireless communication is somewhat slower than wired communication. Industry tests indicate a performance level approximately one-half that of wired 10-Mbps UTP Ethernet. NCR's alternative wireless technology, WaveLAN, is a slow-speed implementation using proprietary communications protocols and hardware. It also is subject to interference by other transmitters, such as remote control electronics, antitheft equipment, and point-of-sale devices.

Ethernet IEEE 802.3

Ethernet is the most widely installed network topology today. Ethernet networks have a maximum throughput of 10 Mbps. The first network interface cards (NICs) developed for Ethernet were much cheaper than corresponding NICs developed by IBM for Token Ring. Until recently, organizations who used non-IBM minicomputer and workstations equipment had few options other than Ethernet. Even today in a heterogeneous environment, there are computers for which only Ethernet NICs are available.

The large market for Ethernet NICs and the complete definition of the specification have allowed over 100 companies to produce these cards.[3] Competition has reduced the price to little more than $100 per unit.

10BaseT Ethernet is a standard that enables the implementation of the Ethernet protocol over telephone wires in a physical star configuration (compatible with phone wire installations). Its robustness, ease of use, and low cost driven by hard competition have made 10BaseT the most popular standards-based network topology. Its pervasiveness is unrivaled: In 1994, new laptop computers will start to ship with 10BaseT built in. IBM is now fully committed to support Ethernet across its product line.

Token Ring IEEE 802.5

IBM uses the Token Ring LAN protocol as the standard for connectivity in its products. In an environment that is primarily IBM hardware and SNA connectivity, Token Ring is the preferred LAN topology option. IBM's Token Ring implementation is a modified ring configuration that provides a high degree of reliability since failure of a node does not affect any other node. Only failure of the hub can affect more than one node. The hub isn't electric and doesn't have moving parts to break; it is usually stored in a locked closet or other physically secure area.

Token Ring networks implement a wire transmission speed of 4 or 16 Mbps. Older NICs will support only the 4-Mbps speed, but the newer ones support both speeds. IBM and Hewlett-Packard have announced a technical alliance to establish a single 100Mbps standard for both Token Ring and Ethernet networks. This technology, called

---

[3] Network World 8, No. 40 (October 7, 1991), p. 43.

100VG-AnyLAN, will result in low-cost, high-speed network adapter cards that can be used in PCs and servers running on either Token Ring or Ethernet LANs. The first AnyLAN products are expected in early 1994 and will cost between $250 and $350 per port. IBM will be submitting a proposal to make the 100VG-AnyLAN technology a part of IEEE's 802.12 (or 100Base-VG) standard, which currently includes only Ethernet. A draft IEEE standard for the technology is expected by early 1994.

100VG-AnyLAN is designed to operate over a variety of cabling, including unshielded twisted pair (Categories 3, 4, or 5), shielded twisted pair, and FDDI.

The entire LAN operates at the speed of the slowest NIC. Most of the vendors today, including IBM and SynOptics, support 16 Mbps over unshielded twisted-pair cabling (UTP). This is particularly important for organizations that are committed to UTP wiring and are considering the use of the Token Ring topology.

Fiber Distributed Data Interface

The third prevalent access method for Local Area Networks is Fiber Distributed Data Interface (FDDI). FDDI provides support for 100 Mbps over optical fiber, and offers improved fault tolerance by implementing logical dual counter rotating rings. This is effectively running two LANs. The physical implementation of FDDI is in a star configuration, and provides support for distances of up to 2 km between stations.

FDDI is a next-generation access method. Although performance, capacity, and throughput are assumed features, other advantages support the use of FDDI in high-performance environments. FDDI's dual counter-rotating rings provide the inherent capability of end-node fault tolerance. By use of dual homing hubs (the capability to have workstations and hubs connected to other hubs for further fault tolerance), highly critical nodes such as servers or routers can be physically attached to the ring in two distinct locations. Station Management Technology (SMT) is the portion of the standard that provides ring configuration, fault isolation, and connection management. This is an important part of FDDI, because it delivers tools and facilities that are desperately needed in other access method technologies.

There are two primary applications for FDDI: first as a backbone technology for interconnecting multiple LANs, and second, as a high-speed medium to the desktop where bandwidth requirements justify it.

Despite the rapid decrease in the cost of Token Ring and 10BaseT Ethernet cards, FDDI costs have been decreasing at a faster rate. As Figure 5.2 illustrates, the cost of 100 Mbps capable FDDI NICs reached $550 by the end of 1992 and is projected to reach $400 by 1995. The costs of installation are dropping as preterminated cable reaches the market. Northern Telecom is anticipating, with its FibreWorld products, a substantial increase in installed end-user fiber driven by the bandwidth demands of multimedia and the availability requirements of business critical applications.

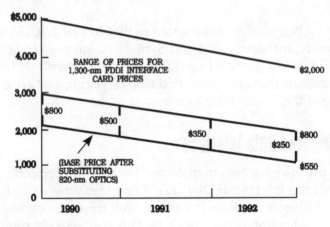

Figure 5.2. Affordable FDDI.

Copper Distributed Data Interface

The original standards in the physical layer specified optical fiber support only. Many vendors, however, have developed technology that enables FDDI to run over copper wiring. Currently, there is an effort in the ANSI X3T9.5 committee to produce a standard for FDDI over Shielded Twisted Pair (IBM compliant cable), as well as Data grade unshielded twisted pair. Several vendors, including DEC, IBM, and SynOptics are shipping an implementation that supports STP and UTP.

Ethernet versus Token Ring versus FDDI

The Ethernet technique works well when the cable is lightly loaded but, because of collisions that occur when an attempt is made to put data onto a busy cable, the technique provides poor performance when the

LAN utilization exceeds 50 percent. To recover from the collisions, the sender retries, which puts additional load on the network. Ethernet users avoid this problem by creating subnets that divide the LAN users into smaller groups, thus keeping a low utilization level.

Despite the widespread implementation of Ethernet, Token Ring installations are growing at a fast rate for client/server applications. IBM's commitment to Ethernet may slow this success, because Token-Ring will always cost more than Ethernet.

Figure 5.3 presents the results of a recent study of installation plans for Ethernet, Token Ring, and FDDI. The analysis predicts a steady increase in planned Token Ring installations from 1988 until the installed base is equivalent in 1996. However, this analysis does not account for the emergence of a powerful new technology which has entered the marketplace in 1993, Asynchronous Mode, or ATM. It is likely that by 1996 ATM will dominate all new installations and will gradually replace existing installations by 1999.

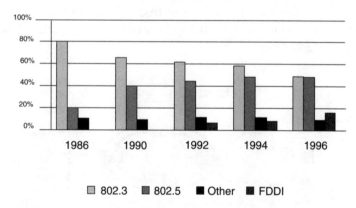

Figure 5.3. LAN-host connections.

As Figure 5.4. illustrates, Token Ring performance is slightly poorer on lightly loaded LANs but shows linear degradation as the load increases, whereas Ethernet shows exponential degradation after loading reaches 30 percent capacity.

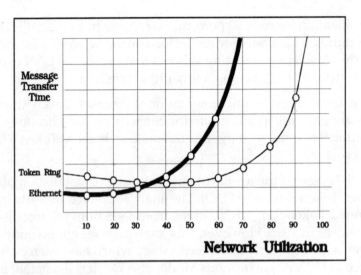

Figure 5.4. Ethernet, Token Ring utilization.

Figure 5.5 illustrates the interoperability possible today with routers from companies such as Cisco, Proteon, Wellfleet, Timeplex, Network Systems, and 3-Com. Most large organizations should provide support for the three different protocols and install LAN topologies similar to the one shown in Figure 5.5. Multiprotocol routers enable LAN topologies to be interconnected.

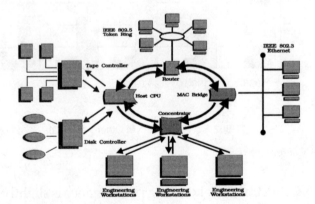

Figure 5.5. FDDI interoperability.

Asynchronous Transfer Mode (ATM)

ATM has been chosen by CCITT as the basis for its Broadband Integrated Services Digital Network (B-ISDN) services. In the USA, an ANSI-sponsored subcommittee also is investigating ATM.

The integrated support for all types of traffic is provided by the implementation of multiple classes of service categorized as follows:

- Constant Bit Rate (CBR): connection-oriented with a timing relationship between the source and destination, for applications such as 64 kbits voice or fixed bit rate video

- Variable Bit Rate (VBR): connection-oriented with a timing relationship between the source and destination, such as variable bit rate video and audio

- Bursty traffic: having no end-to-end timing relationship, such as computer data and LAN-to-LAN

ATM's capability to make the "computing aywhere" concept a reality is made possible because ATM eventually will be implemented seamlessly both in the LAN and in the WAN. By providing a single network fabric for all applications, ATM also gives network managers with the required flexibility to respond promptly to business change and new applications. (See Figure 5.6.)

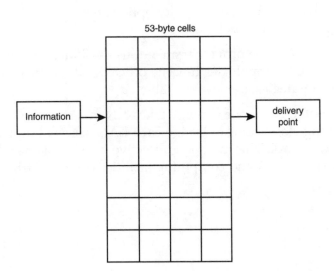

Figure 5.6. ATM Cells.

Hubs

One of the most important technologies in delivering LAN technology to mainstream information system architecture is the intelligent hub. Recent enhancements in the capabilities of intelligent hubs have changed the way LANs are designed. Hubs owe their success to the efficiency and robustness of the 10BaseT protocol, which enables the implementation of Ethernet in a star fashion over Unshielded Twisted Pair. Now commonly used, hubs provide integrated support for the different standard topologies (such as Ethernet, Token-Ring, and FDDI) over different types of cabling. By repeating or amplifying signals where necessary, they enable the use of high-quality UTP cabling in virtually every situation.

These intelligent hubs provide the necessary functionality to distribute a structured hardware and software system throughout networks, serve as network integration and control points, provide a single platform to support all LAN topologies, and deliver a foundation for managing all the components of the network.

There are three different types of hubs. *Workgroup hubs* support one LAN segment and are packaged in a small footprint for small branch offices. *Wiring closet hubs* support multiple LAN segments and topologies, include extensive management capabilities, and can house internetworking modules such as routers or bridges. *Network center hubs*, at the high end, support numerous LAN connections, have a high-speed backplane with flexible connectivity options between LAN segments, and include fault tolerance features.

Hubs have evolved to provide tremendous flexibility for the design of the physical LAN topologies in large office buildings or plants. Various design strategies are now available.

The distributed backbone strategy takes advantage of the capabilities of the wiring closet hubs to bridge each LAN segment onto a shared backbone network. This method is effective in large plants where distances are important and computing facilities can be distributed. (See Figure 5.7.)

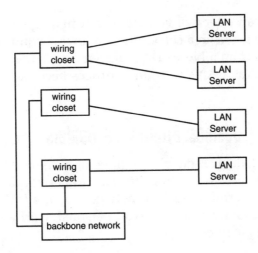

***Figure 5.7.** Distribution of LAN servers.*

The collapsed backbone strategy provides a cost-effective alternative that enables the placement of all LAN servers in a single room and also enables the use of a single high-performance server with multiple LAN attachments. This is particularly attractive because it provides an environment for more effective LAN administration by a central group, with all servers easily reachable. It also enables the use of high-capacity, fault-tolerant internetworking devices to bridge all LAN segments to form an integrated network. (See Figure 5.8.)

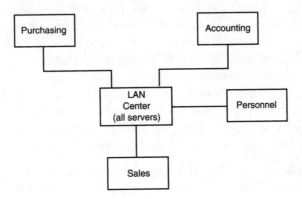

***Figure 5.8.** Bridging LAN segments.*

Hubs are also an effective vehicle to put management intelligence throughout the LANs in a corporation, allowing control and monitoring capabilities from a Network Management Center. This is particularly important as LANs in branch offices become supported by a central group.

Internetworking Devices: Bridges and Routers

Internetworking devices enable the interconnection of multiple LANs in an integrated network. This approach to networking is inevitably supplanting the terminal-to-host networks as the LAN becomes the preferred connectivity platform to all personal, workgroup, or corporate computing facilities.

Bridges provide the means to connect two LANs together—in effect, to extend the size of the LAN by dividing the traffic and enabling growth beyond the physical limitations of any one topology. Bridges operate at the data link layer of the OSI model, which makes them topology-specific. Thus, bridging can occur between identical topologies only (Ethernet-to-Ethernet, Token Ring-to-Token Ring). Source-Route Transparent bridging, a technology that enables bridging between Ethernet and Token-Ring LANs, is seldom used.

Although bridges may cost less, some limitations must be noted. Forwarding of broadcast packets can be detrimental to network performance. Bridges operate promiscuously, forwarding packets as required. In a large internetwork, broadcasts from devices can accumulate, effectively taking away available bandwidth and adding to network utilization. "Broadcast storms" are rarely predictable, and can bring a network completely to a halt. Complex network topologies are difficult to manage. Ethernet bridges implement a simple decision logic that requires that only a single path to a destination be active. Thus, in complex meshed topologies, redundant paths are made inoperative, a situation that rapidly becomes ineffective as the network grows.

Routers operate at the network layer of the OSI model. They provide the means to intelligently route traffic addressed from one LAN to another. They support the transmission of data between multiple standard LAN topologies. Routing capabilities and strategies are inherent to each network protocol. IP can be routed through the OSPF routing algorithm, which is different than the routing strategy for Novell's IPX/SPX protocol. Intelligent routers can handle multiple protocols; most leading vendors carry products that can support mixes of Ethernet, Token Ring, FDDI, and from 8 to 10 different protocols.

Transmission Control Protocol/Internet Protocol

Many organizations were unable to wait for the completion of the OSI middle-layer protocols during the 1980s. Vendors and users adopted the Transmission Control Protocol/Internet Protocol (TCP/IP), which was developed for the United States military Defense Advanced Research Projects Agency (DARPA) ARPANET network. ARPANET was one of the first layered communications networks and established the precedent for successful implementation of technology isolation between functional components. Today, the Internet is a worldwide interconnected network of universities, research, and commercial establishments; it supports thirty million US users and fifty million worldwide users. Additional networks are connected to the Internet every hour of the day. In fact growth is now estimated at 15 percent per month. The momentum behind the Internet is tremendous.

The TCP/IP protocol suite is now being used in many commercial applications. It is particularly evident in internetworking between different LAN environments. TCP/IP is specifically designed to handle communications through "networks of interconnected networks." In fact, it has now become the de facto protocol for LAN-based Client/Server connectivity and is supported on virtually every computing platform. More importantly, most interprocess communications and development tools embed support for TCP/IP where multiplatform interoperability is required. It is worth noting that IBM has followed this growth and not only provides support for TCP/IP on all its platforms, but now enables the transport of its own interoperability interfaces (such as CPIC, APPC) on TCP/IP.

TCP/IP's Architecture

The TCP/IP protocol suite is composed of the following components: a network protocol (IP) and its routing logic, three transport protocols (TCP, UDP, and ICMP), and a series of session, presentation and application services. The following sections highlight those of interest.

Internet Protocol

IP represents the network layer and is equivalent to OSI's IP or X.25. A unique network address is assigned to every system, whether the system is connected to a LAN or a WAN. The system comes with its associated routing protocols and lower level functions such as network-to-physical address resolution protocols (ARP). Commonly used routing protocols include RIP, OSPF, IGRP, and Cisco's proprietary protocol. OSPF has been adopted by the community to be the standards-based preferred protocol for large networks.

Transport Protocols

TCP provides Transport services over IP. It is connection-oriented, meaning it requires a session to be set up between two parties to provide its services. It ensures end-to-end data transmission, error recovery, ordering of data, and flow control. TCP provides the kind of communications that users and programs expect to have in locally connected sessions.

UDP provides connectionless transport services, and is used in very specific applications that do not require end-to-end reliability such as that provided by TCP.

Telnet

Telnet is an application service that uses TCP. It provides terminal emulation services and supports terminal-to-host connections over an internetwork. It is composed of two different portions: a client entity that provides services to access hosts and a server portion that provides services to be accessed by clients. Even workstation operating systems such as OS/2 and Windows can provide telnet server support, thus enabling a remote user to log onto the workstation using this method.

File Transfer Protocol (FTP)

FTP uses TCP services to provide file transfer services to applications. FTP includes a client and server portion. Server FTP listens for a session initiation request from client FTP. Files may be transferred in either direction, and ASCII and binary file transfer is supported. FTP provides a simple means to perform software distribution to hosts, servers, and workstations.

Simple Network Management Protocol (SNMP)

SNMP provides intelligence and services to effectively manage an internetwork. It has been widely adopted by hub, bridge, and router manufacturers as the preferred technology to monitor and manage their devices.

SNMP uses UDP to support communications between agents—intelligent software that runs in the devices—and the manager, which runs in the management workstation. Two basic forms of communications can occur: SNMP polling (in which the manager periodically asks the agent to provide status and performance data) and trap generation (in which the agent proactively notifies the manager that a change of status or an anomaly is occurring).

Network File System (NFS)

The NFS protocol enables the use of IP by servers to share disk space and files the same way a Novell or LAN Manager network server does. It is useful in environments in which servers are running different operating systems. However, it does not offer support for the same administration facilities that a NetWare environment typically provides.

Simple Mail Transfer Protocol (SMTP)

SMTP uses TCP connections to transfer text-oriented electronic mail among users on the same host or among hosts over the network. Developments are under way to adopt a standard to add multimedia capabilities (MIME) to SMTP. Its use is widespread on the Internet, where it enables any user to reach millions of users in universities, vendor organizations, standards bodies, and so on. Most electronic mail systems today provide some form of SMTP gateway to let users benefit from this overall connectivity.

TCP/IP and Internetworks

Interestingly, the interconnected LAN environment exhibits many of the same characteristics found in the environment for which TCP/IP was designed. In particular

- *Routing*: Internetworks need support for routing; routing is very efficient in TCP/IP environments with efficient protocols such as OSPF.

- *Connections versus Connectionless*: LAN activity includes both; the TCP/IP protocol suite efficiently supports both within an integrated framework.
- *Administrative Load Sensitivity*: A LAN administrative support is usually limited; contrary to IBM's SNA, TCP/IP environments contain a tremendous amount of dynamic capabilities, in which devices and networks are dynamically discovered, and routing tables are automatically maintained and synchronized.
- *Networks of Networks*: TCP/IP provides extreme flexibility as the administrative approach to the management of federations of networks. Taking advantage of its dynamic nature, it enables very independent management of parts of a network (if appropriate).

Vendor Products

One of the leading vendors providing TCP/IP support for heterogeneous LANs is FTP Software of Wakefield, Massachusetts, which has developed the Clarkson Packet Drivers. These drivers enable multiple protocols to share the same network adapter. This is particularly useful, if not necessary, for workstations to take advantage of file and print services of a NetWare server, while accessing a client/server application located on a UNIX or Mainframe server.

IBM and Digital both provide support for TCP/IP in all aspects of their products' interoperability. Even IBM's LU6.2/APPC specification can now run over a TCP/IP network, taking advantage of the ubiquitous nature of the protocol. TCP/IP is widely implemented, and its market presence will continue to grow.

Interprocess Communication

At the top of the OSI model, interprocess communications (IPCs) define the format for application-level interprocess communications. In the client/server model, there is always a need for interprocess communications. IPCs take advantage of services provided by protocol stacks such as TCP/IP, LU6.2, Decnet or Novell's IPX/SPX. In reality, a great deal of IPC is involved in most client/server applications, even where it is not visible to the programmer. For example, a programmer programming using ORACLE tools ends up generating code that uses

IPC capabilities embedded in SQL*net, which provide the communications between the client application and the server.

The use of IPC is inherent in multitasking operating environments. The various active tasks operate independently and receive work requests and send responses through the appropriate IPC protocols. To effectively implement client/server applications, IPCs are used that operate equivalently between processes in a single machine or across machine boundaries on a LAN or a WAN.

IPCs should provide the following services:

- Protocol for coordinating sending and receiving of data between processes
- Queuing mechanism to enable data to be entered asynchronously and faster than it is processed
- Support for many-to-one exchanges (a server dealing with many clients)
- Network support, location independence, integrated security, and recovery
- Remote procedure support to invoke a remote application service
- Support for complex data structures
- Standard programming language interface

All these features should be implemented with little code and excellent performance.

Peer-to-Peer Protocols

A peer-to-peer protocol is a protocol that supports communications between equals. This type of communication is required to synchronize the nodes involved in a client/server network application and to pass work requests back and forth.

Peer-to-peer protocols are the opposite of the traditional dumb terminal-to-host protocols. The latter are hierarchical setups in which all communications are initiated by the host. NetBIOS, APPC, and Named Pipes protocols all provide support for peer-to-peer processing.

NetBIOS

The Network Basic I/O System (NetBIOS) is an interface between the transport and session OSI layers that was developed by IBM and Sytek in 1984 for PC connectivity. NetBIOS is used by DOS and OS/2 and is commonly supported along with TCP/IP. Many newer UNIX implementations include the NetBIOS interface under the name RFC to provide file server support for DOS clients.

NetBIOS is the de facto standard today for portable network applications because of its IBM origins and its support for Ethernet, Token Ring, ARCnet, StarLAN, and serial port LANs, and its IBM origins.

The NetBIOS commands provide the following services:

- *General*: Reset, Status, Cancel, Alert, and Unlink. The general services provide miscellaneous but essential administrative networking services.

- *Name*: Add, Add Group, Delete, and Find. The naming services provide the capability to install a LAN adapter card with multiple logical names. Thus, a remote adapter can be referred to by a logical name such as Hall Justice, R601 rather than its burned-in address of X'1234567890123456'.

- *Session*: Call, Listen, Send, Chain Send, Send No-Ack, Receive, Receive Any, Hang Up, and Status. Sessions provide a reliable logical connection service over which a pair of network applications can exchange information. Each packet of information that gets exchanged over a session is given a sequence number, through which it is tracked and individually acknowledged. The packets are received in the order sent and blocked into user messages. Duplicate packets are detected and discarded by the sessions services. Session management adds approximately five percent overhead to the line protocol.

- *Datagram*: Send, Send-Broadcast, Receive, and Receive-Broadcast. Datagrams provide a simple but unreliable transmission service, with powerful broadcast capabilities. Datagrams can be sent to a named location, to a selected group (multicast) or to all locations on the network (broadcast). There is no acknowledgment or tracking of the datagram. Applications requiring a guarantee of delivery and successful processing must devise their own schemes to support such acknowledgment.

Application Program-to-Program Communication

The application program-to-program communication (APPC) protocol provides the necessary IPC support for peer-to-peer communications across an SNA network. APPC provides the program verbs in support of the LU6.2 protocol. This protocol is implemented on all IBM and many other vendor platforms. Unlike NetBIOS or Named Pipes, APPC provides the LAN and WAN support to connect with an SNA network, that may interconnect many networks.

Standards for peer-to-peer processing have evolved and have been accepted by the industry. IBM defined the LU6.2 protocol to support the *handshaking* necessary for cooperative processing between intelligent processors. Most vendors provide direct support for LU6.2 protocols in their WAN and the OSI committees and have agreed to define the protocol as part of the OSI standard for peer-to-peer applications. A recently quoted comment, "The U.S. banking system would probably collapse if a bug were found in IBM's LU6.2," points out the prevalence of this technology in highly reliable networked transaction environments.[4]

Programmers have no need or right to work with LU6.2 directly. Even with the services provided by APIs, such as APPC, the interface is unreasonably complex, and the opportunities for misuse are substantial. Vendors such as PeerLogic offer excellent interface products to enable programs to invoke the functions from COBOL or C. High-level languages, such as Windows 4GL, access network transparency products such as Ingres Net implemented in the client and server (or SQL*Net in Oracle's case).

These network products basically map layers five and six of the OSI model, generate LU6.2 requests directly to access remote SQL tables, and invoke remote stored procedures. These products include all the necessary code to handle error conditions, build parameter lists, maintain multiple sessions, and in general remove the complexity from the sight of the business application developer.

The power of LU6.2 does not come without complexity. IBM has addressed this with the definition of a Common Programmers Interface

---

[4] *Mohsen Al-Ghosein, Consultant for Microsoft Consulting Services, personal communication (1992).*

for Communications (CPI-C). Application program-to-program communication (APPC) is the API used by application programmers to invoke LU6.2 services. Nevertheless, a competent VTAM systems programmer must be involved in establishing the connection between the LAN node and the SNA network. The APPC verbs provide considerable application control and flexibility. Effective use of APPC is achieved by use of application interface services that isolate the specifics of APPC from the developer. These services should be built once and reused by all applications in an installation.

APPC supports conversational processes and so is inherently half-duplex in operation. The use of parallel sessions provides the necessary capability to use the LAN/WAN connection bandwidth effectively. In evaluating LU6.2 implementations from different platforms, support for parallel sessions is an important evaluation criterion unless the message rate is low.

LU6.2 is the protocol of choice for peer-to-peer communications from a LAN into a WAN when the integrity of the message is important. Two-phase commit protocols for database update at distributed locations will use LU6.2 facilities to guarantee commitment of all or none of the updates. Because of LU6.2 support within DECNET and the OSI standards, developers can provide message integrity in a multiplatform environment.

Named Pipes

Named Pipes is an IPC that supports peer-to-peer processing through the provision of two-way communication between unrelated processes on the same machine or across the LAN. No WAN support currently exists. Named Pipes are an OS/2 IPC. The server creates the pipe and waits for clients to access it. A useful compatibility feature of Named Pipes supports standard OS/2 file service commands for access. Multiple clients can use the same named pipe concurrently. Named Pipes are easy to use, compatible with the file system, and provide local and remote support. As such, they provide the IPC of choice for client/server software that do not require the synchronization or WAN features of APPC.

Named Pipes provide strong support for many-to-one IPCs. They take advantage of standard OS/2 and UNIX scheduling and synchronization services. With minimal overhead, they provide the following:

- A method of exchanging data and control information between different computers
- Transparency of the interface to the network
- API calls that facilitate the use of remote procedure calls (RPCs)

The use of an RPC across a named pipe is particularly powerful because it enables the requester to format a request into the pipe with no knowledge of the location of the server. The server is implemented transparently to the requester on "some" machine platform, and the reply is returned in the pipe. This is a powerful facility that is very easy to use. Named Pipes support should become widespread because Novell and OSF have both committed the necessary threads support.

One of the first client/server online transaction processing (OLTP) products on the market, Ellipse, is independent of any communications method, although it requires networking platforms to have some notion of sessions. One of the major reasons Cooperative Solutions chose OS/2 and LAN Manager as the first Ellipse platform is OS/2 LAN Manager's Named Pipes protocol, which supports sessions using threads within processes.

Ellipse uses Named Pipes for both client/server and interprocess communications on the server, typically, between the Ellipse application server and the database server, to save machine instructions and potentially reduce network traffic. Ellipse enables client/server conversations to take place either between the Ellipse client process and the Ellipse server process or between the Ellipse client process and the DBMS server, bypassing the Ellipse server process. In most applications, clients will deal with the DBMS through the Ellipse server, which is designed to reduce the number of request-response round trips between clients and servers by synchronizing matching sets of data in the client's working storage and the server DBMS.

Ellipse uses its sessions to establish conversations between clients and servers. The product uses a named pipe to build each client connection to SQL Server. Ellipse uses a separate process for Named Pipes links between the Ellipse server and the SQL Server product.

Ellipse also uses sessions to perform other tasks. For example, it uses a named pipe to emulate cursors in an SQL server database management system (DBMS). Cursors are a handy way for a developer to step through a series of SQL statements in an application. (Sybase doesn't have cursors.) Ellipse opens up Named Pipes to emulate this function, simultaneously passing multiple SQL statements to the DBMS. An SQL server recognizes only one named pipe per user, so Ellipse essentially manages the alternating of a main session with secondary sessions.

On the UNIX side, TCP/IP with the Sockets Libraries option appears to be the most popular implementation. TCP/IP supports multiple sessions but only as individual processes. Although UNIX implements low-overhead processes, there is still more overhead than incurred by the use of threads. LAN Manager for UNIX is an option, but few organizations are committed to using it yet.

Windows 3.x client support is now provided with the same architecture as the OS/2 implementation. The Ellipse Windows client will emulate threads. The Windows client requires an additional layer of applications flow-control logic to be built into the Ellipse environment's Presentation Services. This additional layer will not be exposed to applications developers, in the same way that Named Pipes were not exposed to the developers in the first version of the product.

The UNIX environment lacks support for threads in most commercial implementations. Cooperative Solutions hasn't decided how to approach this problem. Certainly, the sooner vendors adopt the Open Software Foundation's OSF/1 version of UNIX, which does support threads, the easier it will be to port applications, such as Ellipse, to UNIX.

The missing piece in UNIX thread support is the synchronization of multiple requests to the pipe as a single unit of work across a WAN. There is no built-in support to back off the effect of previous requests when a subsequent request fails or never gets invoked. This is the scenario in which APPC should be used.

Anonymous Pipes

Anonymous pipes is an OS/2 facility that provides an IPC for parent and child communications in a spawned-task multitasking environment. Parent tasks spawn child tasks to perform asynchronous processing. It provides a memory-based, fixed-length circular buffer, shared with the use of read and write handles. These handles are the OS/2 main storage mechanism to control resource sharing. This is a high-performance means of communication when the destruction or termination of a parent task necessitates the termination of all children and in-progress work.

Semaphores

Interprocess synchronization is required whenever shared-resource processing is being used. It defines the mechanisms to ensure that concurrent processes or threads do not interfere with one another. Access to the shared resource must be serialized in an agreed upon manner. *Semaphores* are the services used to provide this synchronization.

Semaphores may use disk or D-RAM to store their status. The disk is the most reliable and slowest but is necessary when operations must be backed out after failure and before restart. D-RAM is faster but suffers from a loss of integrity when there is a system failure that causes D-RAM to be refreshed on recovery. Many large operations use a combination of the two-disk to record start and end and D-RAM to manage in-flight operations.

Shared Memory

Shared memory provides IPC when the memory is allocated in a named segment. Any process that knows the named segment can share it. Each process is responsible for implementing synchronization techniques to ensure integrity of updates. Tables are typically implemented in this way to provide rapid access to information that is infrequently updated.

Queues

Queues provide IPC by enabling multiple processes to add information to a queue and a single process to remove information. In this way, work requests can be generated and performed asynchronously. Queues can operate within a machine or between machines across a LAN or WAN. File servers use queues to collect data access requests from many clients.

Dynamic Data Exchange

Through a set of APIs, Windows and OS/2 provide calls that support the *Dynamic Data Exchange* (DDE) protocol for message-based exchanges of data among applications. DDE can be used to construct hot links between applications in which data can be fed from window to window without interruption intervention. For example, a hot link can be created between a 3270 screen session and a word processing document. Data is linked from the 3270 window into the word processing document. Whenever the key of the data in the screen changes, the data linked into the document changes too. The key of the 3270 screen transaction Account Number can be linked into a LAN database. As new account numbers are added to the LAN database, new 3270 screen sessions are created, and the relevant information is linked into the word processing document. This document then can be printed to create the acknowledgment letter for the application.

DDE supports warm links created so the server application notifies the client that the data has changed and the client can issue an explicit request to receive it. This type of link is attractive when the volume of changes to the server data are so great that the client prefers not to be burdened with the repetitive processing. If the server link ceases to exist at some point, use a warm rather than hot link to ensure that the last data iteration is available.

You can create request links to enable direct copy-and-paste operations between a server and client without the need for an intermediate clipboard. No notification of change in data by the server application is provided.

You define execute links to cause the execution of one application to be controlled by another. This provides an easy-to-use batch-processing capability.

DDE provides powerful facilities to extend applications. These facilities, available to the desktop user, considerably expand the opportunity for application enhancement by the user owner. Organizations that wish to integrate desktop personal productivity tools into their client/server applications should insist that all desktop products they acquire be DDE-capable.

Remote Procedure Calls

Good programmers have developed modular code using structured techniques and subroutine logic for years. Today, these subroutines should be stored "somewhere" and made available to everyone with the right to use them. RPCs provide this capability; they standardize the way programmers must write calls to remote procedures so that the procedures can recognize and respond correctly.

If an application issues a functional request and this request is embedded in an RPC, the requested function can be located anywhere in the enterprise the caller is authorized to access. Client/server connections for an RPC are established at the session level in the OSI stack. Thus, the RPC facility provides for the invocation and execution of requests from processors running different operating systems and using different hardware platforms from the caller's. The standardized request form provides the capability for data and format translation in and out. These standards are evolving and being adopted by the industry.

Sun RPC, originally developed by Netwise, was the first major RPC implementation. It is the most widely implemented and available RPC today. Sun includes this RPC as part of their Open Network Computing (ONC) toolkit. ONC provides a suite of tools to support the development of client/server applications.

The Open Software Foundation (OSF) has selected the Hewlett-Packard (HP) and Apollo RPC to be part of its distributed computing environment (DCE). This RPC—based on Apollo's Network Computing System (NCS)—is now supported by Digital Equipment Corporation, Microsoft, IBM, Locus Computing Corp., and Transarc. OSI also has proposed a standard for RPC-like functions called Remote Operation Service (ROSE). The selection by OSF likely will make the HP standard the de facto industry standard after 1994. Organizations wishing to be compliant with the OSF direction should start to use this RPC today.

The evolution of RPCs and message-based communications is detailed in Figure 5.9.

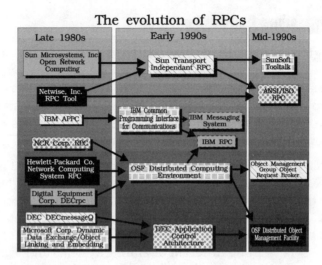

The evolution of RPCs

Figure 5.9. The evolution of RPCs.

Organizations that want to build applications with the capability to use RPCs can create an architecture as part of their systems development environment (SDE) to support the standard RPC when it is available for their platform. All new development should include calls to the RPC by way of a standard API developed for the organization. With a minimal investment in such an API, the organization will be ready to take advantage of the power of their RPC as it becomes generally available, with very little modification of applications required.

When a very large number of processes are invoked through RPCs, performance will become an issue and other forms of client/server connectivity must be considered. The preferred method for high-performance IPC involves the use of peer-to-peer messaging. This is not the store-and-forward messaging synonymous with e-mail but a process-to-process communications with an expectation of rapid response (without the necessity of stopping processing to await the result).

The Mach UNIX implementation developed at Carnegie Mellon is the first significant example of a message-based operating system. Its performance and functionality have been very attractive for systems that require considerable interprocess communications. The NeXT operating system takes advantage of this message-based IPC to implement an object-oriented operating system.

The advantage of this process-to-process communication is evident when processors are involved in many simultaneous processes. It is evident how servers will use this capability; however, the use in the client workstation, although important, is less clear. New client applications that use object-level relationships between processes provide considerable opportunity and need for this type of communication. For example, in a text-manipulation application, parallel processes to support editing, hyphenation, pagination, indexing, and workgroup computing may all be active on the client workstation. These various tasks must operate asynchronously for the user to be effective.

A second essential requirement is object-level linking. Each process must view the information through a consistent model to avoid the need for constant conversion and subsequent incompatibilities in the result.

NeXTStep, the NeXT development environment and operating system, uses PostScript and the Standard Generalized Markup Language (SGML) to provide a consistent user and application view of textual information. IBM's peer-to-peer specification LU6.2 provides support for parallel sessioning thus reducing much of the overhead associated with many RPCs, that is, the establishment of a session for each request. IBM has licensed this technology for use in its implementation of OSF/1.

RPC technology is here and working, and should be part of every client/server implementation. As we move into OLTP and extensive use of multitasking workgroup environments, the use of message-based IPCs will be essential. DEC's implementation is called DECmessageQ and is a part of its Application Control Architecture. The OSF Object Management Group (OMG) has released a specification for an object request broker that defines the messaging and RPC interface for heterogeneous operating systems and networks. The OMG specification is based on several products already in the marketplace, specifically HP's NewWave with Agents and the RPCs from HP and Sun. Organizations that want to design applications to take advantage of these facilities as they become available can gain considerable insight by analyzing the NewWave agent process. Microsoft has entered into an agreement with HP to license this software for inclusion in Windows NT.

Object Linking and Embedding

OLE is designed to let users focus on data—including words, numbers, and graphics—rather than on the software required to manipulate the data. A document becomes a collection of objects, rather than a file; each object remembers the software that maintains it. Applications that are OLE-capable provide an API that passes the description of the object to any other application that requests the object.

Wide Area Network Technologies

WAN bandwidth for data communications is a critical issue. In terminal-to-host networks, traffic generated by applications could be modeled, and the network would then be sized accordingly, enabling effective use of the bandwidth. With LAN interconnections and applications that enable users to transfer large files (such as through e-mail attachments) and images, this modeling is much harder to perform.

"Bandwidth-on-demand" is the paradigm behind these emerging technologies. Predictability of applications requirements is a thing of the past. As application developers get tooled for rapid application development and as system management facilities enable easy deployment of these new applications, the lifecycle of network redesign and implementation is dramatically shortened. In the short term, the changes are even more dramatic as the migration from a host-centric environment to a distributed client/server environment prevents the use of any past experience in "guessing" the actual network requirements.

Network managers must cope with these changes by seeking those technologies that will let them acquire bandwidth cost effectively while allowing flexibility to serve these new applications. WAN services have recently emerged that address this issue by providing the appropriate flexibility inherently required for these applications.

Distance-insensitive pricing seems to emerge as virtual services are introduced. When one takes into account the tremendous amount of excess capacity that the carriers have built into their infrastructure, this is not as surprising as it would seem. This will enable users and systems architects to become less sensitive to data and process placement when designing an overall distributed computing environment.

Frame Relay

Frame Relay network services are contracted by selecting two components: an access line and a *committed information rate* (CIR). This CIR speed is the actual guaranteed throughput you pay for. However, Frame Relay networks enable you, for example, to exceed this throughput at certain times to allow for efficient file transfers.

Frame Relay networks are often qualified as *virtual private networks*. They share a public infrastructure but implement virtual circuits between the senders and the receivers, similar to actual circuits. It is therefore a connection-oriented network. Security is provided by defining closed user groups, a feature that prevents devices from setting up virtual connections to devices they are not authorized to access.

Figure 5.10 illustrates a typical scenario for a frame relay implementation. This example is being considered for use by the Los Angeles County courts for the ACTS project, as described in Appendix A.

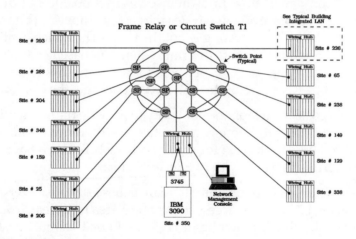

Figure 5.10. Frame relay implementation.

Switched Multimegabit Data Service (SMDS)

SMDS is a high-speed service based on cell relay technology, using the same 53-byte cell transmission fabric as ATM. It also enables mixed data, voice, and video to share the same network fabric. Available from selected RBOCs as a wide-area service, it supports high speeds well over 1.5 Mbps, and up to 45 Mbps.

SMDS differs from Frame Relay in that it is a connectionless service. Destinations and throughput to those destination do not have to be predefined. Currently under trial by major corporations, SMDS—at speeds that match current needs of customers—is a precursor to ATM services.

ATM in the Wide Area Network

The many advantages of ATM were discussed earlier in the chapter. Although not available as a service from the carriers, ATM will be soon be possible if built on private infrastructures.

Private networks have traditionally been used in the United States for high-traffic networks with interactive performance requirements. Canada and other parts of the world have more commonly used public X.25 networks, for both economic and technical reasons. With the installation of digital switching and fiber-optic communication lines, the telephone companies now find themselves in a position of dramatic excess capacity. Figure 5.11 illustrates the cost per thousand bits of communication. What is interesting is not the unit costs, which continue to decline, but the ratio of costs per unit when purchased in the various packages. Notice that the cost per byte for a T1 circuit is less than 1/5 the cost of a 64-Kbps circuit. In a T3 circuit package, the cost is 1/16.

In reality, it costs the telephone company to provide the service, initiate the call, and bill for it. There is no particular difference in the cost for distance and little in the cost for capacity. British Telecom has recently started offering a service with distance-insensitive pricing.

LANs provide a real opportunity to realize these savings. Every workstation on the LAN shares access to the wide-area facilities through the router or bridge. If the router has access to a T1 or T3 circuit, it can provide service on demand to any of the workstations on the LAN. This means that a single workstation can use the entire T1 for the period needed to transmit a document or file.

$/KB 1990

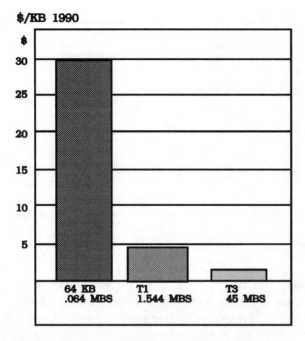

Figure 5.11. Communication bandwidth trends. (Source: PacTEL tariffs, 1992.)

As Figure 5.12 illustrates, this bandwidth becomes necessary if the transmission involves electronic documents. The time to transmit a character screen image is only 0.3 seconds with the 64-Kbps circuit. Therefore, increasing the performance of this transmission provides no benefit. If the transmission is a single-page image, such as a fax, the time to transmit is 164 seconds. This is clearly not an interactive response. Using a T1 circuit, the time reduces to only 5.9 seconds, and with a T3, to 0.2 seconds. If this image is in color, the times are 657 seconds compared to 23.5 and 0.8 seconds. In a client/server database application where the answer set to a query might be 10M, the time to transmit is 1,562 seconds (compared to 55.8 and 1.99 seconds).

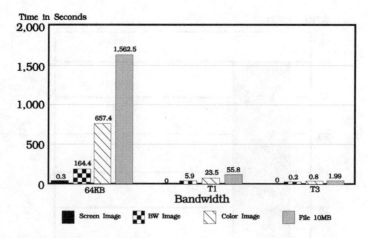

Figure 5.12. Communications throughput.

When designing the architecture of the internetwork, it is important to take into account the communications requirements. This is not just an issue of total traffic, but also of instantaneous demand and user response requirements. ATM technologies will enable the use of the same lines for voice, data, or video communications without preallocating exclusive portions of the network to each application.

Integrated Services Digital Network

ISDN is a technology that enables digital communications to take place between two systems in a manner similar to using dial-up lines. Connections are established over the public phone network, but they provide throughput of up to 64 Kbps. ISDN has two basic components:

- *B-Channel*: These two channels (hence the name of 2B+D for basic rate ISDN) provide communication services for either voice or data switched service. Data can be transmitted in any communications protocol.

- *D-Channel Signaling*: This channel is used by the terminal equipment to control call setup and disconnection. It is much more efficient than call control of a dial-up line; the time required to set up a call is typically less than three seconds.

ISDN Applications

ISDN can provide high quality and performance services for remote access to a LAN. Working from the field or at home through ISDN, a workstation user can operate at 64 Kbps to the LAN rather than typical modem speeds of only 9.6 Kbps. Similarly, workstation-to-host connectivity can be provided through ISDN at these speeds. Help desk support often requires the remote help desk operator to take control of or share access with the user workstation display. GUI applications transmit megabits of data to and from the monitor. This is acceptable in the high-performance, directly connected implementation usually found with a LAN attached workstation; but this transmission is slow over a communications link.

Multimedia applications offer considerable promise for future use of ISDN. The capability to simultaneously send information over the same connection enables a telephone conversation, a video conference, and integrated workstation-to-workstation communications to proceed concurrently. Faxes, graphics, and structured data all can be communicated and made available for all participants in the conversation.

Network Management

When applications reside on a single central processor, the issues of network management assume great importance but often can be addressed by attentive operations staff. With the movement to client/server applications, processors may reside away from this attentiveness.

If the data or application logic necessary to run the business resides at a location remote from the "glass house" central computer room, these resources must be visible to some network managers. The provision of a network control center (NCC) to manage all resources in a distributed network is the major challenge facing most large organizations today. Figure 5.13 illustrates the various capabilities necessary to build this management support. The range of services is much greater than services traditionally implemented in terminal connected host applications. Many large organizations view this issue as the most significant obstacle to successful rollout of client/server applications.

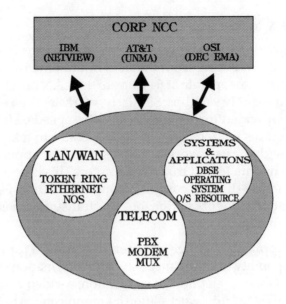

Figure 5.13. Network management.

Figure 5.13 illustrates the key layers in the management system architecture:

1. *Presentation* describes the management console environment and the tools used there.

2. *Reduction* refers to distributed intelligence, which acts as an intermediary for the network management interface. Reduction enables information to be consolidated and filtered, allowing the presentation service to delegate tasks through the use of an emerging distributed program services such as RPC, DME, or SMP. These provide the following benefits: response to problems and alerts can be executed locally to reduce latency and maintain availability, distributed intelligence can better serve a local environment—because smaller environments tend to be more homogeneous and such intelligence can be streamlined to reflect local requirements, scalability with regards to geography and political or departmental boundaries allows for local control and bandwidth optimization, reduction in management traffic overhead (because SNMP is a polling protocol), and placing distributed facilities locally reduced the amount of polling over a more expensive wide-area internet.

3. Gathering of information is done by device agents. Probably the greatest investment in establishing a base for the management network is through device management. Device management can represent the smallest piece of information, which may be insignificant in the overall picture. However, as network management tools evolve, the end result will be only as good as the information provided. These device agents provide detailed diagnostics, detailed statistics and precise control

OSF defines many of the most significant architectural components for client/server computing. The OSF selection of HP's Openview, combined with IBM's commitment to OSF's DME with its Netview/6000 product, ensures that we will see a dominant standard for the provision of network management services. There are five key OSI management areas:

- Fault management
- Performance management
- Inventory management
- Accounting management
- Configuration management

The current state of distributed network and systems management illustrate serious weaknesses when compared to the management facilities available in the mainframe world today. With the adoption of Openview as the standard platform and including products such as Remedy Corporation's Action Request System for problem tracking/process automation, Tivoli's framework for system administration, management and security, and support applications from vendors such as Openvision, it is possible to implement effective distributed network and systems management today. The required integration will create more difficulties than mainframe operations might.

Standards organizations and the major vendors provide their own solution to this challenge. There is considerable truth in the axiom that "the person who controls the network controls the business." The selection of the correct management architecture for an organization is not straightforward and requires a careful analysis of the existing and planned infrastructure. Voice, data, application, video, and other nonstructured data needs must all be considered.

Client/Server Systems
Development—
Software

6

Client/Server Systems
Development
Software

Executive Summary

If the selling price of automobiles had kept with the selling price of computer hardware, in 1992 dollars, a Geo would sell for $500. If the productivity improvement of telephone operators had kept pace with the productivity improvement in systems development, 60 percent of the adult U.S. population would need to work as telephone operators to handle the current volume of calls compared to the volume of the 1920s.

An Index Group survey found that up to 90 percent of information technology (IT) departments' budgets are spent maintaining and enhancing existing systems.[1] This maintenance and enhancement continues to be done using old, inefficient, and undisciplined processes and technology. Figure 6.1 documents the change in maintenance effort measured in Fortune 1000 companies from the 1970s until today. As the number of installed systems increases, organizations find more of their efforts being invested in maintenance. Ed Yourdon claims that the worldwide software asset base is in excess of 150 billion lines of code. Most of this code was developed in the 1960s and 1970s with older technologies. Thus, this code is unstructured and undocumented, leading to what the Gartner Group is calling the "Maintenance Crisis." We simply must find more effective ways to maintain systems.

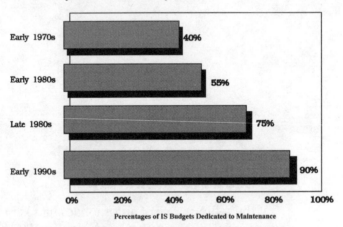

Figure 6.1. Percentage of IS budgets dedicated to maintenance.

Business Process Reengineering (BPR) techniques help organizations achieve competitive advantage through substantive improvements in quality, customer service and costs. BPR must be aligned with technology strategy to be effective. Organizations must use technology to enable the business change defined by the BPR effort. In too many organizations technology is inhibiting change. Many CIOs are finding that their careers are much shortened when they discover that the business strategy identified by their organization cannot be realized because the technical architecture employed lacks the openness to support the change.

---

[1]*Index Group Survey, Fortune 1000, December 1990.*

Senior executives look for new applications of technology to achieve business benefit. New applications must be built, installed, and made operational to achieve the benefits. Expenses incurred in maintenance and enhancement are not perceived to produce value. Yet, most measurements show that 66 percent of the cost of a system is incurred after its initial production release during the maintenance and enhancement phases. In this period of tight budgets it is increasingly difficult to explain and justify the massive ongoing investment in maintenance of systems that do not meet the current need.

Figure 6.2 illustrates how demand for new systems is increasing as technology costs decline and performance improves. Our challenge is to change the expenditures from ongoing maintenance to new development. Buying off-the-shelf application solutions frequently will meet the need. However, unless the packaged solution perfectly matches the needs of the organization, additional and expensive maintenance will be required to modify the package to make it fit.

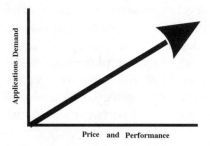

Figure 6.2. *Systems development demand.*

Clearly, the solution is to design and build systems within a systems development environment (SDE). Applications and systems within an SDE are built to be maintained and enhanced. The flexibility to accept enhancements is inherent in the design. A methodology defines the process to complete a function. The use of a systems integration life cycle methodology ensures that the process considers the ramifications of all decisions made from business problem identification through and including maintenance and operation of the resultant systems. The changes implied by BPR and the movement from mainframe-centered development to client/server technology requires that you adopt a methodology that considers organizational transformation. Object-oriented technologies (OOTs) can now be used to define the necessary methodology and development environment to dramatically improve our ability to use technology effectively.

With effective use of OO technologies productivity improvements of 10:1 are being measured. Systems are being built with error rates that are one-third that of traditionally developed systems. The creation and reuse of objects supports the enterprise on the desk through the reuse of standard technology to support the user and developer. OO technology allows business specialists to work as developers assembling applications by reusing objects previously constructed by more technical developers.

Factors Driving Demand for Application Software Development

Strategic planning, development, and follow-on support for applications software is a vital,—albeit expensive—process, that may yield enormous benefits in terms of cost savings, time to market for new products, customer satisfaction, and so on. There are opportunities to influence and compress application development planning time—through the use of an existing enterprise-wide architecture strategy or the adoption of a transformational outsourcing strategy. BPR and total quality management (TQM) programs demand software development and enhancements. A competitive market insists that companies demonstrate their value to a skeptical buyer through increasing the value of product and services.

Rising Technology Staff Costs

Coincident with the increasing demand for systems development, enrollment in university-level technology programs is declining, and the pool of available technical talent is shrinking relative to the exploding demand. As a result, technology personnel costs are rising much faster than inflation. In 1994, we see a 22-percent increase in demand for computer technologists. Many organizations find that technology professionals, in whom much organization specific application and technology knowledge has been invested, change jobs every three to five years. This multiplies the burden of reinvestment and retraining in organ-izations that are struggling to reduce costs. If organizations are to maximize their return on technology investments, they must develop a continuous learning program to ensure reuse of training programs, standard development procedures, developer tools and interfaces built for other systems.

Pressure to Build Competitive Advantage by Delivering Systems Faster

There is tremendous pressure on organizations to take advantage of new technology to build competitive advantage. This can be most easily accomplished by bringing innovative service offerings to market sooner than a competitor does. In most cases, new service offerings are required just to keep pace with competitors. The application backlog is horrific. Studies show that 80 to 90 percent of the traditional host-based MIS shop's staff time is devoted to maintaining or enhancing existing—often technically obsolete—applications. Some portion of the relatively small amount of time remaining is available for development of new applications.

For many organizations, implementing systems that not only increase efficiency and effectiveness but also transform fundamental processes to create a competitive advantage is absolutely essential to survival. For many companies, the prospects of global competition and uncertain recessionary times add fuel to the fire to succeed. Companies that cannot find inventive ways to refine their business process and streamline the value chain quickly will fall behind companies that can.

Need to Improve Technology Professionals' Productivitiy

The Index Group reports that the Computer-Aided Software Development (CASE) and other technologies that speed software development are cited by 70 percent of the tope IT executives surveyed as the most critical technologies to implement. The CASE market is growing at a rate of 30 percent per year, and Index's estimates predict it will be a $5 billion market by 1995, doubling from 1990 figures.

This new breed of software tools helps organizations respond more quickly by cutting the time it takes to create new applications and making them simpler to modify or maintain. Old methods, blindly automating existing manual procedures, can hasten a company's death knell.

Companies need new, innovative mission-critical systems to be built quickly, with a highly productive, committed professional staff partnered with end-users during the requirements, design, and construction phases. The client/server development model provides the means to develop horizontal prototypes of an application as it is designed. The user will be encouraged to think carefully about the implications of design elements. The visual presentation through the workstation is much more real than the paper representation of traditional methods.

Yourdon reports that less than 20 percent of development shops in North America have a methodology of any kind, and even a lower percentage actually use the methodology. Input Research reports that internally developed systems are delivered on time and within budget about 1 percent of the time. They compare this result to those outsourced through systems integration professionals who use high-productivity environments, which are delivered on time and within budget about 66 percent of the time.

The use of a proven, formal methodology significantly increases the likelihood of building systems that satisfy the business need and are completed within their budgets and schedules. Yourdon estimates that 50 percent of errors in a final system and 75 percent of the cost of error removal can be traced back to errors in the analysis phase. CASE tools and development methodologies that define systems requirements iteratively with high and early user involvement have been proven to significantly reduce analysis phase errors.

Need for Platform Migration and Reengineering of Existing Systems

Older and existing applications are being rigorously reevaluated and in some cases terminated when they don't pay off. A 15-percent drop in proprietary technology expenditures was measured in 1993 and this trend will continue as organizations move to open systems and workstation technology. BPR attempts to reduce business process cost and complexity by moving decision making responsibility to those individuals who first encounter the customer or problem. Organizations are using the client/server to bring information to the workplace of empowered employees.

The life of an application tends to be 5 to 15 years, whereas the life of a technology is much shorter—usually one to three years. Tremendous advances can be made by reengineering existing applications and preserving the rule base refined over the years while taking advantage of the orders-of-magnitude improvements that can be achieved using new technologies.

Need for a Common Interface Across Platforms

Graphical user interfaces (GUIs) that permit a similar look and feel and front-end applications that integrate disparate applications are on the rise.

A 1991 *Information Week* survey of 157 IT executives revealed that ease of use through a common user interface across all platforms is twice as important as the next most important criteria as a purchasing criterion for software. This is the single-system image concept.

Of prime importance to the single-system image concept is that every user from every workstation have access to every application for which they have a need and right without regard to or awareness of the technology.

Developers should be equally removed from and unconcerned with these components. Development tools and APIs isolate the platform specifics from the developer. When the single-systems image is provided, it is possible to treat the underlying technology platforms as a commodity to be acquired on the basis of price-performance without concern for specific compatibility with the existing application. Hardware, operating systems, database engines, communication protocols—all these must be invisible to the application developer.

Increase in Applications Development by Users

As workstation power grows and dollars-per-MIPS fall, more power is moving into the hands of the end user. The Index Group reports that end users are now doing more than one-third of application development; IT departments are functioning more like a utility. This is the result of IT department staff feeling the squeeze of maintenance projects that prevent programmers from meeting critical backlog demand for new development.

This trend toward application development by end-users will create disasters without a consistent, disciplined approach that makes the developer insensitive to the underlying components of the technology. End-user application developers also must understand the intricacies of languages and interfaces.

Object-oriented technologies embedded in SDE have regularly demonstrated to produce new development productivity gains of 2 to 1 and maintenance productivity improvements of 5 to 1 over traditional methods—for example, process-driven or data-driven design and development. More recently mature OO SDEs with a strong focus on object reusability are achieving productivity gains of 10 to 1 over traditional techniques.

Production-capable technologies are now available to support the development of client/server applications. The temptation and normal practice is to have technical staff read the trade press and select the best products from each category, assuming that they will combine to provide the necessary development environment. In fact, this almost never works. When products are not selected with a view as to how they will work together, they do not work together.

Thus, the best Online Transaction Processing (OLTP) package may not support YOUR best database. Your security requirements may not be met by any of your tools. Your applications perform well, but it may take forever to change them. Organizations must architect an environment that takes into account their particular priorities and the suite of products being selected. The selection of tools will provide the opportunity to be successful.

An enterprise-wide architecture strategy must be created to define the business vision and determine a transformation strategy to move from the current situation to the vision. This requires a clear understanding of industry standards, trends, and vendor priorities. Combining the particular business requirements with industry direction it is possible to develop a clear strategy to use technology to enable the business change. Without this architecture strategy, decisions will be made in a vacuum with little business input and usually little clear insight into technology direction.

The next and necessary step is to determine how the tools will be used within your organization. This step involves the creation of your SDE. Without the integration of an SDE methodology, organizations will be unable to achieve the benefits of client/server computing. Discipline and standards are essential to create platform-independent systems. With the uncertainty over which technologies will survive as standards, the isolation of applications from their computing platforms is an essential insurance policy.

Client/Server Systems Development Methodology

The purpose of a methodology is to describe a disciplined process through which technology can be applied to achieve the business objectives. Methodology should describe the processes involved through the entire life cycle, from BPR and systems planning through and including maintenance of systems in production. Most major systems integrators and many large in-house MIS groups have their own life cycle management methodology. Andersen Consulting, for example, has its Foundation, BSG has its Blueprint, and SHL Systemhouse has its own SHL Transform—the list goes on and on. These companies offer methodologies tuned for the client/server computing environment. However, every methodology has its own strengths, which are important to understand as part of the systems integration vendor selection process.

Figure 6.3 shows the processes in a typical systems integration life cycle. It is necessary to understand and adhere to the flow of information through the life cycle. This flow allows the creation and maintenance of the systems encyclopedia or electronic repository of data definitions, relationships, revision information, and so on. This is the location of the data models of all systems. The methodology includes a strict project management discipline that describes the deliverables expected from each stage of the life cycle. These deliverables ensure that the models are built and maintained. In conjunction with CASE tools, each application is built from the specifications in the model and in turn maintains the model's where-used and how-used relationships.

Table 6.1 details the major activities of each stage of the systems integration life cycle methodology. No activity is complete without the production of a formal deliverable that documents, for user signoff, the understanding gained at that stage. The last deliverable from each stage is the plan for the next stage.

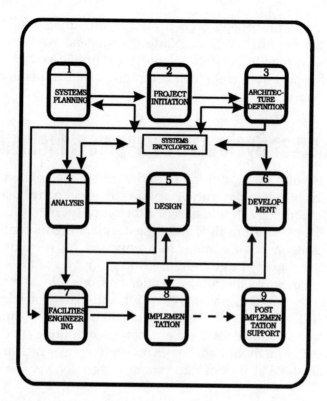

Figure 6.3. *Systems integration life cycle.*

Table 6.1. SILC phases and major activities.

SILC Phase	Major Activities
Systems Planning	Initiate systems planning
	Gather data
	Identify current situation
	Describe existing systems
	Define requirements
	Analyze applications and data architectures
	Analyze technology platforms
	Prepare implementation plan

SILC Phase	Major Activities
Project Initiation	Screen request
	Identify relationship to long-range systems plan
	Initiate project
	Prepare plan for next phase
Architecture Definition	Gather data
	Expand the requirements to the next level of detail
	Conceptualize alternative solutions
	Develop proposed conceptual architecture
	Select specific products and vendors
Analysis	Gather data
	Develop a logical model of the new application system
	Define general information system requirements
	Prepare external system design
Design	Perform preliminary design
	Perform detailed design
	Design system test
	Design user aids
	Design conversion system
Development	Set up the development environment
	Code modules
	Develop user aids
	Conduct system test

continues

Table 6.1. continued

SILC Phase	Major Activities
Facilities Engineering	Gather data
	Conduct site survey
	Document facility requirements
	Design data center
	Plan site preparation
	Prepare site
	Plan hardware installation
	Install and test hardware
Implementation	Develop contingency procedures
	Develop maintenance and release procedures
	Train system users
	Ensure that production environment is ready
	Convert existing data
	Install application system
	Support acceptance test
	Provide warranty support
Post-implementation Support	Initiate support and maintenance services
	Support hardware and communication configuration
	Support software
	Perform other project completion tasks as appropriate

Project Management

Many factors contribute to a project's success. One of the most essential is establishing an effective project control and reporting system. Sound project control practices not only increase the likelihood of achieving planned project goals but also promote a working environment where the morale is high and the concentration is intense. This is particularly critical today when technology is so fluid and the need for isolating the developer from the specific technology is so significant.

The objectives of effective project management are to

1. Plan the project:
   - Define project scope
   - Define deliverables
   - Enforce methodology
   - Identify tasks and estimates
   - Establish project organization and staffing
   - Document assumptions
   - Identify client responsibilities
   - Define acceptance criteria
   - Define requirements for internal quality assurance review
   - Determine project schedules and milestones
   - Document costs and payment terms
2. Manage and control project execution:
   - Maintain personal commitment
   - Establish regular status reporting
   - Monitor project against approved milestones
   - Follow established decision and change request procedures log and follow up on problems
3. Complete the project:
   - Establish clear, unambiguous acceptance criteria
   - Deliver a high-quality product consistent with approved criteria
   - Obtain clear acceptance of the product

New technologies such as client/server place a heavy burden on the architecture definition phase. The lack of experience in building client/server solutions, combined with the new paradigm experienced by the user community, leads to considerable prototyping of applications. These factors will cause rethinking of the architecture. Such a step is reasonable and appropriate with today's technology. The tools for prototyping in the client/server platform are powerful enough that prototyping is frequently faster in determining user requirements than traditional modeling techniques were.

When an acceptable prototype is built, this information is reverse engineered into the CASE tool's repository. Bachman's Information Systems' CASE products provide among the more powerful available tools to facilitate this process.

Architecture Definition

The purpose of the architecture definition phase in the methodology is to define the application architecture and select the technology platform for the application. To select the application architecture wisely, you must base the choice on an evaluation of the business priorities. Your organization must consider and weight the following criteria:

- Cost of operation—How much can the organization afford to pay?

- Ease of use—Are all system users well-trained, computer literate, and regular users? Are some occasional users, intimidated by computers, users with little patience, or familiar with another easy to use system? Will the system be used by the public in situations that don't allow for training or in which mistakes are potentially dangerous?

- Response time—What is the real speed requirement? Is it less than 3 seconds 100 percent of the time? What is the impact if 5 percent of the time the response lag is up to 7 seconds?

- Availability—What is the real requirement? Is it 24 hours per day, 7 days per week, or something less? What is the impact of outages? How long can they last before the impact changes?

- Security—What is the real security requirement? What is the cost or impact of unauthorized access? Is the facility secure? Where else can this information be obtained?

- Flexibility to change—How frequently might this application change? Is the system driven by marketing priorities, legislative changes, or technology changes?

- Use of existing technology—What is the existing investment? What are the growth capabilities? What are the maintenance and support issues?

■ System interface—What systems must this application deal
with? Are these internal or external? Can the systems being
interfaced be modified?

These application architecture issues must be carefully evaluated and
weighed from a business perspective. Only after completing this process can managers legitimately review the technical architecture options.
They must be able to justify the technology selection in the way it supports the business priorities. Figure 6.4 illustrates the conundrum we
face as we move from application architecture to technical architecture.
There is always a desire to manage risk and a corresponding desire to
use the best technology. A balance must be found between the two ex-
tremes of selecting something that fits the budget and is known to work
versus the newest, best, and unproven option. Cost is always a consideration.

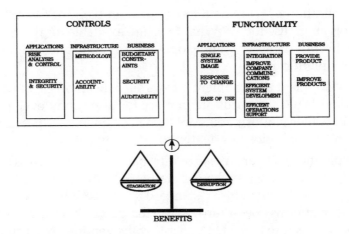

Figure 6.4. The objectives of an architecture.

Once managers understand the application architecture issues, it becomes appropriate to evaluate the technical architecture options. Notice that staff are not yet selecting product, only architectural features.
It is important to avoid selecting the product before purchasers understand the baseline requirements.

The following is a representative set of technical architecture choices:

■ Hardware (including peripherals)—Are there predefined standards for the organization? Are there environmental issues, such
as temperature, dirt, and service availability?

- Distributed versus centralized—Does the organization have a requirement for one type of processing over the other? Are there organizational standards?

- Network configuration—Does the organization have an existing network? Is there a network available to all the sites? What is the capacity of the existing network? What is the requirement of the new one?

- Communications protocols—What does the organization use today? Are there standards that must be followed?

- System software—What is used today? Are there standards in place? What options are available in the locale and on the anticipated hardware and communications platforms?

- Database software—Is there a standard in the organization? What exists today?

- Application development tools (for example, CASE)—What tools are in use today? What tools are available for the candidate platforms, database engine, operating system, and communications platforms?

- Development environment—Does such an environment exist today? What standards are in place for users and developers? What other platform tools are being considered? What are the architectural priorities related to development?

- Application software (make or buy, package selection, and so on)—Does the organization have a standard? How consistent is this requirement with industry-standard products? If there is a product, what platforms does it run on? Are these consistent with the potential architecture here? How viable is the vendor? What support is available? Is source code available? What are the application architecture requirements related to product acquisition?

- Human interface—What are the requirements? What is in place today? What are users expecting?

Figure 6.5 illustrates the layering of technical architecture and applications architecture. One should not drive the other. It is unrealistic to assume that the application architects can ignore the technical platform, but they should understand the business priorities and work to see that these are achieved. Interfaces must isolate the technical platform from the application developers. These interfaces offer the assurance that changes can be made in the platform without affecting functioning at the application layer.

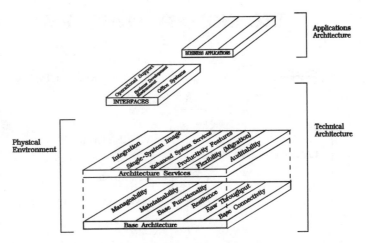

Figure 6.5. *Components of the technical and applications architectures.*

With the technical architecture well defined and the application architecture available for reference, you're prepared to evaluate the product options. The selection of the technology platform is an important step in building the SDE. There will be ongoing temptation and pressure to select only the "best products." However, the classification of "best product in the market," as evaluated in the narrow perspective of its features versus those of other products in a category, is irrelevant for a particular organization. Only by evaluating products in light of the application and technical architecture in concert with all the products to be used together can you select the best product for your organization.

Figure 6.6 details the categories to be used in selecting a technology platform for client/server applications. Architectures and platforms should be organizational. There is no reason to be constantly reevaluating platform choices. There is tremendous benefit in developing expertise in a well-chosen platform and getting repetitive benefit from reusing existing development work.

TECHNOLOGY PLATFORM

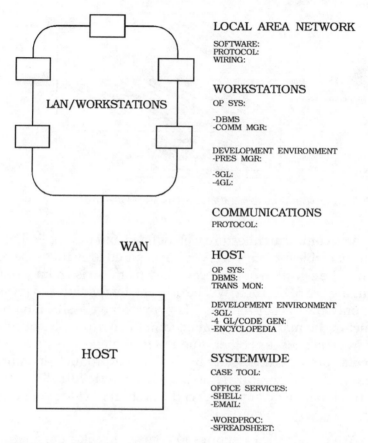

LOCAL AREA NETWORK

SOFTWARE:
PROTOCOL:
WIRING:

WORKSTATIONS

OP SYS:

-DBMS
-COMM MGR:

DEVELOPMENT ENVIRONMENT
-PRES MGR:

-3GL:
-4GL:

COMMUNICATIONS
PROTOCOL:

HOST

OP SYS:
DBMS:
TRANS MON:

DEVELOPMENT ENVIRONMENT
-3GL:
-4 GL/CODE GEN:
-ENCYCLOPEDIA

SYSTEMWIDE

CASE TOOL:

OFFICE SERVICES:
-SHELL:
-EMAIL:

-WORDPROC:
-SPREADSHEET:

Figure 6.6. Building the technology platform.

Systems Development Environment

Once your organization has defined its application and technical architectures and selected its tools, the next step is to define how you'll use these tools. Developers do not become effective system builders because they have a good set of tools; they become effective because their development environment defines how to use the tools well.

An SDE comprises hardware, software, interfaces, standards, procedures, and training that are selected and used by an enterprise to optimize its information systems support to strategic planning, management, and operations.

- An architecture definition should be conducted to select a consistent technology platform.
- Interfaces that isolate the user and developer from the specifics of the technical platform should be used to support the creation of a single-system image.
- Standards and standard procedures should be defined and built to provide the applications with a consistent look and feel.
- Reusable components must be built to gain productivity and support a single-system image.
- Training programs must ensure that users and developers understand how to work in the environment.

IBM defined its SDE in terms of an application development cycle, represented by a product line it called AD/Cycle, illustrated in Figure 6.7. Another way of looking at the SDE is illustrated in Figures 6.8 and 6.9. The SDE must encompass all phases of the systems development life cycle and must be integrated with the desktop. The desktop provides powerful additional tools for workstation users to become self-sufficient in many aspects of their information-gathering needs.

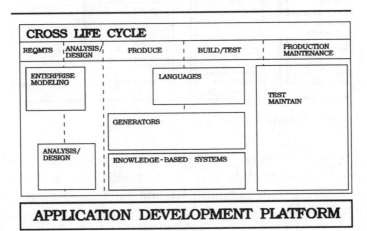

Figure 6.7. *IBM AD/Cycle model.*

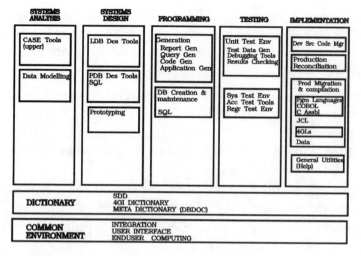

Figure 6.8. An SDE architecture.

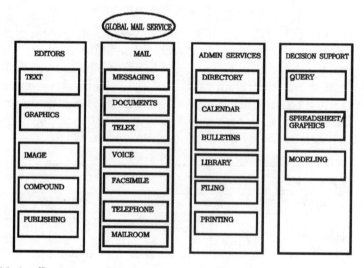

Figure 6.9. An office systems architecture.

The most significant advantages are obtained from an SDE when a conscious effort is made to build reusable components. These are functions that will be used in many applications and will therefore improve productivity. Appendix A's case studies illustrate the benefits of projects built within the structure of an SDE. With the uncertainty surrounding product selection for client/server applications today, the benefits of using an SDE to isolate the developers from the technology are even more significant. These technologies will evolve, and we can build applications that are isolated from many of the changes. The following components should be included in any SDE established by an organization:

- Built-in navigation—Every process uses the same methods to move among processes. For every process a default next process is identified, and all available processes are identified. This navigation definition is done by a business analyst and not the developer. Every user and every developer then views navigation in the same way.

- Standardized screen design—Well-defined standards are in place for all function types, and these screens are generated by default based on the business process being defined. Users and developers become familiar with the types of screens used for help, add, change, delete, view, and table management functions.

- Integrated help—A standardized, context-sensitive help facility should respond to the correct problem within the business process. No programmer development is required. The help text is provided by the end-user and analyst who understand how the system user will view the application. Help text is user maintainable after the system is in production.

- Integrated table maintenance—Tables are a program design concept that calls for common reference data, such as program error codes, printer control codes, and so on, to be stored in a single set of files or databases. A single table maintenance function is provided for all applications in the organization. Programmers and users merely invoke its services. Thus, all applications share standard tables.

- Comprehensive security—A single security profile is maintained for each authorized user. Navigation is tied to security; thus, users only see options they are eligible to use. Every programmer and user see the same security facilities. Security profiles are maintained by an authorized user and use the table maintenance facilities.

- Automatic view maintenance—Screens are generated, navigation is prescribed, and skeleton programs are generated based on the security profile and business requirements defined for a process. The developer does not have to write special code to extract data from the database. All access is generated based on the defined business processes and security.

■ Standard skeleton programs—An analyst answers a set of questions to generate a skeleton program for each business process. This feature includes standard functions that the programmer will require.

Every platform includes a set of services that are provided by the tools. This is particularly true in the client/server model, because many of the tools are new and take advantage of object-oriented development concepts. It is essential for an effective SDE to use the facilities and not to redevelop these because of elegance or ego.

Figure 6.10 illustrates the development environment architecture built for a project using Natural 4GL from Software AG. Software AG has successfully ported its Natural product from a mainframe-only environment to the workstation, where it can be used as part of a client/server architecture.

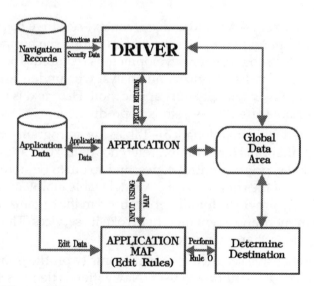

Figure 6.10. Software AG's natural architecture.

The ACTS example shown in Appendix A uses this SDE architecture with Easel and Telon. Users and developers can move between these environments with minimal difficulty because there is such a high degree of commonalty in the look and feel and in the services provided. Development within the justice application (of which ACTS is a part) included the Software AG products, Easel, and Telon. The same developers were productive throughout because of the common architecture. This occurred despite the fact that portions of the application were traditional mainframe, portions were mixed workstation-to-mainframe programs, and portions were pure client/server.

The advantages of building an SDE and including these types of components are most evident in the following areas:

- Rapid prototyping—The development environment generates skeleton applications with embedded logic for navigation, database views, security, menus, help, table maintenance, and standard screen builds. This framework enables the analyst or developer to sit with a user and work up a prototype of the application rapidly. In order to get business users to participate actively in the specification process, it is necessary to show them something real. A prototype is more effective for validating the process model than are traditional business modeling techniques. Only through the use of an SDE is such prototyping possible. Workstation technology facilitates this prototyping. The powerful GUI technology and the low cost of direct development at the workstation make this the most productive choice for developing client/server applications.

- Rapid coding—Incorporating standard, reusable components into every program reduces the number of lines of custom code that must be written. In addition, there is a substantial reduction in design time, because much of the design employs reusable, standard services from the SDE. The prototype becomes the design tool.

- Consistent application design—As mentioned earlier, much of the design is inherent in the SDE. Thus, by virtue of the prototype, systems have a common look and feel from the user's and the developer's perspectives. This is an essential component of the single-system image.

- Simplified maintenance—The standard code included with every application ensures that when maintenance is being done the program will look familiar. Because more than 50 percent of most programs will be generated from reusable code, the maintenance programmer will know the modules and will be able to ignore them unless global changes are to be made in these service functions. The complexity of maintenance corresponds to the size of the code and the amount of familiarity the programmer has with the program source. The use of reusable code provides the programmer with a common look and much less new code to learn.

■ Enhanced performance—Because the reusable components are written once and incorporated in many applications, it is easier to justify getting the best developers to build the pieces. The ability to make global changes in reusable components means that when performance problems do arise, they can often be fixed globally with a single change.

Productivity Measures

It is difficult to accurately quantify productivity gains obtained by using one method versus another, because developers are not willing to build systems twice with two different teams with the same skill set. However, a limited number of studies have been done estimating the expected cost of developing and maintaining systems without a formal SDE compared to the actual results measured with an SDE. One such analysis studied U.S. competitiveness. The researchers determined that, on average, a Japanese development team produces 170 percent of the debugged lines of code per year that a U.S. development team does. Japanese literature describes the Japanese approach to building systems as very consistent with the SDE approach described here. The necessity for Japanese developers to deal with U.S. software and a Japanese script language user interface has taught them the value of software layers. This led naturally to the development of reusable software components. Measurements by the researchers of errors in systems developed by Japanese and United States development teams showed that the Japanese had only 44 percent of the errors measured in the U.S. code.

Japanese developers work in a disciplined style that emphasizes developing to standards and reuse of common components. Our experience with SDE-based development is showing a 100-percent productivity improvement for lines of debugged source code per work year for new development and a 400-percent productivity increase for maintenance of existing systems. It's easy to understand the new code improvement rate from the facts noted earlier, but it is not as clear why the maintenance improvement is so great.

A significant reason for better productivity appears to be the reduction in testing effort that results from fewer errors. It is difficult to make changes to a production application. The cost and effort involved in changing production code is dramatically greater than changes to a test system. Developers and testers are careful about changes to production products. If you eliminate half the errors, you not only have happier users but also a substantial reduction in effort to correct the problems. The ability to make global changes and the reduction in complexity that comes from the familiar environment also improve maintenance productivity.

CASE

CASE tools are built on an "enterprise model" of the processes to be automated; that is, systems integration and software development. This underlying enterprise model or "metamodel" used by CASE is crucial to the tool's usefulness. Tools based on a poor model suffer from poor integration, are unable to handle specific types of information, require duplicate data entry, cannot support multiple analyst-developer teams, and are not flexible enough to handle evolving new techniques for specifying and building systems solutions. Tools with inadequate models limit their users' development capabilities.

All the leading CASE products operate and are used in a client/server environment. Intel 486-based workstations operating at 50MHz or faster, with 16-24 Mbytes of memory and 250Mbyte hard disks and UNIX workstations of similar size are typically required. Thus, combining hardware and CASE software costs, CASE costs up to $20,000 per user workstation/terminal.

Unfortunately, a thorough review of the available CASE products shows that none adequately provide explicit support for development of client/server applications and GUIs. This lack of support occurs despite the fact that they may operate as network-based applications that support development of host-based applications. There is considerable momentum to develop products that support the client/server model. The Bachman tools are in the forefront in this area because of their focus on support for business process reengineering. With many client/server applications being ported from a minicomputer or mainframe, the abilities to reuse the existing models and to reverse engineer the databases are extremely powerful and time-saving features.

It seems likely that no single vendor will develop the best integrated tool for the entire system's life cycle. Instead, in the probable scenario, developers mix the best products from several vendors. This scenario is envisioned by IBM in their AD/Cycle product line, by Computer

Associates in their CA90 products, and by NCR in their Open Cooperative Computing series of products.

As an example, an organization may select Bachman, which provides the best reengineering and reusability components and the only true enterprise model for building systems solutions for their needs. This model works effectively in the LAN environment and supports object-oriented reuse of specifications. The organization then integrates the Bachman tools with ParcPlace Parts product for Smalltalk code generation for Windows, UNIX or OS/2 desktops and server applications and with Oracle for code generation in the UNIX, OS/2, and Windows NT target environment. The visual development environments of these products provide the screen painting, business logic relationship, and prototyping facilities necessary for effective systems development.

A more revolutionary development is occurring as CASE tools like the Bachman products are being integrated with development tools from other vendors. These development tools, used with an SDE, allow applications to be prototyped and then reengineered back into the CASE tool to create process and data models. With the power of GUI-based development environments to create and demonstrate application look and feel, the prototyping approach to rapid application design (RAD) is the only cost-effective way to build client/server applications today.

Users familiar with the ease of application development on the workstation will not accept paper or visual models of their application. They can only fully visualize the solution model when they can touch and feel it. This is the advantage of prototyping, which provides a "real touch and feel." Except in the earliest stages of solution conceptualization, the tools for prototyping must be created using the same products that are to be used for production development.

Not all products that fall into the CASE category are equally effective. For example, some experts claim that the information engineering products—such as Texas Instruments' product, IEF—attempt to be all things to all people. The criticism is that such products are constrained by their need to generate code efficiently from their models. As a result, they are inflexible in their approach to systems development, have primitive underlying enterprise models, may require a mainframe repository, perform poorly in a team environment, and provide a physical approach to analysis that is constrained by the supported target technologies (CICS/DB2 and, to a lesser extent, Oracle). Critics argue that prototyping with this class of tool requires developers to model an unreasonable amount of detail before they can present the prototype.

Object-Oriented Programming (OOP)

OOP is a disciplined programming style that incorporates three key characteristics: encapsulation, inheritance, and dynamic binding. These characteristics differentiate OOP from traditional structured programming models, in which data has a type and a structure, is distinct from the program code, and is processed sequentially. OOP builds on the concepts of reuse through the development and maintenance of class libraries of objects available for use in building and maintaining applications.

■ Encapsulation joins procedures and data to create an object, so that only the procedures are visible to the user; data is hidden from view. The purpose of encapsulation is to mask the complexity of the data and the internal workings of the object. Only the procedures (methods) are visible to the outside world for use.

■ Inheritance passes attributes to dependent objects, called descendants, or receives attributes from objects, called ancestors, on which the objects depend. For example, the family airplane includes all structures, whereas the descendant jet inherits all the properties of airplane and adds its own, such as being nonpropeller-driven; the child F14 inherits all the properties of airplane and jet and adds its own properties—speed greater than 1,400 mph and climbing rate greater than 50 feet per second.

■ Dynamic binding is the process whereby linking occurs at program execution time. All objects are defined at runtime, and their functions depend on the application's environment (state) at the time of program execution. For example, in a stock management application, the function called program trading can sell or buy, depending on a large range of economic variables that define the current state. These variables are transparent to the user who invokes the trade process.

- Class library is a mature, tested library of reusable code that provides application-enabling code such as help management, error recovery, function key support, navigation logic, and cursor management. The class library concept is inherent to the SDE concept and—in combination with the standards and training fundamental—is inherent to the productivity and error reductions encountered in projects that use an SDE.

Object-oriented programming is most effective when the reusable components can be cut and pasted to create a skeleton application. Into this skeleton the custom business logic for this function is embedded. It is essential that the standard components use dynamic binding so that changes can be made and applied to all applications in the environment. This provides one of the major maintenance productivity advantages.

Certain programming languages are defined to be object-oriented. C++, Objective C, SmallTalk, MacApp, and Actor are examples. With proper discipline within an SDE it is possible to gain many of the advantages of these languages within the more familiar environments of COBOL and C. Because the state of development experience in the client/server world is immature, it's imperative for organizations to adopt the discipline of OOP to facilitate the reuse of common functions and to take advantage of the flexibility of global changes to common functions.

Objects are easily reused, in part because the interface to them is so plainly defined and in part because of the concept of inheritance. A new object can inherit characteristics of an existing object "type." You don't have to reinvent the wheel; you can just inherit the concept. Inheritance gives a concise and precise description of the world and helps code reusability, because every program is at the level in the "type hierarchy" at which the largest number of objects can share it. The resulting code is easier to maintain, extend, and reuse.

A significant new component of object-oriented development has been added with the capability to use server objects with RPC requests. During 1994, the introduction of CORBA compliant object stores will dramatically open the client/server paradigm to the "anything anywhere" dimension. Objects will be built and stored on an arbitrary server for use by any client or server anywhere. The earliest implementations of this model are provided by NeXT with its Portable Distributed Objects (PDO) and Suns Distributed Objects Everywhere (DOE) architecture.

And what about object-oriented database management system (OODBMS)? It combines the major object-oriented programming concepts of data abstraction, encapsulation, and type hierarchies with the database concepts of storage management, sharing, reliability, consistency, and associative retrieval.

When is an OODBMS needed, and when will an extended relational data-base management system (DBMS) do? Conventional database management products perform very well for many kinds of applications. They excel at processing large amounts of homogeneous data, such as monthly credit card billings. They are good for high-transaction-rate applications, such as ATM networks. Relational database systems provide good support for ad hoc queries in which the user declares what to retrieve from the database as opposed to how to retrieve it.

As we traverse the 1990s, however, database management systems are being called on to provide a higher level of database management. No longer will databases manage data; they must manage information and be the knowledge centers of the enterprise. To accomplish this, the database must be extended to

- Provide a higher level of information integration
- Store and retrieve all types of data: drawings, documents, fax, images, pictures, medical information, voice, and video

Many RDBMS products already handle binary large objects (BLOBs) in a single field of a relation. Many applications use this capability to store and provide SQL-based retrieval of digital laboratory data, images, text, and compound documents. Digital's Application Driven Database Systems (ADDS) have been established to enable its SQL to handle these complex and abstract data types more explicitly and efficiently.

But applications that require database system support are quickly extending beyond such traditional data processing into computer-aided design (CAD) and CASE, sophisticated office automation, and artificial intelligence. These applications have complex data structuring needs, significantly different data accessing patterns, and special performance requirements. Conventional programming methodologies are not necessarily appropriate for these applications and conventional data management systems may not be appropriate for managing their data.

Consider for a moment the factors involved in processing data in applications such as CAD, CASE, or generally in advanced office automation. The design data in a mechanical or electrical CAD database is heterogeneous. It consists of complex relationships among many types of data. The transactions in a CASE system don't lend themselves to transaction-per-second measurement; transactions can take hours or even days. Office automation applications deal with a hierarchical structure of paragraphs, sentences, words, characters, and character attributes along with page position and graphical images. Database access for these applications is typically a directed graph structure rather than the kind of ad hoc query that can be supported in SQL. Each object contains within its description reference to many other objects and elements. These are automatically collected by the object manager to provide the total view. In typical SQL applications, the developer makes explicit requests for related information.

In trying to manipulate such complex data using a relational system, a programmer writes code to map extremely complex in-memory data structures onto lower-level relational structures using awkward and resource-intensive recursive programming techniques. The programmer finds himself or herself doing database management instead of letting the DBMS handle it. Worse, even if the programmer manages to code the translation from in-memory objects to relational tables, performance is unacceptable.

Thus, relational systems have not been any help for the programmer faced with these complex coding tasks. The object-oriented programming paradigm, on the other hand, has proven extremely useful. The complex data structures CAD and CASE programmers deal with in memory are often defined in terms of C++ or Smalltalk objects.

It would be helpful if the programmer didn't have to worry about managing these objects, moving them from memory to disk, then back again when they're needed later. Some OOP systems provide this object "persistence" just by storing the memory image of objects to disk. But that solution only works for single-user applications. It doesn't deal with the important concerns of multiuser access, integrity, and associative recall.

Persistence means that objects remain available from session to session. Reliable means automatic recovery in case of hardware or software failures. Sharable means that several users should be able to access the data. All of these qualities may require systems that are larger than many that are currently available. In some cases, of course, programmers aren't dealing with overwhelmingly complex data, yet want to combine the increased productivity of object-oriented programming with the flexibility of an SQL DBMS. Relational technology has been extended to support binary large objects (BLOBs), text, image and compound documents, sound, video, graphics, animation, and abstract data types. As a result, organizations will be able to streamline paper-intensive operations to increase productivity and decrease business costs— assuming they use a database as a repository and manager for this data.

7

Client/Server Systems Development— Hardware

Executive Summary

As mentioned in Chapter 2, "Advantages of Client/Server Computing," the cost of powerful hardware for client/server computing has declined dramatically in the last few years. Nevertheless, this power must be packaged properly, and cost still must be considered in the design and purchasing decision. Hardware that provides the client/server, LAN-to-LAN, and LAN-to-WAN connectivity must be acquired for clients, servers, data storage, and the networks.

Entry-level client workstations can range from a basic Intel-based PC to an entry-level Apple Macintosh or an X-Terminal. These entry-level clients start at about $1,000 and use LAN servers for printing, backup, software storage, application execution, and WAN connectivity. High-end client workstations can cost more than $50,000 for engineering stations that provide advanced capabilities such as a gigabyte or more of local storage, high-resolution graphics monitors, 100-MIPS processing, direct WAN connectivity, 1000-dpi color printing, or professional multimedia development tools. The average client workstation has dropped from $5000 to $2000 in the last two years. This buys a configuration with the processing power equivalent to an 8Mbyte Intel 33-MHz 486DX PC with local storage of 250Mbytes, LAN connectivity, and a VGA-equivalent monitor. This cost level is not expected to decline much further, because GUI software and reengineered application requirements will steadily increase the processing power requirements for entry-level machines.

Server hardware offers the largest and most complex set of choices. Servers run the gamut from a $30M+ traditional IBM mainframe, to a 4- to 16-way symmetric segment multiprocessor machine, to a 32- to 32767-processor massively parallel cluster supporting hundreds of users, to a $5,000 PC used to provide file and connectivity services for a small LAN workgroup. Many organizations also have client/server applications that use the services of existing IBM 370 mainframes running VM, MVS, or VSE, DEC VAX minicomputers running VMS or Ultrix, and large RISC-based systems running UNIX—all as high-end servers.

Other mainframe and minicomputer hardware platforms, running proprietary operating systems, are frequently used in terminal emulation mode from the client workstation. The non-IBM and DEC proprietary operating system platforms rarely are used to provide other services, such as database and RPC-invoked application services. There is a lack of tools available in these environments to build or buy client/server applications. Servers based on the IBM, DEC, and UNIX operating systems will provide application services using existing applications through terminal emulation or RPC-invoked application services. These same servers will provide connectivity and database services to the first client/server applications in an organization.

Connectivity requires every client workstation to be connected to a LAN or through a WAN to a remote server. In the usual situation, the workstation is connected through an Ethernet, Token Ring, FDDI, CDDI, or occasionally a parallel or serial interface to the LAN. The primary connection types require a network interface card (NIC) to be inserted in the workstation to provide the protocol processing necessary to establish and maintain the connection. The cost of LAN connectivity has declined rapidly in parallel with the industry reduction in workstation costs.

Cabling costs vary widely, depending on the physical difficulty of installation and whether the network planners choose unshielded twisted-pair (UTP), shielded twisted-pair (STP), or glass-fiber cables. Cable costs without installation run from $1 per foot for UTP, $1.50 per foot for STP, to $3 per foot for glass fiber. Installation costs vary from $1 per foot to $15 per foot, depending on the physical environment and connection requirements. Glass-fiber termination equipment is more costly than twisted-pair, although the costs are declining. Current costs are between $100-200 for Ethernet, $300-500 for Token Ring, $300-700 for CDDI, and $750-1250 for FDDI.

Today, many vendors provide the hardware for these connections. Each vendor offers some advantages in terms of cost, performance, and reliability. Motorola provides wireless Ethernet connectivity at lower speeds and higher costs than wired connections. Wireless connections are an advantage in existing buildings with no cable installed and with relatively low-speed communications requirements.

WAN connectivity requires each workstation to be directly connected to the WAN or to a communications server connected to the WAN. Most new LANs are installed using communications servers. There are cost, performance, and especially network management reasons for using a LAN communications server. A substantial advantage accrues because there is no need to cable each workstation to the WAN. Workstations that are individually connected to the WAN require an embedded controller card for synchronous communications and either a modem or serial connection for asynchronous communications. These typically operate at speeds of 2400-64000 bits per second (bps) through analog or digital modems. Each workstation must have its own cable connecting it to the WAN controller. Workstations connected to the WAN through a communications server share a higher-speed connection, typically 14400 bps, 56000 bps, or 1.54 Mbps.

A major advantage of the communications server is its ability to multiplex a high-speed communications line and provide bandwidth on demand to each client workstation. Only the single LAN cable and LAN controller are needed to provide workstation connectivity in the server implementation.

Data storage can be provided to a client from a local disk or through the file services of the NOS. Local disk storage requires the workstation to have its own disk devices. Server storage involves large shared server disks. In either case, a backup capability must be provided. This can be done through local diskette or tape devices or though a server tape, disk, or optical device.

Hardware/Network Acquisition

Before selecting client hardware for end users, most organizations should define standards for classes of users. This set of standards simplifies the selection of the appropriate client hardware for a user and allows buyers to arrange purchasing agreements to gain volume pricing discounts.

There are a number of issues to consider when selecting the client workstation, including processor type, coprocessor capability, internal bus structure, size of the base unit, and so on. However, of these issues, one of the most overlooked regarding client/server applications is the use of a GUI. GUI applications require VGA or better screen drivers. Screens, larger than the 15-inch PC standard, are required for users who normally display several active windows at one time; the more windows active on-screen, the larger the monitor viewing area requirements. The use of image, graphics, or full-motion video requires a large screen with very high resolution for regular usage. It is important to remember that productivity is dramatically affected by inability to easily read the screen all day. Inappropriate resolution will lead to fatigue and inefficiency.

The enterprise on the desk requires that adequate bandwidth be available to provide responsiveness to the desktop user. If regular access to off LAN data is required, a router based internetworking implementation will be required. If only occasional off LAN access is required, bridges can be used. Routers provide the additional advantage of support for multiprotocol internetworking. This is frequently necessary as organizations install 10BaseT Ethernet into an existing Token Ring environment. Fast Ethernet and FDDI are becoming more prevalent as multimedia applications are delivered.

PC-Level Processing Units

Client/server applications vary considerably in their client processing requirements and their I/O demands on the client processor and server. In general, clients that support protected-mode addressing should be purchased. This implies the use of 32-bit processors—perhaps with a 16-bit I/O bus if the I/O requirement is low. Low means the client isn't required to send and receive large amounts of data, such as images, which could be 100K bytes or larger, on a constant basis.

As multiwindowed and multimedia applications become prevalent during 1994, many applications will require the bandwidth only provided by a 32-bit I/O bus using VESA VL-bus or Intel PCI technology. Windowed applications require considerable processing power to provide adequate response levels. The introduction of application integration via DCE, OLE, and DOE significantly increases the processing requirements at the desktop. The recommended minimum configuration for desktop processors has the processing capacity of a 33Mhz Intel 486SX. By early 1995, the minimum requirement will be the processing capacity of a 50Mhz Intel 486DX or a 33Mhz Intel Pentium.

Macintosh

The Mac System 7 operating system is visually intuitive and provides the best productivity when response time to GUI operations is secondary. The Motorola 68040, 8Mbytes RAM, 120Mbyte disk is recommended. By early 1995, the availability of PowerPC technology and the integration of System 7 with AIX and Windows means that users will need considerably more processor capacity. Fortunately, the PowerPC will provide this for the same or lower cost than the existing Motorola technology.

Notebooks

Users working remotely on a regular basis may find that a notebook computer best satisfies their requirements. The notebook computer is the fastest growing market today. The current technology in this area is available for Intel PC, Apple Macintosh, and SPARC UNIX processors. Because notebooks are "miniaturized," their disk drives are often not comparable to full-size desktop units. Thus, the relatively slower speed of disk I/O on notebooks makes it preferable to install extra RAM, creating "virtual" disk drives.

A minimal configuration is a processor with the equivalent processing power of a 33Mhz Intel 486SX, 8mbytes of RAM and 140Mbytes of disk. In addition, the notebook with battery should weigh less than seven pounds and have a battery life of three hours. Color support is an option during 1994 but will be mandatory for all by 1995. In addition, if the application will run a remote GUI, it is desirable to install software to compress the GUI and V.32 modem communications at 9600 bps or V.32bis at 14400 bps, employing V.42 and V.42bis compression, respectively. The effective throughput is two to three times the baud rate because of compression. The use of MNP4 and V.42 or MNP5 and V.42bis error correction enables these speeds to work effectively even during noisy line conditions. The introduction of PCMCIA technology, credit card size modems, and flash memory are available to upgrade the notebook.

Pen

Pen-based clients provide the capability to operate applications using a pen to point and select or write without the need for a mouse or keyboard. Frequently, they are used for verification, selection, and inquiry applications where selection lists are available. Developers using this technology use object-oriented software techniques that are RAM-intensive.

The introduction of personal digital assistant (PDA) technology in 1993 has opened the market to pocket size computing. During 1994, this technology will mature with increased storage capacity through cheaper, denser RAM and flash memory technology. The screen resolution will improve, and applications will be developed that are not dependent upon cursive writing recognition.

The PDA market is price-sensitive to a $500-$1000 device with the capability to run a Windows-like operating environment in 4MB of RAM, a 20Mhz Intel 486SX processor, and 8MB of flash memory. Devices with this capability will appear in 1994, and significant applications beyond personal diaries will be in use. During 1995, 16MB of RAM and 32MB of flash memory will begin to appear, enabling these devices to reach a mass market beyond 1996. In combination with wireless technology advances, this will become the personal information source for electronic news, magazines, books, and so on. Your electronic Personal Wall Street Journal will follow you for access on your PDA.

UNIX Workstation

UNIX client workstations are used when the client processing needs are intensive. In many applications requiring UNIX, X-terminals connected to a UNIX presentation server will be the clients of choice. A UNIX client workstation will then have more processing power than a PC client.

The introduction of software from SunSoft, Insignia Solutions, and Locus Computing that supports the execution of DOS and Windows 3.x applications in a UNIX window makes the UNIX desktop available to users requiring software from both environments. The PowerPC and Sparc technologies will battle for this marketplace. Both are expected to gain market share from Intel during and after 1994.

X-Terminals

X-terminals provide the capability to perform only presentation services at the workstation. Processing services are provided by another UNIX, Windows 3.x, NT, OS/2 2.x, or VMS server. Database, communications, and applications services are provided by the same or other servers in the network. The minimum memory configuration requirement for an X-terminal used in a client/server application is 4-8 Mbytes RAM, depending on the number of open windows.

Server Hardware

Server requirements vary according to the complexity of the application and the distribution of work. Because servers are multiuser devices, the number of active users is also a major sizing factor. Servers that provide for 32-bit preemptive multitasking operating systems with storage protection are preferred in the multiuser environment.

Intel-based tower PCs and Symmetric Multi-Processors (SMPs) are commonly used for workgroup LANs with file and application service requirements. Most PC vendors provide a 66Mhz Intel 486DX or Intel

Pentium for this market in 1994. SMP products are provided by vendors such as IBM, Compaq, and NetFrame. Traditional UNIX vendors, such as Sun, HP, IBM, and Pyramid provide server hardware for applications requiring UNIX stability and capacity for database and application servers and large workgroup file services.

The SMP products, in conjunction with RAID disk technology, can be configured to provide mainframe level reliability for client/server applications. It is critical that the server be architected as part of the systems management support strategy to achieve this reliability.

Data Storage

Permanent storage requirements are very application-specific. In addition to quantity of disk storage, the issues of performance and reliability must be considered.

Magnetic Disk

Disk storage devices should use the SCSI-2 standard controller interface. This provides the best performance in a standards-based environment. Many vendors provide high-capacity, high-performance, and highly reliable disk devices for this controller.

The use of high-capacity cache storage dramatically improves performance. Most current SCSI-2 controllers are configurable with 256K or more cache. This is an important, yet frequently overlooked component of the architecture. New drives are available in the traditional 3.5 size with 1.0-1.6Gbyte capacity. The use of compression software can easily double this capacity. With the increasing size of GUI software and the introduction of multimedia applications, the demand for disk capacity will increase rapidly during 1994 and beyond.

Mirrored Disk

When applications require high reliability, it may be appropriate to use a configuration that supports mirrored disks. With this configuration, data is automatically written to two disks. This enables the application to continue if a failure occur on one disk. System files and data files should be considered for mirroring. Even though system files are usually read-only, the number of users affected by unavailability of the files may justify this redundancy. In addition, performance can improve since dual reads can be handled in parallel.

RAID-Disk Array

Traditional magnetic disk technology is often referred to as single large expensive disk (SLED). Very high performance and high availability can be achieved through a redundant array of inexpensive drives (RAID). These enable data files to be spread across several physical drives. Data also can be mirrored as part of this configuration. RAID technology provides a considerable performance advantage because many parallel I/O operations can be processed at the same time. High capacity caches must be used in conjunction with RAID to achieve optimum performance. The size will be identified as part of the architecture definition.

Tape

Although most permanently stored data uses disk, tape is a very popular form of low-cost magnetic storage and is used primarily for backup purposes. The standard backup tape device today is digital audio tape (DAT). These tapes provide approximately 1.2 Gbytes of storage on a standard cartridge-size cassette tape. Tape is a sequential medium and does not adequately support direct (random) access to information. If an organization standardizes on a single tape format and technology, distribution of information by mailing tapes can be a cost-effective communications mechanism for large quantities of information that do not require real-time transmission or accessibility.

Optical Disks

Optical disk storage technology provides the advantage of high-volume, economical storage with somewhat slower access times than traditional magnetic disk storage.

CD-ROM

Compact disk-read only memory (CD-ROM) optical drives are used for storage of information that is distributed for read-only use. A single CD-ROM can hold up to 800MB of information. Software and large reports distributed to a large number of users are good candidates for this media. CD-ROM also is more reliable for shipping and distribution than magnetic disks or tapes.

By 1995, it is expected that all software and documentation will be distributed only on CD-ROM. The advent of multimedia applications and the resulting storage requirements will further drive the demand for CD-ROM.

In 1993, the speed of CD-ROM technology was doubled through a doubling of the rotation of the drive. Newer drives will triple-spin and quad-spin. The speed of the drive is very critical for applications that use the CD-ROM interactively. The addition of large cache SCSI-2 controllers can also significantly improve performance. The architecture definition must look at the business requirement in determining the appropriate configuration. Poor selection will result in unacceptable performance, excessive cost, or both.

WORM

Write once, read many (WORM) optical drives are used to store information that is to be written to disk just once but read many times. This type of storage is frequently used to archive data that should not be modified. Traffic tickets issued by police departments are scanned and stored on WORM drives for reference on payment or nonpayment. The WORM technology guarantees that the image cannot be tampered with. A magnetic drive can be used to store an index into the data on the WORM drive. Data can be effectively erased from a WORM by removing reference to it from the index. This can be useful when a permanent audit trail of changes is required.

Erasable Optical

Erasable optical drives are used as an alternative to standard magnetic disk drives when speed of access is not important and the volume of data stored is large. They can be used for image, multimedia, backup, or high-volume, low-activity storage.

Network Interface Cards (NICs)

Client and server processors are attached to the LAN through NICs. These provide the physical connectivity to the wire and the protocol support to send/receive messages. As discussed in Chapter 5, "Components of Client/Server Applications—Connectivity," the most popular network protocols today are Token Ring, Ethernet, and FDDI. The following paragraphs illustrate key selection issues regarding each technology.

Token Ring

Token Ring NICs were originally IBM-only products but are now provided and supported by many PC and UNIX vendors. The IEEE standard 802.5 defines the standards for the interface. Token Ring NICs are particularly desirable for LANs that are collocated with an IBM mainframe. They are also useful when interactive use is combined on the same LAN with high-volume file transfer or print image communications. Token Ring LANs operate at 4 or 16 Mbps. Shielded twisted-pair (STP) (Type 1 cabling) is required by some vendors for 16-Mbps processing, but unshielded twisted-pair (UTP) cable is supported by many at 16 Mbps and all at 4 Mbps.

The rapid decline in price for 10BaseT Ethernet and the increasing availability of Fast Ethernet means that despite some technical advantages the future of Token Ring is limited.

Ethernet

The existing de facto standard for LAN connection defined by the IEEE standard 802.3, Ethernet is supported by almost every vendor. The large number of vendors providing NICs ensures their competitive pricing. Ethernet works well when interactive-only or file transfer-only communications are present on the LAN. When mixing interactive and file transfer on the same Ethernet system, performance is excellent when LAN loading does not exceed 30 percent of the capacity. Most Ethernet

LANs operate at 10 Mbps. The present standard for Ethernet connectivity 10BaseT operates on STP or UTP. Recent products supporting Fast Ethernet and ATM will provide support for 100Mbit and up to 2.4Gbit on existing Type 5 UTP-cabled network.

FDDI

Fiber Distributed Data Interchange (FDDI) is a protocol originally defined for high-speed communications over glass fiber. FDDI provides 100-Mbps throughput today. NICs for FDDI are becoming available for more processing environments. This throughput is necessary when applications deal with large images, large file transfers, or multimedia using full-motion video. The rapid advances in Fast Ethernet and ATM means that FDDI will see limited rollout except for building internetworking and WANs.

CDDI

Copper Distributed Data Interchange (CDDI) provides support for FDDI communications over copper wire. The same 100-Mbps throughput is supported over Type 1 cabling (STP), and standards are emerging to provide support over Type 3 cabling (UTP) that is carefully selected and installed. This technology is now called Fast Ethernet. ATM is discussed in Chapter 5 and will increasingly be the protocol of choice for LAN/WAN internetworking.

Power Protection Devices

A lot has been written in books, magazines, and journals about computer hardware and software; and a number of computer specialty businesses are dedicated to helping you work through issues of specific concern to your business objectives. Rather than cover the minute details here, this chapter has attempted to highlight a number of areas for you.

However, before closing this chapter, one critical area often overlooked (but is the cause of many serious problems when neglected) is power protection.

Uninterruptible Power Supply (UPS)

Prices for UPS have declined to the point where they are widely used for LAN server protection. These units contain battery backups to enable at least a graceful power-down sequence. All buffers can be purged and files closed so that no information is lost. Other units provide 15-90 minutes of power backup to handle most power failure situations.

Surge Protectors

The electronics in computer systems are affected by power fluctuations. Protection can be obtained through the use of surge protection equipment. Every client and server processor, and all peripherals should be wired through a surge protector. Most UPS systems include integrated surge protectors.

Client/Server Systems
Development
Service and Support

Client/Server Systems Development—Service and Support

8

Executive Summary

Users of mainframe-based applications may grumble about costs, response time, inflexibility, lack of user friendliness, bureaucracy, and their particular piques in a specific environment. One thing they should not complain about is data loss. Mainframe users expect that when a host transaction completes, the data is reliably stored. Any subsequent application, system, hardware, or power failure will not cause data loss. In some sites a fire, flood, hurricane, or other natural disaster will cause minimal or no data loss.

Personal computer users historically have had different expectations. In the past, if after an hour working on a spreadsheet the system hangs up, power fails, or a virus reboots the machine, users certainly feel annoyed but not really surprised.

Likewise, even with companies that have moved beyond single-user PC applications and have embraced networking, users historically have been more tolerant of less rigorous standards. For example, Forester Research projects that the costs to manage distributed networks of PCs and servers will be 10 to 30 percent more than to manage minicomputers and mainframes. Other studies have claimed costs are double. This higher cost is the case when LANs evolve and applications are built without an architectural view and without appropriate standards to support the design.

With the movement to client/server computing, demand for mainframe-like performance from client/server architectures increases. If firms are going to move the business of the corporation into the client/server world, mainframe-like expectations will prevail and mainframe-like support must be provided.

Recent experience with remotely-managed LAN applications is demonstrating that costs are equal to or less than costs for traditional mainframe applications. Effective remote management requires systems and application architectures that anticipate the requirement for remote management.

Systems Administration

Like many things in life, the principle of "do it right the first time" applies to the long-term success of your client/server application. Thus, it is important to ensure that client/server hardware is specified and assembled according to organizational standards and tested prior to implementation. Software should be loaded by trained staff and tested to ensure that it is installed according to standards and works as expected. The largest number of user problems are caused by incorrect installation and equipment that is faulty at installation. Most LAN administration problems can be prevented by proper architecture supported by trained installers.

Availability

Availability means system uptime—or the capability of the system to be available for processing information and doing its expected work whenever called on. Minicomputer and mainframe data centers should provide at least 99.8-percent availability with today's technology. To achieve this level of availability, a combination of technological and procedural steps are followed. Most availability failure today is caused by human error. To minimize this, data centers implement rigid procedures to manage change.

Whether the change is hardware, network, system, or application software, stringent procedures to request, validate, test, and implement the change are defined and adhered to. Backout procedures are defined and tested to ensure that if a failure occurs after implementation of the change, the data center can fall back to its previous status.

Technological features such as separate electrical power sources, backup diesel generator and battery power sources, redundant processors, and magnetic disk devices all are used to ensure that failure of a single component will not take down the data center. Very critical systems use fault-tolerant processors from vendors such as Tandem and Stratus to ensure that availability approaches 100 percent.

Data centers use highly skilled professionals in the central location. They are expected to be able to recover the site quickly after any failure. Vendor service contracts are used to guarantee that repair can be accomplished in one, four, or eight hours as necessary.

Client/server applications must be able to provide the appropriate level of availability demanded by the business need. Certain features, such as redundant power supplies and battery backup, are relatively easy to provide. In large cities, vendor service-level agreements can be purchased to ensure that failures can be repaired quickly. In smaller cities, repair by replacement will be necessary if the required service levels cannot be provided because of the travel time.

The provision of highly qualified technical staff at each site is sometimes physically and rarely economically feasible. Remote LAN management is the only way to make effective use of scarce resources. Remote management requires a central site connected through WAN services to each LAN. Network management service levels are defined through reasonability levels. This enables comparative interrogation of the availability of individual devices, of performance, and even of server magnetic disk space use.

Products such as Openvison, Sun Connect, HP Openview, IBM's NetView and SystemView can be integrated through industry-standard network management protocols to provide the desired level of availability for reasonable cost. The OSF has defined a standard Distributed Management Environment (DME) for management of its Distributed Computing Environments (DCE) standard, which is evolving as the definition for an object technology based management platform. Although this technology is less mature than the DCE standard, experienced systems from integrators are demonstrating effective remote systems management network operations centers.

Reliability

All current technology minicomputer and mainframe operating systems provide basic services to support system reliability. Reliability first requires availability factors to be resolved. Reliability requires applications to be protected from overwriting each other and requires shared memory to be accessed only by authorized tasks. Security must be implemented to allow access to resources only by authorized users. Database management software must ensure that either the entire set of updates requested by a unit-of-work be completed or that none be completed. Specifically, the software must automatically handle multiple user contention, provide full recovery after failure of in-flight updates, and provide utility functions to recover a damaged magnetic disk.

Serviceability

Most minicomputer and mainframe operating systems and hardware provide diagnostic services that pinpoint the location of failures. Transient errors are noted so that preventive maintenance can correct problems before they affect availability. The central location of the equipment allows trained technicians to institute regular preventive maintenance programs. For this reason, many organizations install their first servers in the glass room until they have more experience with remote LAN management.

Products based on standard protocols such as the Simple Network Management Protocol (SNMP) provide the necessary feedback of event alerts to support the remote systems management function. It is necessary that the architecture design take into account the issues of standards and products to be serviceable.

Software Distribution

The centralized minicomputer and mainframe environment shares executable software from a single library. Software maintenance and enhancement are accomplished by changes to a single location. In the distributed client/server model, executable software is resident on servers located throughout the organization. Changes to system and application software must be replicated across the organization. This presents a tremendous complication in serviceability of these applications.

An additional complexity is incurred in the UNIX world when several different hardware platforms are used. Despite the fact that the source level of the software is compatible across the various platforms, the executable binary form of the software is not compatible. An HP 9000 and an IBM RS 6000 may run the same application and use the same Ingres Windows 4GL development software, but the same generated applications cannot be distributed to each location.

The executable libraries must be created on a machine with the same physical hardware. This causes serious problems for distribution of software throughout a large network of disparate computer platforms. Testing should also be done on each platform before changes are distributed. Most organizations have addressed this requirement by installing one of each of the hardware platforms from the field in a central support location.

The solution to this problem is a properly designed client/server architecture supported by effective software management tools. This problem is certainly solvable but only through design and planning. It will not be solved in an ad hoc fashion after implementation.

There are special requirements in supporting distributed technology. An advantage of the personal computer is that it is easy to modify. This is of course a disadvantage for production environments. Remote support personnel must be able to discover the hardware and software configuration of the remote technology. With this discovery they can determine which software versions to send and provide educated support for problems.

Performance

In the centralized minicomputer and mainframe environment, trained technical support personnel and operations staff monitor performance on an ongoing basis. Sophisticated monitoring tools, such as Candle Corporation's Omegamon MVS, and analysis tools, such as RMF from IBM, track the system's day-to-day performance. IBM and Digital Equipment Corporation include features in their large computers' operating systems that provide considerable dynamic tuning capabilities. If trends show performance degrading, systems managers can add hardware or make adjustments to improve performance before it affects the user community.

Additional tools, such as Crystal from BBN and TPNS from IBM, are available to simulate new applications before they move into production. This means that the organization learns in advance the resource requirements of new applications. Changes can be made to the operating environment to ensure that performance will be acceptable.

In the client/server environment, neither UNIX, Windows NT, nor OS/2 yet provides these sophisticated performance-monitoring tools. Certain tools, such as Network General's Sniffer, are available to remotely monitor the LAN traffic. UNIX, Windows NT and OS/2 provide limited capabilities to define task priorities. Many vendors are now marketing products to support this need. At present, though, the design expertise of enterprise architects is essential to avoid performance shortcomings. Fortunately the cost of hardware for client workstations or Windows NT, OS/2, and UNIX servers is such that adding extra capacity to improve performance is usually not a major cost factor for a client/server system.

Network Management

Network management tools such as those from OpenVision, IBM's NetView, AT&T's UNMA, and Digital Equipment Corporation's EMA products, to name a few, all provide a level of remote monitoring that can track response time and network loading. None of these products provides the type of analysis of the remote server that RMF provides or the tuning tools that are provided within MVS and VMS. Products such as ESRA from Elegant Computing, are available to do remote analysis of UNIX servers in order to monitor disk usage, error logs, and user profiles. This product is used extensively to manage remote UNIX servers.

Other products, such as Microcoms LANlord, provide significant capabilities for remote access to Windows and OS/2 PC LAN desktops. It is impossible to provide adequate support for distributed client/server applications without the capability to support the desktop and the server remotely. This is an area of intense focus by the industry, and during 1993, a number of major systems integrators implemented NOS to provide desktop support for Novell, LAN Manager, LAN Server, and NFS client/server environments. During 1994, this capability will become essential to all organizations.

Help Desk

The most efficient and effective way to provide support to client/server users is through the use of the *help desk*. A help desk is a set of systems and procedures used by technical and applications staff to provide support to end-users in areas ranging from basic how to do and problem determination to advanced troubleshooting and diagnosis. This type of support may be provided using remote PCs, voice-only assistance over the telephone, or in-person assistance via an on-site help request. This provides immediate feedback for simple problems and an early and complete audit trail of problems. Proper follow-up is essential to provide users with confidence in the help desk function.

A professional help desk is one of the keys to successful implementation of the client/server model. Remote users require immediate access to assistance. Effective implementation of a client/server application depends on the availability of immediate support when problems occur.

Experience with distributed client/server implementations demonstrates that successful implementation requires that 80 percent of problems be solved while the user is on the phone. A further 10 percent must be solved within an hour of the call. The remainder should be resolved or a workaround found within 24 hours.

Users familiar with PC software expect ease of use and intuitive navigation and recovery in their software. If a client/server application lacks these features internally, it is critical for a help desk to be available at the first sign of trouble. The help desk support personnel must take over control of the client workstation in order to assess the situation well. This process called *over the shoulder* helps enable the remote help desk to work as if they were working over the shoulder of the user. The help desk is able to see the screen, execute software on the user workstation, review local data files and make software changes as necessary. Centralized help desks must identify and track problems and then ensure that corrective action is provided to the user as soon as possible. They are the lifeline that explains discovered problems and ways to work around them.

Help desk personnel must be able to identify with the frustration of a user working remotely from any personal support. They must be sympathetic and clear in their explanation of solutions.

The help desk must provide one-stop shopping for help. Help must be available whenever a user is working. The Royal Bank of Canada has over 45,000 users of an interactive voice response (IVR) system that enables the caller to select the type of help needed and to be in contact with a help desk analyst in less than 90 seconds.[1] The value of this capability is so great that many organizations are outsourcing this function to help desk specialty organizations. Computerland Canada has implemented this service for several of the largest organizations in Canada. Help services are one of the fastest growing segments of that company's business.

Help desks provide feedback to the developers not only on all application errors but also in the critical areas of usage complexity and additional training needs. More than 75 percent of the 1,200 organizations surveyed in a 1991 survey by the Help Desk Institute expect to expand their current help desk operations over the next five years by increasing staff and expanding operating hours.[2]

Help desk personnel require trouble-ticket support software to be effective. Remedy software provides an effective implementation. All calls are logged, and the collective expertise of the help desk is available. All previous calls, problems, and solutions can be searched to help solve the current problem. Remedy records each problem and implements escalation procedures to ensure problems are solved in a timely

---

[1] Julia King, *"Executive Report: Help Desks,"* Computerworld 25, No. 45 (*November 11, 1991*), p. 74.

[2] Ibid., p. 73.

manner. In addition, and more importantly, the software provides management with the capability to review problems and determine what changes are necessary to ensure that problems do not occur again.

Most calls in new implementations are caused by software that is awkward to use. Correcting these problems will greatly improve user efficiency. Many organizations who outsource help desk services do so at a declining cost each year—and will continue to do so—because as usage problems are resolved, calls will decline.

Remote Systems Management

LAN administrators should be able to connect remotely to and then manage the workstation of any user who has a problem. LANlord from Microcom provides support for the Windows 3.x desktop. Microsoft's Hermes product will provide support for Windows NT desktops in late 1994. The products DCAF from IBM, PolyMod2 from Memsoft and Remote OS from Menlo provide support for the OS/2 environment. DCAF requires an OS/2 workstation but can control a user DOS or Windows workstation. Network General provides Distributed Sniffer, which operates both locally and remotely. It provides excellent support to a LAN administrator with a graphical user interface (GUI) to display results.

Because UNIX provides support for remote login, all UNIX environments provide good tools for remote systems management. Sun Connect, IBM Netview 6000, HP Openview, and OpenVisons products all provide good support dependent on the specific requirements of the distributed computing environment.

Each of these products provides an accurate record of performance and traffic loading at the point of analysis. If these analyses are done regularly, LAN administrators can detect problems as they arise. If the exploratory programs are infrequently run or trend lines are not created, problems will sneak up with no warning.

Security

In any application environment, managers must assess the security requirements. It is necessary to walk a thin line between enough security and overbearing security measures. Users should find security to be invisible when they are authorized for a function and impenetrable when they are unauthorized. Security of the server should start by placing physical barriers around unauthorized access. Because users do not need physical access to the database and application servers, both should be placed in a locked room. Frequently the existing host computer room can be used to hold workgroup servers.

Every user of a client/server application should be assigned a personal ID and password. The ID can be used to assign authority and track access. Customized procedures can be built for each individual ID to manage backup, access times, and prompting. The DCE-defined Kerberos standard is preferred for UNIX servers. SunSoft provides Kerberos as an option to Secure RPC and Secure NFS, its C2-securable networking features available in Solaris, Version 2.1. Security is now recognized as an essential element in next-generation operating systems. Microsoft for NT and Novell with NetWare 4.x are both building security to meet the U.S. government C2 specifications.

Physical network security standards are being defined by several groups including the IEEE. SNMP-2 is being enhanced to support greater security. Operating systems designed from the ground up with security in mind form a trusted computing base (TCB) that incorporates encryption of passwords, safeguards against bypassing the logon system and the capability to assign privileges to user groups. NetWare 4.0 and Windows NT can also log attempted security breaches and trigger alarms that notify a network manager.

The new operating systems require that each account specifically be granted rights for remote access or encrypt passwords during remote access. Effective security must be defined as part of the enterprise-wide architecture put in place as an organization moves to the client/server model. In addition, effective administrative procedures for user definition, password maintenance, physical security, and application design must be instituted.

When maximum security is required, network and permanently stored data should be encrypted. Products such as Beaver Computer Company's DES coprocessor plug into sockets on its SL007 Notebook Computer to intercept data moving to and from the hard disk. The data encryption standard (DES) algorithm uses a personal key to make data unusable to anyone who lacks that key. This data is encrypted when it's stored and decrypted on retrieval. Only when the correct DES key is provided is the information meaningful. The U.S. government has attempted to define a standard data encryption algorithm for which they would possess a back door key. It is unlikely that this algorithm will be adopted by any other organizations.

Diskless workstations can prevent information from being copied to a floppy and removed or from being left where someone might break into the workstation to access the hard disk. No sensitive data should be stored on the client workstation or on an unprotected workgroup server.

LAN and Network Management Issues

As companies integrate LANs into their enterprise networks, the network administrator's role is changing drastically—gaining complexity and growing in importance, according to a market research report from Business Research Group (BRG) of Newton, Massachusetts.[3]

LAN management has changed from managing an isolated LAN to managing a LAN that's part of an enterprise network. The challenges of managing local networks, remote networks, and interconnections among them are complicated by the lack of global network administration software. Several studies have determined that network administration is the major priority of most organizations.

LAN administrators are working more closely with the existing host systems support group—the management information systems (MIS) department. Although workstations were once seen as the nemesis of MIS, they are now a key part of the strategic information technology direction of many companies. MIS departments must see their survival as dependent on integration of LANs into the enterprise system.

Integrating different technologies from different vendors requires a lot of work, and frequently the tools to build multivendor, multiprotocol networks are missing. Lack of knowledge of these new technologies is yet another stumbling block for LAN administrators.

Although the network administrator's job is becoming more difficult, it also is becoming increasingly important as the network plays a more strategic role in business-critical applications.

---

[3]*Elizabeth Doughtery, "Who's Behind the LAN," LAN Magazine 6, No. 10 (October 1991), pp. 73-78.*

The shift from running business-critical applications on mainframes to workstation LANs has elevated the influence of workstation users and, subsequently, LAN administrators. Because of that shift from terminals to workstations, the people who reside between the data and the workstation—the LAN administrators—have an increasingly important role.

The LAN administrator should be responsible to both the MIS network management and the user community. Nearly three-quarters of respondents to the BRG survey agreed that department managers should control LAN applications, but MIS should control other aspects of LANs. The services that MIS departments provide for LANs typically are traditional MIS services carried over to the LAN environment. These services include:

- Network maintenance (91.1 percent of the sites)
- Network integration (87 percent)
- Capacity planning (82.3 percent)
- Equipment maintenance (80.4 percent)
- Help desks (79.7 percent)

Other services include:

- Security administration (77.5 percent)
- Network cabling and installation (76.3 percent)
- Network application administration (73.1 percent)
- Server backup (66.1 percent)
- Network application development (62.3 percent)
- PC data backup (41.8 percent)

Despite the growing complexity of networks, only 37 percent of the surveyed sites use a LAN management package. This lack of management tools is an impediment to enterprise-wide applications. Lack of security on LANs is another roadblock. Respondents tended to define a LAN management package as an umbrella enterprise-wide management system, such as IBM's NetView, rather than as an integration of tools that manage specific devices.

Many companies do not have the diagnostic devices or the expertise to effectively manage network hardware. Very few maintain historical records for ongoing comparative analysis. Only 41 percent of the respondents use protocol analyzers; about the same percentage use cable activity testers and tracers. Only 28 percent use time domain reflectometers. Learning to operate such diagnostic tools is relatively easy; understanding what the results mean is not so simple.

In another recent survey, this time by Infonetics, Fortune 500 companies were asked to determine the reliability of their LANs and the costs related to unavailability. The survey produced statistics to which organizations making the move to client/server computing must be sensitive.

The first question evaluated the average length of time the LAN was unavailable after a failure. More than 50 percent of respondents noted that the LAN was unavailable for more than two hours. In fact 19 percent of the respondents noted that each failure took more than eight hours to repair. A failure meant the system was unavailable for the remainder of the working day. This will be an unacceptably long time if the business requires LAN availability in order to operate.

The second question determined the number of failures per year. More than 50 percent of the respondents noted more than 10 failures per year. In fact, 20 percent noted more than 50 per year, or one per week. Clearly, if each failure takes more than two hours to fix, the amount of downtime is well beyond acceptable levels.

The third question attempted to quantify the cost of lost productivity per year caused by LAN failure. In 36 percent of the organizations, more than $100,000 in lost productivity occurred in one year. Amazingly, in 7 percent of the organizations, the lost productivity exceeded $15 million. Clearly, there is an opportunity for substantial cost savings by reducing the frequency of errors and the mean time to repair. In critical applications such as the Fire Department dispatch systems described in Appendix A, the cost of downtime is measured in human lives as well as property damage.

The final question looked at lost revenue caused by failures. In 10 percent of organizations, more than $100,000 in losses were caused by system failures. Again amazingly, in 4 percent of the organizations, the loss exceeded $1 million. In the 25 percent of organizations where lost revenue was less than $100 and lost productivity was less than $5,000 per year, we can assume that the LAN is not integral to running the business.

Licensing

Mini- and mainframe software licensing costs have traditionally been based on the processing capability of the computers involved. The costs are based on the model of hardware and on the number of users typically supported by that equipment. The more powerful the machine and the more simultaneous users it can support, the higher the software license fee. UNIX software continues to be licensed in the LAN arena on this basis. DOS, Windows, and OS/2 personal computer software licensing agreements were developed when software was being acquired for single-user use on a dedicated personal computer. The dramatic increase in processing power of personal computers and the advent of LANs have created a licensing cost issue for software vendors.

Three charging algorithms are used today: single use, LAN use, and site license. Single use requires that every workstation acquire its own license. LAN use typically allows up to a maximum number of simultaneous users for a fixed fee. Site licenses allow unlimited usage by an organization, either at a single site or across an entire organization. Because organizations have increasing standardization of software products, more site-licensing agreements are being signed.

The Software Publishers' Association (SPA) has raised the visibility of licensing recently by filing lawsuits against organizations that appear to be using software without proper licensing agreements. Many of these organizations are LAN users. Buyer organizations such as the Software Managers' Interest Group, and other user/vendor associations such as the Open User Recommended Solutions (OURS) organization, are working to define standards for licensing that reflect the way software is used.

Products such as BrightWork's SiteLock, DEC's License Management Facility (LMF) and Hewlett-Packard's Network Licensing System (NetLS) allow software licensing that reflects software usage. In many organizations, hundreds of users may have access to a software product but only tens of users may be active with it at any one time.

With single-user licensing, many LAN users are obligated to buy hundreds of licenses. Organizations are usually willing to restrict the number of active users to substantially fewer than the maximum possible. In return, they expect a reduction in the license.

Client/Server Systems
Development
Training

Client/Server Systems Development— Training

9

Executive Summary

What trips up IS spending planners most when they initiate rightsizing? "Training, training, and training," says Henry Leingang, vice-president and CIO at Viacom Inc., the New York entertainment and broadcasting firm.[1] It is easy to overlook the training effort required when organizations attempt to reengineer their business processes. Managers become accustomed to people doing their jobs in a certain way and overlook the effort that has been expended to get them to that level of competence. Reengineering means change—change that is fundamental and not transparent. Change requires people to

---

[1] *John P. McPartlin, Bob Violino, Peter Krass, "The Hidden Costs of Downsizing,"* Information Week, *No. 347 (November 18, 1991), p. 36.*

be learning to work effectively within the changed environment. Continuous change means that a continuous program of learning must be in place to allow people to work effectively.

Client/server computing provides an opportunity to reengineer the business process by using technology earlier and in a more integrated manner. It does not eliminate the need to train for the new process.

Training Advantages of GUI Applications

A major training benefit of the graphical user interface (GUI) is the opportunity to provide an intuitive interface. Each time standard functions are used in a GUI platform, they are invoked in the same way. Each new business application does not require user retraining in the use of help, error correction, menu navigation, or security measures. The basic business process functionality to view, add, change, and delete information appears and works consistently from application to application. These processes are implemented as part of an organizational "view" implemented with a systems development environment (SDE) and incorporated into every application.

Because of GUIs, users can be trained once to properly use these features, and this knowledge can be reused for every new application. With standardized training on these fundamentals, new applications need only provide training on the new business processes. This will reduce costs, reduce stress on trainees, and decrease the time it takes to move new applications into production.

Reduced Training Costs

Forrester Research predicts that the use of GUIs will cut user training costs by 30 to 40 percent.[2] In the Los Angeles Fire Department project described in Appendix A, the department has determined that training time has been reduced from the previous 10 weeks to only 4 weeks. Chief Rudd credits this to the ease of use provided by the GUI compared to the previous character mode implementation.

---

[2]*Forrester Research,* Professional Systems Report *(Cambridge, MA: Forrester Research, 1990).*

Adding a common front end to a mixture of existing applications dramatically reduced training costs for a major telephone company in another project. A reduction in staff turnover, attributed to the ease of use, further reduced training costs because of fewer new employees. In fast food restaurants, staff turnover may exceed 300 percent per year. Training costs could overwhelm profitability. The use of ergonomically engineered GUIs, with touch screen interfaces, enables new staff to be trained in less than one hour.

Although end-user training is the most costly and therefore receives the most benefit from the use of GUIs in client/server computing, there is still a need to train the technical support organization. Without proper training the system administrators, systems programmers, technicians, and developers will not build effective systems or support the system's users effectively. It costs about $300 to install the networking components to set up a workstation, but the salary cost for the maintenance staff can be $1,000 per machine if LAN Administration is done on a "learn as you do it" basis.[3]

Training the Technical Staff

With the critical nature of many client/server applications, downtime is a sensitive issue. Training of support personnel becomes a major concern for organizations moving forward with client/server applications. Many of the same techniques available to train users can be used in training the technical support organization. An SDE, consistent standards, multimedia, integrated help features, readable documentation, and training/test systems all have a place in the training of technical staff.

Technicians moving from a mainframe environment are challenged to overcome their culture shock and view these workstation-based systems as powerful equipment. These technicians must be trained to respect the knowledge possessed by the user community. In a client/server implementation, it is common for technical support personnel to deal with users who are very familiar with the technology and who may occasionally be more sophisticated about the technology than the technician. This is a major culture shock for technical personnel familiar with the complexities of the host environment and the relative lack of sophistication of the mainframe user community.

---

[3]*These figures are cited by Larry Orenstein, Assistand Chief Engineer, IT Division, Stone & Webster Engineering.*

Training in product specifics may be obtained from many sources: product vendors, professional trainers, colleges, user groups, and hands-on, in-house tutorials. Each organization should assess the degree and type of training pertinent to its particular situation. Novell, Microsoft, and IBM have extensive training programs available for technical support personnel and network administrators. And they have created active programs to certify trainers to provide training for their products.

Experience indicates that technical personnel in a business get the most benefit from product vendor training. Most personnel in the business will benefit more from training that is tailored to the specifics of an organization's SDE and business priorities. The single-system image concept is best implemented when detailed technical training reflects the need to know. Training systems incorporated into the SDE and tailored to an organization frequently provide the most optimal training environment because the sessions use terminology and business language that the trainees are familiar with.

A well-implemented Help Desk, using a product such as Remedy's Action Request System, is the best training vehicle for technical support personnel. This is the vehicle to capture the corporate experience and through workgroup computing techniques, to share this knowledge throughout the support organization, and to leverage the experience and expertise of the organization.

Systems Administrator Training

One of the first steps in training systems administration personnel to support client/server technology must be to teach the importance and reality of the applications. There is a prevalent attitude that workstations provide only personal productivity services. The implication of this attitude is that the organization doesn't really care about availability of the LANs. Insufficient training in this area will doom all other training efforts.

Once system administration personnel accept the requirements for system availability, the next steps are much easier. Administrators must understand the level of performance and ease of use their users require. Engineers and clerical users do have different needs, expectations, and technical abilities. Management should direct training into the areas that are of concern to the organization. In small workgroup LANs, many performance and automation issues are not nearly as significant as ease of use and ease of maintenance. In large LANs, performance and automated procedures may be sufficiently critical to justify the use of complex installation and maintenance procedures.

The cost of training expert administrators and technicians is such that most organizations will need to provide remote LAN and WAN management and support. It often is impractical to have highly technical support personnel at every workgroup location. Thus, as part of their training personnel, they should be made aware of both the technical and human-interaction protocols of working remotely. The lack of eye contact inherent in a remote support situation means that the person providing support to a frustrated user must be able to build and maintain a rapport over the telephone or through e-mail. This is a challenge that many organizations have not addressed in their training. The inability to deal with this situation has led some organizations to use outsourced support with professionally trained help desk and technical support personnel.

LAN Administration

The first step in system administration training is to understand the organization's conventions. Naming, security, help procedures, and so on must be understood and implemented uniformly between applications and products. Large systems rolled out in many locations should develop administrator training as well as user training. This training will ensure that each installation operates the same way and that remote support personnel can communicate with local administrators.

The administrator should receive thorough software product training. Word processors, spreadsheets, databases, graphics, and other complex products should be installed with uniform default settings across all sites. In order to properly select these options and support requests for help, the administrator should be an expert in the use of the product. Remote support will be much easier when products are installed with consistent defaults.

Disk space management is an important issue for the administrator. Proper file naming conventions and defaults will ensure that each user's or workgroup's data is localized for backups and archiving. If everyone stores data files in random locations, it will be extremely difficult to manage space usage. The administrator must understand what the product requirements are and arrange to have temporary and backup files created on volumes that can be cleaned up regularly. This is an often-overlooked aspect of training in product usage.

Products such as Network General's Sniffer enable LAN administrators to monitor the network for capacity and problems without the need for detailed knowledge of the applications. Contributing to the power of these products is their capability to be used without prior detailed training on the specific technologies employed on the LAN. Sniffer captures LAN traffic, analyzes the data, and recommends actions based on its assessment of the data's meaning. Internal LAN message formats are interpreted by the software so that the LAN administrator can take action based on the recommendations without the need for detailed knowledge of these message formats. This feature is particularly critical with remote LANs, for which it is not possible to have the most highly trained LAN administrative personnel resident.

WAN Issues

All the same WAN network issues associated with remote terminal access to host systems exist in the client/server-to-WAN access. Additional complexities arise when data is distributed to the remote LAN. Application programs that are distributed to remote servers present many of the same problems as do distributed databases. Administrators must be trained in the software and in procedures to handle network definition, network management, and remote backup and recovery. Many of the WAN problems appear as unrelated incidents to remote users who don't understand the WAN issues. It is imperative to train the WAN administrator in the use of remote management tools. Tools such as IBM's NetView and Cabletron's Spectrum enable administrators to remotely manage the LAN-to-WAN environment needed for many client/server applications.

Training developers in WAN issues is also critical because of the WAN's impact on communication issues. Where data is stored and how it is to be retrieved must be considered in the development of applications. The conversations will be quite different for a WAN rather than a LAN.

WANs are particularly complex to understand and optimize because of the many configuration options available. Training WAN administrators to understand all of the options available to establish an optimal topology is more expensive than many organizations can justify. Tools such as IBM's NetView, Sunsoft's Sun/Connect, HP's Openview, and various products from BBN and Openvision can be used to provide recommendations and assessments to the WAN administrator. Training in the tools is frequently more valuable than extensive training in the WAN technologies.

Operating System Issues

Administrators must be expertly trained in the operating system (OS) used by clients and servers in the client/server application. Networks frequently run several OSs—such as DOS, Windows 3.x, Windows NT, OS/2, and UNIX—within the supported client/server implementations. This diversity of platforms challenges the administrators to have expertise not only in the particulars of a single OS but also in the interaction of the various OSs.

New releases of OSs introduce additional challenges as new interactions and incompatibilities appear. In the UNIX arena, an additional challenge arises when the hardware platforms are not homogeneous and several UNIX derivatives, each with minor variations, are being used simultaneously. The costs and implications of training in this area must not be overlooked. In the design and planning for a new client/server application, the training requirements should be carefully considered before an organization establishes too many OS configurations.

PC/Workstation Issues

Administrators must be trained in the basic hardware components of the workstation. Many problems that occur in the field can be fixed remotely by a user with direction from the remote administrator. Common problems such as unplugged devices, loose cards, or lost configurations, can often be repaired by a user with some willingness to follow directions. Support personnel should be trained in software to support remote PC/workstation logins. Software such as Checkit PRO for the PC and ESRA for UNIX can be used to diagnose more complex hardware problems.

Application Issues

Administrators must be well-versed in the application to enable rapid and effective communication with remote users. They should be trained in both the functionality and technology of the applications. It is common to designate a sophisticated user as the support administrator for an application. Because most problems are related to applications, the application support administrator should be an expert in how business users utilize the application. It is especially important with the first applications being rolled out for remote usage, that support administrators be able to rapidly determine whether a problem is related to application usage or truly technical.

Programmers' Resistance to New Technologies

The major problem facing organizations in training developers for the client/server model is the staff's resistance to such a radical change. Many computer industry personnel are now middle-aged, and many are reluctant to undertake a challenging relearning process. Many feel they have invested the best years of their lives in attaining excellence in their technologies and the business of their corporations and are reluctant to see this knowledge diminished in value by radically new and different technologies. The movement from host-centered COBOL programming to distributed C and graphical, object-oriented development requires a rethinking of the fundamentals of system development. Windowing systems require the layout skills more commonly found in a graphic designer than in a programmer. Training seasoned minds for this new environment is a challenging undertaking.

One solution is to provide training that enables developers to work effectively in the new environment. The problems indicate there is a real need to market the advantages of the new environment to these people. Training for programmers should be built into the SDE. Success in building client/server applications is more dependent on the use of standards and reusable objects than it was in the host environment. It is important for the SDE team to appreciate this mandate and to develop training that addresses the natural objections of the existing staff and highlights the advantages of the new tools. The SDE objects must be seen as an integral part of the development tools, not as optional components. With the rapid changes taking place in the tools of client/server development, the developers may see as many new tools in a single project as they have encountered in their careers. Ongoing training to gain proficiency in these new tools will create the demand for a new training approach that focuses on teaching only the differences within the common framework laid out by the SDE.

Technology components, such as communications and database access, use the same underlying technologies that most host developers are familiar with. In most cases, these technologies are masked by high-level interfaces, so training all personnel, except the technical support staff, can be restricted to the use of the interface software. This is an important feature of the SDE and a necessary step in protecting the single-system image.

Training for debugging in the client/server technologies is both simpler and more difficult. The single-user workstation usually provides responsive debugging information. Frequently, this feature is integrated with windowed debugging tools that enable staff to monitor the application output in conjunction with the application execution status. The complexity comes with the mass of new technologies implemented in a distributed environment. This complexity will be greatly simplified with careful attention in the SDE to building reusable objects that manage all interfaces. Database functions to support the building of test environments, back up of logical rather than physical components, recovery in shared environments, and views of before-and-after images all will reduce the training effort and improve productivity.

Database Administrator Training

Database administrators face additional challenges in a client/server implementation when data is distributed. Even in single-site, shared database applications, the client/server model typically leads to ad hoc end-user access. Most current host implementations operate in an environment where trained operations and technical support staff are operating and supporting the applications. This ensures that standard operating procedures will be followed and that problems can be solved quickly by experienced technical support personnel.

In the client/server environment, distributed data implies that data may be stored where no skilled staff are available to provide support. In addition, the additional complexity of the new environment requires new training for existing database administration staff. Design issues are particularly critical here because performance can be dramatically affected by the location of data. Remote control of utility functions is mandatory, and training existing staff to handle these procedures presents real challenges, especially when they continue to operate existing systems. Once again, the use of SDE-developed standard procedures that are reused between applications will allow this training to be provided once and applied to all new client/server applications.

End-User Training

End users should be trained once in the user interface standards defined by the organization as part of the SDE. The best time to provide this training is in conjunction with the first applications. It is likely that users will already know how to use a workstation for personal productivity. The new standards will not be dramatically different from those currently used unless a very different technology is being employed.

Workstation Operations

It is important to train in the shared use of the workstation for personal productivity and client/server application functionality. Users will be very unhappy if their existing valued capabilities are lost as a result of the new system. This training should include such standard features as security, help, navigation (how to get from one function to the next), table management and scrolling, as well as standard business processes such as viewing, adding, changing, and deleting information.

Applications and New Technologies

When the standard environment is understood, the particular application processes can be trained within this environment. In the future, new applications should require only training in the new business processes. The training should take place on a test system that replicates the production environment with training databases. This method ensures that the training environment matches production and can act as an acceptance test for the application. Training cannot take place on software that is faulty. User confidence and concentration will be lost if errors are regularly encountered. Version releases of the software should enable training to be provided on portions of the application as it is ready, without the need to wait for products to be completed.

Training Delivery Technology

Taking advantage of the many new training technologies is an integral part of a successful client/server training plan. For example, integrated context-sensitive help can provide users with information when they are in doubt. These facilities are provided as part of an SDE. Help details are provided by knowledgeable users during the development of the application. Formal user instruction should use a training version of the software that provides all of the functionality of the production system and uses training databases.

Integration of video and audio presentations into the training program will make it enjoyable for the trainee. These technologies can be integrated into the training program so that full-motion video training can be invoked to demonstrate a scenario on the workstation at any time the user requires. This training can be integrated in a context-sensitive manner so that the training system recognizes the point in the business process at which a request for training is issued and begins the training on that topic. For example, a user that is unfamiliar with the steps required to enter a contract in a new customer information management system would press a key that starts a video sequence illustrating the contract process. This form of training enables casual users of a system to be productive without the need for constant formal retraining. All training is provided directly at the workstation on demand.

The use of multimedia technologies can be an effective means of improving attentiveness to the training. This technology enables trainers to illustrate explanations of the business process with sound and video examples at the request of the trainee. When the user feels confident, he or she can recall the production environment and proceed. Integrating this facility into the SDE can dramatically reduce training costs for organizations with new employees or an application with casual users.

10

The Future of Client/ Server Computing

Executive Summary

The single-system image is a reality. In the future, cheap and powerful workstation technology will be available to everyone—with truly distributed applications using processing power wherever it is available and providing information wherever it is needed. In the future, information will be available for use by owners and authorized users, without the constant need for professional systems developers and their complex programming languages. The future will bring information captured at its source and available immediately to authorized users.

The future will provide information from data in its original form: image, video, audio, graphics, document, spreadsheet, or structured data, without the need to be aware of specific software for each form. Successful organizations of the future—those that are market-driven and competitive—will be ones using client/server as an enabling technology to add recognized value to their product or service. The future is now for early adopters of technology. By the turn of the century, the enterprise on the desk will be the norm for all successful organizations. Laggards will not be price competitive, will not provide competitive customer services, and soon will cease to exist.

What's in Store for Networking— Everyone's a Peer!

Trends in computer hardware clearly indicate that D-RAM and processor MIPS are going to become very cheap. Object technologies based on the CORBA model and represented today by Sun's DOE project will enable the resources of a network of machines—each processor available as client and server—to participate in providing business solutions. Networked computing provides an opportunity for whole new classes of client/server computing. OS/2, various versions of UNIX, and Windows NT provide the necessary components-shared memory, preemptive multitasking, database servers, communications servers, and GUI services. Suddenly, because of the conjunction of these components, truly distributed, peer-to-peer computing is a reality. Applications will find their servers without the need for application developers help. This new environment has been intriguingly labeled the post-scarcity personal computing environment by two IBM OS/2 architects, Robert Orfali and Dan Harkey.[1]

The power available on each processor enables architects to layer software through application program interfaces (APIs) that hide the underlying platform hardware and software from the developer. APIs show the developer a single-system image across a heterogeneous network of processors. Platforms will be selected for their cost effectiveness in meeting a particular business need rather than as upgrades to existing installed equipment. Hardware and software vendors—based on their capability to provide the platform that best meets the business need—will compete. The real competition will revolve around who provides the best user/developer productivity. Effective application maintenance and enhancement will be the primary criteria for product selection.

---

[1]*Robert Orfali and Dan Harkey*, Client-Server Programming with OS/2 (*New York: Van Nostrand Reinhold, 1991), p. 75.*

What's in Store for Software Development— Everything's an Object!

Object-oriented development (OOD) can facilitate the system development environments (SDE) described throughout this book. The premise behind OOD is *code reuse*. The traditional concept of code reuse involves creating repositories of software that can be reused by developers. The object-oriented concept takes this traditional view and recycles it with greater formalism and improved repository management tools. The good news is that code reuse and OOD works; we have measured significant productivity improvements for development and maintenance, compared to standard development methodologies based on sound structured development practices. However, there is a steep learning curve that must be climbed before these gains are realized. OOD is not a new technology; it has been around for more than 15 years. A true OOD standard developing environment has yet to be established. Until this standardization occurs, the full potential of OOD described in this chapter will not be reached.

OOD probably will be accepted for its contribution to zero defect development. The capability to reuse previously tested components is fundamental to most engineering and manufacturing processes. It is now becoming fundamental to the systems development process.

Enabling Technologies

Client/server computing describes a model for building application systems, along with the core hardware and software technology that helps in building these systems. The material in the following paragraphs describes aggregations of these core technologies that have created *enabling technologies*. Enabling technologies are combinations of hardware and software that can be used to assist in creating a particular kind of application system.

Expert Systems

The main business advantage of using *expert systems* technology is the opportunity to protect business know-how. Many organizations are severely short of experts. With the aging of the work force, and as a large number of experienced workers retire together, this shortage will become worse. Encapsulating the rules that describe an expert's response to a business situation into a stored electronic rules base, provides the substantive opportunity for higher productivity and reduced costs as these stored rules are consistently applied.

In applications using expert systems products, such as those from Trinzic Corp., Nexpert, and others, objects are created that include this expert knowledge. These objects can be reused in applications to support decision making throughout the entire organization. Figure 10.1 illustrates the benefits organizations can obtain by using expert systems technology.

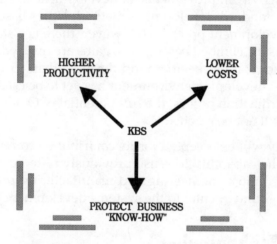

Figure 10.1. *A knowledge-based system (KBS).*

Many expert systems products are merely glitz. They are simplified to enable trivial applications to be developed but are not useful because they do not have the capacity to handle the complexity of real-life business processes. A major flaw in many products is their inability to integrate with a company's information systems and databases. If a product cannot be integrated into the organizational SDE or cannot use the organization's databases directly, it is not useful. It isn't practical to create multiple development environments and copies of data to support real-time decision making. Some expert systems products are used for after-the-fact analysis, but the best products are integrated into the business. Figure 10.2 illustrates a typical integrated architecture.

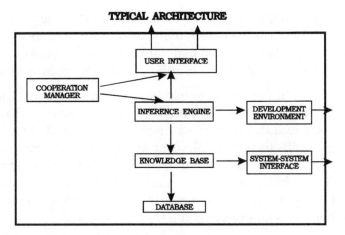

Figure 10.2. *Architecture of a typical expert systems application.*

Expert systems applications are well-suited to the client/server model. In addition to the advantages offered by the user interface component, the rules base benefits from the processing power and ease of use at the workstation. In most implementations, rules should be managed by a knowledgeable user and not by a professional programmer, because the user is the only one intimately familiar with how his or her job works—a job the expert system must emulate.

The rules are enforced by the inference engine, a CPU-intensive process that takes advantage of the low-cost processing and RAM available with client/server technology. Most applications will be implemented using existing databases on host-based DBMSs. The client/server model provides the necessary connectivity and services to support access to this information.

Expert systems currently are used mainly in government and financial organizations. In the government sphere, knowledgeable personnel create rule bases to determine people's eligibility for programs such as welfare aid. Welfare programs, in particular, change these rules rapidly, and an expert system that manages and applies these rules can improve the fairness and decrease the cost of adjudication for the program.

The financial community has built loan determination rules that can significantly reduce the time required to analyze loan application and determine the loan's risk of default. A new application of expert systems is network management. In particular, remote LAN management is an ideal application for expert systems technology. The network alerts are processed by a rules-based analyzer to help diagnose problems. Historical data is captured and maintained for subsequent comparison. The rules base also can invoke regular preventive maintenance.

The retail sector is beginning to use expert systems for real-time management. In an ideal scenario, a manager uses a rules base to describe the expected results for products as they are introduced or repackaged. The system audits the reality against the expectation in real time. Only when results are different than the defined expectation is the manager notified. This allows unexpected results, good or bad, to be detected early and allows the manager to concentrate on customers or new programs when expectations are being met.

Geographic Information Systems

Geographic information systems (GISs) provide the capability to view the topology of a landscape, including features such as roads, sewers, electrical cables, and mineral and soil content. GIS is a technology that has promised much and finally is beginning to deliver. As with the expert systems technology, GISs are truly useful when they integrate with the business process. From a technological perspective, GISs must operate on standard technologies, integrate with the organization SDE, and directly access the organizational databases.

Conceptually, GISs enable users to store virtually unlimited geographic information as a series of layers. Some layers, such as street layouts, compose the *base map*. Other layers, such as wetlands and subterranean water sources, are *thematic* layers that serve a specific, sometimes narrow purpose. A GIS user can custom design a printed map to fill a particular need by simply selecting the relevant layers. Selecting the street layer and the wetlands layer would produce a map of wetlands and their relationship to the streets. Selecting the subterranean water sources layer and the wetlands layer would show the wetlands superimposed on the features of the underlying aquifer.

Each line, curve, and symbol in a map is fixed in space by a series of numbers, called the *spatial data*. Spatial data describes the precise positioning of map objects in three-dimensional space.

Besides storing map objects such as street segments and wetland boundaries, GISs enable designers to specify attributes the users want to associate with any map object. Such attributes may be descriptive data, detailed measurements of any kind, dates, legal verbiage, or other comments. When viewing a map on-screen, the user can click any map object, and a data-entry window will open to display the attributes associated with that object. Attribute information is usually stored in RDBMS tables, and each map layer can draw attributes from multiple tables.

GIS applications are naturals for client/server technology. Powerful workstations manage the mapping. Connectivity enables shared access to the layers maintained by various departments. The GIS database is related to attributes stored in other databases that provide considerably more value in combination. For example, combining the voters list with the street maps allows polling booths to be located with easy access for all and ensures that no natural or artificial barriers are blocking the way.

Point-of-Service (POS)

Point-of-service (POS) technologies—traditionally known as point-of-sale technologies—are ubiquitous. Every restaurant, supermarket, most department stores, and even auto service stations use POS technology at the site for pricing, staff management, accounting, product distribution, and inventory control. POS is one of the most widely installed examples of client/server technology. Implementations use an intelligent cash register, bar code scanner, scale, or gas pump as the client working with a UNIX or OS/2 server.

The integration of technology, business process, and management information in POSs is a model for the implementation of client/server applications. Some older implementations continue to use dumb client devices, but lower technology costs and the growing use of object-oriented development techniques are moving more processing to the client. These applications have a specific set of characteristics; namely, they run in a large number of distributed sites and are frequently used by users with little training in a business environment demanding rapid change. Appendix A describes a large POS application built and implemented for the United States Post Office.

There is a growing demand for POSs, such as applications, to improve service and reduce costs. Self-service customs and excise processing, postal counters, help services, libraries, and even vending machines are demanding the processing power and ease of use that can be provided by this technology.

Imaging

Imaging is the conversion of documents from a physical medium (for example, paper) to a digital form where they can be manipulated by computers. Imaging should be viewed as an enabling technology. Information that is available in machine-readable form never should be converted to paper and scanned back into machine-readable form. The business process should strive to maintain and use information in machine-readable form from the earliest moment.

There is an unfortunate tendency to automate existing processes by converting recycled paper to digital form without considering whether the information printed on the form can be captured elsewhere and used without rekeying. *Optical character recognition* (OCR) is an existing technology that offers powerful capabilities to convert the image of typed information on a form to text. *Intelligent character recognition* (ICR) enables handwritten input to be recognized. Our experience in text form processing shows this technology to be capable of a high degree of reliability. Even more efficiency can be gained, whether through EDI or capture-at-source techniques, so the information on the form can be maintained in machine-readable form at all times and communicated electronically where needed.

Figure 10.3 shows a typical document imaging system. Information is entered into the system from a scanner. The scanner, similar to a fax machine, converts the paper image into digital form. This image is stored on a permanent medium, such as a magnetic or optical disk. Information must be indexed on entry so it can be located after it is stored. The index usually is stored in a relational database on a high-speed magnetic disk. Access to stored images is always initiated by an index search. High-resolution screens enable users to view the images after storage. Laser printers are used to recreate the image on paper as required.

Document images are stored and accessed through standard data access requests. The only difference between the image of an application form and the textual information keyed from the form is the amount of space required to store the image. Typically, a black-and-white image occupies 35K of storage space. The keyed data from a form typically occupies less than 2K of storage space.

As Figure 10.3 illustrates, images can be accessed by any workstation with access to the image server. Note that the image server replaces the filing cabinet but provides the additional advantage of allowing multiple access to the same documents or folders. The movement toward standards for the creation, distribution, indexing, printing, display, and revision of images has enabled a large number of vendors to enter the market with products. This has led to a dramatic reduction in the price of these components. Figure 10.4 plots this price change.

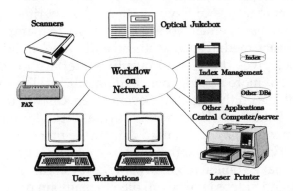

Figure 10.3. *A typical document imaging system.*

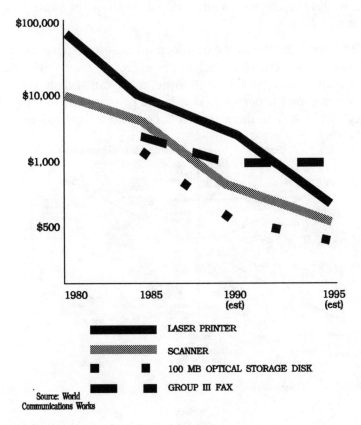

Figure 10.4. *Declining costs of imaging peripherals.*

Electronic Document Management—Multimedia

The concepts of electronic image management relate to the manipulation of information contained in forms, blueprints, x-rays, microfilm, fingerprints, photographs, and typewritten or handwritten notes. Electronic document management adds the capability to manipulate information from other media, such as audio and video. In addition, the "folder" device gives the user an intuitive interface to information equivalent to, but more flexible than, a filing cabinet. The information is always available on the desktop. Several users can use the folder simultaneously. Folders are always refiled in the correct location. Billions of these documents exist and are used daily in the process of providing government services. Consider that the Los Angeles County municipal hospitals alone have 5 billion pieces of paper, x-rays, scans, photographs, audio reports, and videos (and so on) filed to maintain patient records. Currently, the cost of this technology is prohibitively high for most organizations, but these systems will come down in price as all computer components do.

Figure 10.5 illustrates the range of information sources that can be manipulated digitally. To make efficient and effective use of this information, the means must exist for rapid filing, retrieval, and sharing of this information among all persons. This is the principle of making information available only to those with a "need and a right to know."

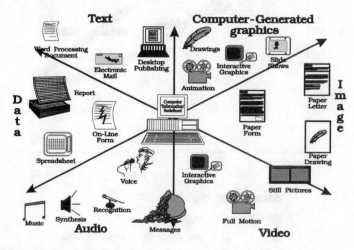

Figure 10.5. Multimedia technologies.

Electronic mail can be delivered routinely in seconds anywhere in the United States. Consumers can have direct access to suppliers. Goods can be ordered and paid for electronically. A retired engineer in Northern California can teach algebra to disadvantaged children in Compton, located in the southern part of the state. A parent can deliver office work to an employer in downtown Los Angeles while he cares for children at home. Library and museum materials can be explored at the users' own pace, with their personal interests in mind, to tap into a rich assortment of interactive, graphical how-to lessons. The community library can provide the conduit to government services: taking drivers' photographs and producing drivers' licenses on-site, producing birth certificates, or searching the titles on properties. Lawyers can file case data, review their calendars, or locate their clients' criminal records all from the law office and under the safeguards provided by electronic passwords, user auditing, and caller ID validation.

Each of these functions can be conveniently provided to citizens and consumers without them having to travel to an office location. The cost savings and environmental impact of this convenience are important considerations in today's society. Businesses no longer need to rent or buy expensive office space close to clients and suppliers. Individuals can live where they want and commute electronically to work. It is easy to imagine how the provision of these services in such a convenient manner can generate significant revenues that more than offset the cost of providing the service.

High-speed communications networks can provide the capability to distribute information other than voice conversations throughout a county, state, or country. With the advent of fiber-optic cabling, the capacity for information distribution to a location, office, library, or home is essentially infinite. As this technology become readily available, we will be able to consider where best to store and use information without concern for transmission time or quality. This is particularly true within a small geographical area, such as a county where the "right of way" is owned and private fiber-optic networks can be installed. High-speed networks in conjunction with new standards for data integrity ensure that information can be stored throughout the network and properly accessed from any point in the network.

Electronic documents can be transmitted and received just like any other digital information. The same networks and personal computers can send and receive. The major stumbling blocks to widespread sharing of electronic documents have been the incompatible formats in which various vendors store and distribute the digital image and the lack of a central repository of indexes to the documents. These indexes should describe the document content to enable users to select the correct folder and document.

Most information used by business and government today is contained in formats that are not manipulatable through traditional data-processing techniques. This is consistent with the "need and a right to know," mentioned earlier. Los Angeles County, for example, decided to overcome these problems through the definition of standards that must be adhered to by all products acquired for county projects.

Full-Text Retrieval

An area of explosive growth, coincident with the availability of high-powered workstations and RISC servers, is *full-text retrieval*. Originally a technology used by the military to scan covert transmissions and media communications, full-text retrieval is now a mainstream technology. Vendors such as Fulcrum and PLS have packaged their technology to be used in more traditional business applications. Northern Telecom bundles a product, Helmsman, with all its switch documentation to facilitate document access. All major news services provide an electronic feed of their information. This information is continuously scanned by reporters, businesses, and government offices to identify significant events or locate trends. Dow Jones provides their news retrieval system with access to $10**12$bytes (that's three billion pages) of textual data. Many criteria searches can be run against all this text in a few seconds. Figure 10.6 illustrates the flow of information in a full-text retrieval application.

The major hardware and software technologies that have made this technology production viable are Optical Character Recognition (OCR), ICR, optical storage, powerful workstations, large D-RAM, software algorithms, and high-resolution monitors. OCR and ICR technologies convert the paper documents to text files. Companies such as Colera provide software to convert typewritten documents directly into WordPerfect format. Recent improvements in these algorithms provide support for most major fonts. Improvements in handwriting recognition promise to enable users to enter data from handwritten documents as well. Colera provides a fax link that enables documents to be entered by way of OCR as they are received from a fax. Mitek provides high-speed ICR engines to be used with document workflow applications. Embedded diagrams are maintained in image format.

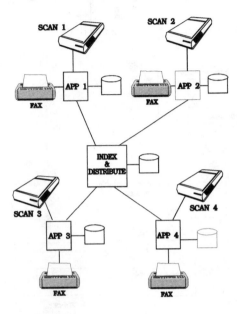

Figure 10.6. *Text management process.*

Full-text indexing of documents is a CPU-intensive function, and the availability of low-cost, high-powered workstations has made the technology viable. (See Figure 10.7.) PC products such as Lotus Magellan enable the casual user to create full-text indexes of all their files. Viewers and launchers within the products enable users to access these files in their native format and manipulate them using a data editor of choice. With the advent of Object Linking and Embedding (OLE 2.x) and CORBA-based object solutions such as DOE, full-text access will become much more common to support capture and inclusion of source material. For high-performance retrievals, the indexes must support boolean search requests. The availability of large and low-cost D-RAM provides the necessary environment. High-resolution monitors are necessary as we move to a multiwindowed environment using facilities such as OLE and DOE. Extensive use of these facilities will not be viable without the appropriate resolution, because eyestrain will discourage use. We recommend Super VGA, a resolution of 1024 by 768, as a minimum for this type of multiwindowed work.

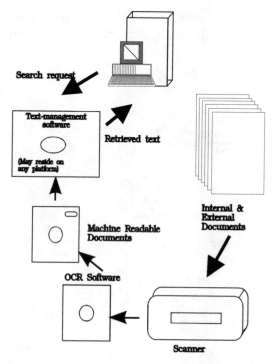

Figure 10.7. Text management process.

Transformational Systems—
The Challenge of the 1990s

In the more than 40 years since the introduction of the stored program computer in 1951, we have seen tremendous advances in the capabilities of this technology. Computers have proven over and over that they can add numbers at mind-numbing rates. We have extrapolated from this capability the functionality to maintain accounts, calculate bills, print checks, and create memos. All this functionality has enabled organizations to grow and do more work with fewer clerical and administrative staff.

As the world economy becomes more integrated, goods and services are provided by companies and individuals from all parts of the world. Consumers can and will buy the most cost-effective quality product and service available. This substantially increases the necessity for organizations to demonstrate their value. Western economies, with their higher salaries and cost of plant, are particularly threatened by this trend. However, Western economies have the advantage of a highly educated population. Educated staff are willing to accept decision-making responsibility and are better able to adapt to change. The challenge is to find ways in which technology can enable the West to capitalize on these advantages.

Many organizations and industries are finding solutions that use client/server technology to truly transform the working environment. The following are brief examples of business solutions and technology partnerships that apply this technology to fundamentally change the business process. Several of these examples are further described in Appendix A, along with other client/server project examples.

Emergency Public Safety

Emergency (E911) dispatch operators are responsible for sending the right emergency response vehicles to an incident as quickly as possible and at the same time dealing with the crisis being reported over the telephone. This functionality must be provided 24-hours-per-day, 365-days-per-year, with the maximum possible performance.

As you can imagine, most 911 callers are in a state of anxiety. The telephone switch provides the caller's telephone number and address to the dispatcher workstation. Traditional technical design of a 911 system involves the use of redundant minicomputers connected to character-based terminals. This design solution provides the benefits of fault tolerance and high performance with the costs of complex user interfaces, considerable redundancy, and excess capacity.

Through the use of client/server computing, it is now possible to duplicate all of the functionality of such an existing traditional design with the additional advantages of better performance, a graphical user interface (GUI), a single point of contact, higher reliability, and lower costs. With a client/server-based system, the dispatch operator is empowered to oversee how staff and equipment are allocated to each incident. The operator uses a GUI to dynamically alter vehicle selection and routing. Maps may be displayed that show the location of all incidents, emergency response centers, and vehicles. Vehicles are tracked using automatic vehicle locator (AVL) technology. Obstacles, such as traffic congestion, construction, and environmental damage (such as earthquakes) are shown on the map so the dispatcher can see potential problems at a glance.

The implementation of such an E911 service can dramatically improve the rate at which emergency calls can be answered and reduce the incidence of unnecessary dispatches. Workstation technology provides the dispatcher with a less stressful and more functional user interface. The dispatcher can respond quickly to changes in the environment and communicate this information immediately to the vehicle operator. The system is remarkably fault-tolerant. If a single workstation is operating, the dispatcher can continue to send emergency vehicles to the incident. This architecture is general enough to apply to any application that has reasonable quantities of transient data.

Electronic Data Interchange

Electronic data interchange (EDI) technology enables unrelated organizations to conduct their business computer to computer without the need to use the same computer applications or technology in all locations. Combining *just in time* (JIT) manufacturing with EDI truly transforms the process:

1. A salesperson accepts an order through a laptop computer system.
2. Using the electronic mail facilities of the organization, the order is shipped to the order entry system.
3. The component parts are determined, and electronic purchase orders are generated to each supplier.
4. The EDI link routes the order, which is processed by the supplier's order system.
5. An EDI link is used to validate the purchaser's credit worthiness.
6. The paperless invoice is sent by way of EDI back to the purchaser.
7. When it is time for payment, an EDI link is used to generate the electronic funds transfer (EFT) to pay.

With EDI, a single entry by the person closest to the customer causes the facilities of the manufacturer and its suppliers to schedule appropriate production, shipping, and billing. The maximum possible time is allowed for all parties to process the order, thus reducing their need to carry inventory. A further advantage comes when production is driven by orders, because only those products that will actually be sold are manufactured. Manufacturers are able to offer more flexibility in product configuration, because they are manufacturing to order. The use of EDI standards allows organizations to participate in this electronic dialog regardless of differences among their individual technologies or application systems.

Financial Analysis

Financial analysts are overloaded with data. It is impossible for them to process all the data received. They must read it, looking for gems of information. Powerful workstation technology enables these analysts to specify personal filters to be applied against the data in order to present only information of likely interest and to present it in order of most likely interest. These filters provide search criteria specific to each analyst and provide only information satisfying the filter criteria to the analyst.

Improvements in technology enable the data to be scanned in real time. Alerts can be generated to the analyst whenever a significant event is detected. In this way, the analyst's job is transformed. He or she is now concerned with developing the rules to drive the filters and with understanding how to react to the significant events that are detected. Meaningful and useful data is available to support the analyst's decision making. He or she has more time to make informed decisions.

Conclusion

This book discussed the vision of an application of technology that provides a single-system image view to all users of the technology. In the single-system model, each user has access to all applications for which he or she has a "need and right" of access, without regard to the technology of the workstation, the network, or the location of the business data and logic. In this model, technology is treated as a commodity to be chosen for its price, performance, and functionality—not for the color of its box.

Achieving this vision requires the system developer to be equally insensitive to the technology. If the developer is aware of the specific technology, he or she will develop in a manner specific to that technology. In the single-system image model, the developer needs to know only the syntax in which the business logic is specified. Through client/server technology available today, it is possible for developers to design and develop systems to support this single-system image concept.

Attention to industry standards and the creation and use of a development environment that isolates the user from the technology is mandatory to enable platform technology to become a commodity. Object-oriented technology recognizes this fact and offers the future promise of systems that are generated for an arbitrary target platform. Technology buyers will now be in control of their purchasing decisions and not subject to the whim of their current supplier. Applications can be developed in a scalable manner and implemented on a platform appropriate for the workload at a particular location.

Appendix A

Case Studies

Executive Summary

The 16 examples of successful client/server and system automation projects given in this chapter are introduced in this section. Most of the examples include figures that summarize the system configurations of the environments. Later sections provide technology discussions about these organizations and explore systems development and maintenance issues.

Major Pipeline Company Nominations, Scheduling, and Allocations (NSA) System

A major pipeline company transports around 1.1 MMCF of natural gas a day at all times, day and night, to ensure that Californians have enough electricity to live their lives in relative comfort. This wholly owned subsidiary of a $13.5 billion energy company—the nation's largest provider of natural gas—found itself examining a changing marketplace, redefining its business goals, and determining how to support its new focus.

After focusing on business and operational changes, the company began to define what it would take to become a world-class servicer of natural gas shippers. They knew they needed to improve pipeline processes by optimizing gas volume and monitoring throughput to prevent imbalances. They wanted to change their invoicing process and simplify other functions. This process of business reengineering would serve them well. An obvious next step was to review the company's computer systems.

At a time when the pipeline company needed improvement in quality and service, it needed flexibility in its systems. The existing systems ran on a number of IBM and DEC platforms—with some redundancies and delay between critical activities and information availability. Review of their systems also revealed that technology had come a long way since these systems were developed in 1987. What this gas pipeline transportation company needed was streamlined systems for streamlined business processes.

Using a LAN running Novell NetWare Version 3.11, Microsoft Windows 3.0 with Powersoft's PowerBuilder 1.0 development package, a Sybase database engine, and a UNIX operating system for the database server, the company has implemented a transportation contract system; a nominations, scheduling, and allocations system; and a customer service interface system (see Figure A.1).

United States Postal Service Comprehensive Tracking and Tracing (CTT) System

The United States Postal Service (USPS) competes with commercial companies for provision of expedited mail service. The Comprehensive Tracking and Tracing (CTT) system's primary purpose is to track Express Mail to improve the competitive position of this product for USPS.

CTT is used to monitor the movement of an individual piece of Express Mail from the time it enters the postal system (acceptance) through final delivery. Whenever a significant action occurs with a piece of mail, an event is generated to record that action. Events occur at acceptance, as mail moves through intermediate points (enroute events), when the mail arrives at the postal unit for delivery, and finally when the mail is delivered (or a delivery has been attempted). (See Figure A.1.)

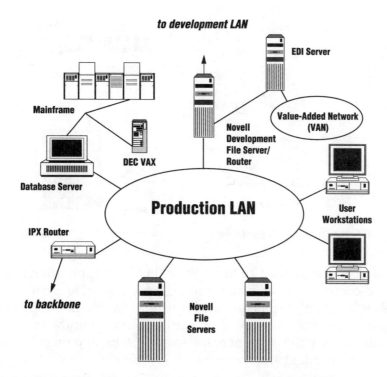

Figure A.1. *The technical architecture of a major pipeline company's NSA system.*

The heart of the data collection system is a series of handheld laser scanners, located in 16,000 postal locations, which read the bar-coded label identifications contained on each Express Mail piece. When fully deployed, scanners will capture almost all event data.

CTT is a high-volume transaction system that uses client/server technology. The handheld scanners (client component) collect and then send data to an IBM mainframe host. The data on the host is stored in a DB2 database for inquiry and control. Figure A.2 depicts a high-level view of the system components.

Los Angeles Fire Department Fire Command and Control System

The Los Angeles Fire Department (LAFD) is a full-service metropolitan fire department. The LAFD responds to emergency medical service (EMS) calls as well as to fire and rescue incidents. Approximately 75 percent of all calls for service are for EMS incidents. LAFD's 55 rescue ambulances transport patients to hospitals and provide paramedic services to patients.

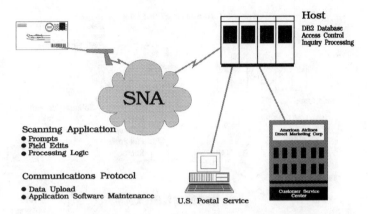

Figure A.2. The components of the postal system's Comprehensive Tracking and Tracing Service.

The Fire Command and Control System (FCCS) II application is a customized computer-aided dispatch (CAD) program. The system is designed to fulfill all dispatch-related functions for the fire department. These include, among many other features, recording the initial incident, dispatching the incident to the various units, and ongoing monitoring of the incident and the units.

FCCS II is a large system that encompasses workstation technology, client/server technology, and a DB2 back-end database. It is particularly interesting because it implements a fault-tolerant application using the client/server model and standard PC workstation technology. In particular, the client workstations provide the capability of full-function dispatching without requiring the mainframe host to be available.

The system uses 70 IBM PS/2 workstations with Token Ring networking, 400 Motorola Digital Terminals (MDTs) and Travel Pilots (portable computers) located in the vehicles, and the Fireworks CAD software package from Lynx Graphics. Various interfaces to an emergency service (E911)—SL-1/Positron, a Metromedia public pager system, a Centracom II radio system, an ADT 4504 display clock, a Veritrac 60-track voice recorder system, a digitized voice system, and communications to the city's IBM 3090 mainframe and to 114 separate fire station locations—are controlled by a set of IBM PS/2 Model 95 workstations.

Los Angeles County Automated Case Tracking System

The Superior Court of the County of Los Angeles has approximately 250 courtrooms located in the central courthouse and in the nine district courthouses around the county. The court employs approximately 300 judges for a system of day and night court sessions. Its current load of more than 45,000 felony cases per year makes the court among the busiest in the world.

The Automated Case Tracking System (ACTS) is being designed and developed to provide automated support for the Los Angeles County Superior Court. The support provides an environment that standardizes and streamlines the workflow. This standardization eliminates redundant manual effort and duplication of data entry, and reduces paper flow. The automated support also enhances the accuracy, consistency, and timeliness of management information reports. ACTS provides the court, staff, and litigants with quick access to case information.

ACTS is a large system that uses client/server technology. Each court location contains multiple workstations attached to multiple Token Rings. Data is exchanged between these locations and the host IBM system via an extensive communications network. Figure A.3 provides a high-level view of the system components.

Los Angeles County Department of Public Social Services— GAIN Employment Activity Reporting System

The Los Angeles County Department of Public Social Services administers county, state, and federal welfare programs to local residents, including Aid to Families with Dependent Children (AFDC), food stamps, Medi-Cal, General Relief, and Greater Avenues of Independence (GAIN).

GAIN Employment Activity Reporting System (GEARS) was designed and developed to support the GAIN welfare program. The purpose of the program is to provide a source of education and training to enable welfare recipients to find employment. During the education and training programs, GAIN provides supportive services in the areas of transportation, child care, and ancillary expense payments. GEARS supports 250 GAIN case managers who coordinate an active caseload of 30,000 participants and a total caseload of 220,000 participants.

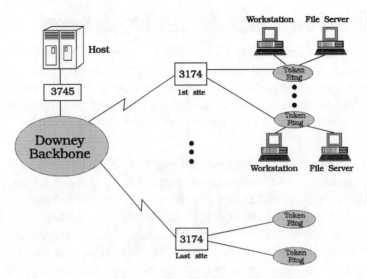

Figure A.3. *The components of the Los Angeles Automated Case Tracking System.*

GAIN represents a large system that was developed under a very aggressive schedule. Although GAIN does not yet use client/server technology, it was developed using a systems development environment and uses remote network management servers that are applicable in a client/server environment.

California Telco Service Order Load and Retrieval (SOLAR) System

A public telephone communications supplier provides service to 4 million customers in a service area that covers approximately 40 percent of southern California and portions of northern California.

The objective of the Service Order Load and Retrieval (SOLAR) project was to provide a user-friendly, online order system that would simplify telephone service order processing and provide accurate and timely order information without rewriting the existing systems. The major benefits of the system are an overall improvement in the quality of service to customers, a reduction in the number of order-processing personnel, and a dramatic reduction in the degree of training required for order-processing personnel to become effective.

SOLAR handles the data entry requirements of the order-processing centers (OPCs), business service order centers (BSOCs), and customer service order centers (CSOCs). SOLAR automates service order issuance, routing, rate calculations, and file maintenance, and also provides interfaces to many related systems.

SOLAR is an example of a large system that was built in a time-compressed schedule using a systems development environment. This system was designed to front-end existing batch systems to provide the end user with a better interface to the old systems, without rewriting them. Figure A.4 depicts the conceptual view of the system.

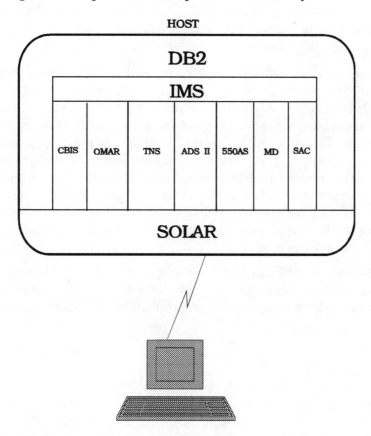

Figure A.4. *The components of the Service Order Load and Retrieval project.*

Winnipeg Fire and Ambulance Departments' Fire and Ambulance Command and Control System (FACCS)

The Winnipeg Fire and Ambulance Departments are separate organizations, each with its own dispatch and operational characteristics and requirements. FACCS is designed to allow the departments to share some common dispatch processing, although they remain separate entities.

The Fire and Ambulance Command and Control System (FACCS) is a computer-aided dispatch (CAD) system that uses workstation processing, graphical user interfaces (GUIs), and client/server technology integrated with relational databases to support administrative and reporting requirements in the same platform.

The primary FACCS token ring is composed of 10 IBM PS/2 workstations that provide the CAD functions, interfaces to existing fire and ambulance LANs, and communications to 27 fire stations and nine ambulance stations. Dispatching is done from workstations running on a standard Token Ring LAN using a proprietary messaging protocol. The protocol implements a fault-tolerant application in which all workstations contain the same data. Data from the workstations is passed to an Oracle server for use by the fire department and the billing administration. The Ambulance Department uses the IBM PC Database Manager product for its records. This data is then usable from workstations on the fire and ambulance LANs.

Dispatchers on the FACCS LAN may query data that exists on either the Oracle or Database Manager server and display this information on their workstations. Figure A.5 depicts the major components of FACCS.

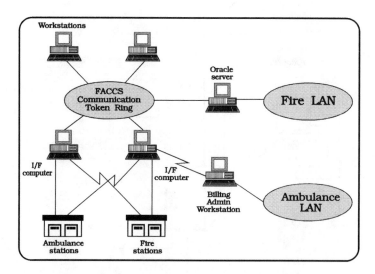

Figure A.5. *The components of the Fire and Ambulance Command and Control System.*

Esso Chemical Canada System for Customer Appreciation and Marketing Potential

The Agricultural Chemical division of Esso Chemical Canada (ECC) is located in Redwater, Alberta, with a Marketing office in Edmonton. The division produces approximately 1.6 million tons of fertilizer products annually, marketing and distributing to customers around the world. Peak demand for products in the spring and fall seasons places tremendous strain on the marketing and distribution resources of the organization.

The System for Customer Appreciation and Marketing Potential (SCAMP) provides the operational components and the information environment required for ECC's marketing and sales business area. The system provides a dual operational-informational environment that improves the quality of and access to information.

The development and operation of the system uses a client/server architecture, with Sun and IBM workstations and Sun servers. ECC uses the Oracle DBMS on the Sun servers. Figure A.6 provides a high-level view of the platforms.

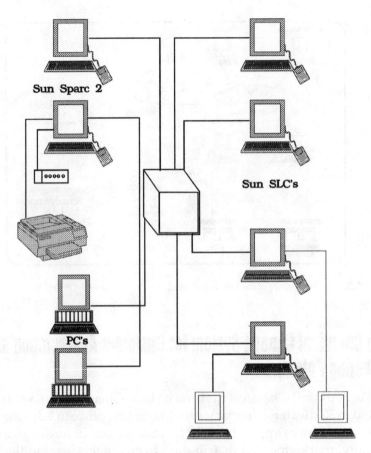

Figure A.6. The technical environment of Esso's System for Customer Appreciation and Marketing Potential.

Syncrude Canada Limited Slope Inclinometer System

Syncrude Canada Limited is an integrated operation that produces synthetic crude oil from an oil sand deposit. The operation—consisting of an open pit mine, an extraction plant, a bitumen upgrader, and a utilities plant—can produce 55 million barrels of synthetic crude oil per year.

The Slope Inclinometer System (SLOPE) was developed to assist the geotechnical engineers in determining ground movement near the edge of the pit in order to ensure the safety and productivity of the huge draglines used in the extraction of ore from the mine. This is accomplished through the capture, analysis, and reporting of ground movement data in a responsive LAN environment, using intelligent workstations equipped with a graphical user interface (GUI). SLOPE uses a client/server architecture and a mainframe DB2 database for data archiving. Figure A.7 provides a high-level view of the system components.

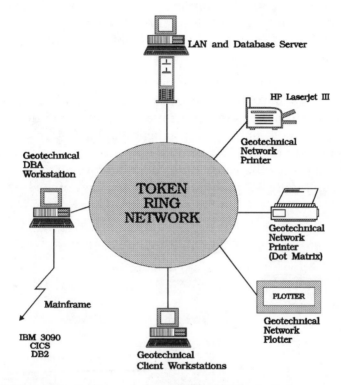

Figure A.7. *The components of Syncrude Canada's Slope Inclinometer System.*

Life Assurance Company "Model Office"

The parent corporation of this large North American firm maintains a base of approximately 650,000 customers. During the spring of 1988, a staff of five senior executives left the home office. Their mission was to reengineer the business processes for accidental death insurance and develop innovative ways and means to satisfy the parent company's clients' needs for insurance products and services, enabling the company to meet aggressive financial growth objectives.

This project took a new approach in meeting the company's data processing requirements for customer service. The project's mission was to build a customer service prototype and a fulfillment and billing system. To accomplish this, it was determined that a model office should be created off-site as a research and development tool. This small-scale office was used to prototype concepts and was then able to implement proven new ideas incrementally in a "roll-out" mode in the home office. The selected technical platform consisted of an Apple Macintosh/DEC VAX platform, using Oracle as the DBMS and Hypercard to build an object-oriented prototype.

The model office environment was designed to test new ideas for communications with the parent company. The overall application environment was meant to be very conceptual, dynamic, and iterative. The previous system did not provide statistics and therefore did not provide suitable information for comparison with the model office. The model office is now the vehicle to generate information on future capacity needs. Figure A.8 provides a high-level view of the system components.

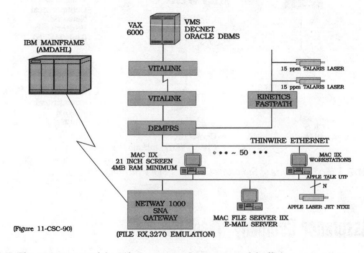

Figure A.8. *The components of the Life Assurance Company model office.*

Blue Cross of Atlantic

In January 1991, Blue Cross of Atlantic began making the transition from developing and maintaining its business applications on an IBM 3090

M200 mainframe (at a very high cost in CPU cycles) to developing and maintaining them on IBM PS/2 workstations in an OS/2 client/server networked environment. Blue Cross networked PS/2 Model 50s, 55s, and 70s. The transition took place using a two-phased approach over a course of eight months. Figure A.9 shows the development environment platform.

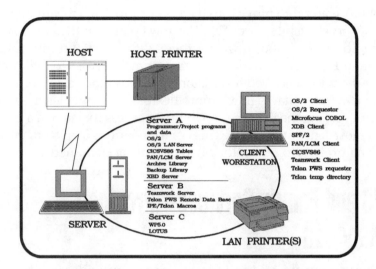

Figure A.9. *The components of the Blue Cross of Atlantic client/server network.*

In the first phase, a workbench environment was set up to assist in migrating OS/VS COBOL programs from the mainframe to workstations for maintenance activities. After maintenance was completed, the programs were remigrated back to the mainframe into production.

LINCS—Liquor Information and Networking Computer System, Saskatchewan Liquor and Gaming Authority

A fundamental problem the Saskatchewan Liquor Board, SLGA, faced was obsolescence. NCR was no longer manufacturing the point of sale hardware in their retail operation. Servicing of this hardware consisted of cannibalizing older machines to keep the existing machines running.

As well, the VAX hardware used in their head office was operating at capacity. SLGA gave consideration to several alternatives before choosing a client/server architecture. This architecture fits well with the business goal of giving each of the 84 retail stores more autonomy and, in the process, gives the SLGA the state-of-the-art in Liquor Boards.

The SLGA wanted to move into the new world. This meant moving to a client/server architecture. The Windows platform they are using for the head office functions provides them with a very intuitive access to their data. This also provides for a more timely access to their data allowing them to make better decisions. This interface also presents the data in a manner that is much more flexible. This enables user-driven reporting, giving the user the capability to access the data in a way that makes most sense at the time. This is a tremendous step from the batch reporting process to which they had become accustomed.

Child and Family Services—Province of Manitoba

The Department of Child and Family Services provides family support services throughout the province of Manitoba. As in any jurisdiction, the social workers have the difficult task of tracking the requirements of families dealing with stress, addictions, and other family problems. Social Workers spend most of their time in the field, yet a significant trail of paperwork must follow documenting the actions taken by the case worker, teacher, and police. This provides an audit trail of case notes in the event that the case requires legal action at a later date. Either participants asking for help or a concerned agency may initiate activity in the Child and Family Services system.

Historically, the various jurisdictions have been very protective of the information maintained by the case workers. Significant problems arise caused by large number of families in need of support services being transient. This causes cases to "fall through the cracks" as information remains local to a jurisdiction. It was often a problem to identify people previously in contact with agencies in different jurisdictions, accessing data, or establishing a dialog with the former case worker.

The new system demands improvements in several areas. One of the key features in the new system is the standardization of program delivery. Through automation, the social worker can follow the legislated policies very easily. This provides a consistent program delivery across the province. The process also improves the social workers' effectiveness through the building of workflow management into the system. The sharing of data across jurisdictions enhances the overall effectiveness of the program. By having a clear and concise case record available, case workers are able to identify and track cases that used to fall through the cracks.

The system uses a client/server implementation for several reasons. The system requires data to have a central repository for continual tracking across a wide distribution base of jurisdictions while still enabling access to the data while the system is offline. Client/server architecture provides this capability. The system requires an easy-to-use interface with integration to existing office standards such as WordPerfect. The system requires the central sharing and integration of case management report data and includes this in management reports for online viewing and printing. Client/server architecture provides this capability.

La Hacienda

The Ministry of Finance (Hacienda) in Mexico receives approximately 23,000,000 tax returns annually. Each form required substantial data entry on behalf of both the banks and the Ministry itself. The cost of manual data entry was exceeding $100,000,000 annually, with the banks being paid an average of $1.60 per form.

A scalable client/server architecture was designed to handle varying volume requirements. A base architecture also was established. As site volumes varied, replication of the architecture was able to meet the demand. The site with the greatest volume requirements, Mexico City, duplicated this architecture four times. Each configuration featured data entry through image scanners and optical character recognition. An optical disk autochanger provided the storage of images. In addition, key entry from images provided post-recognition edit checking, and networked access, over both local- and wide-area networks.

The Mexico City site configuration consists of four processing lines networked using an FDDI Backbone. Each line consists of a Ricoh

IS-520 Scanner capable of scanning both sides of a form in two seconds. HNC and Xerox ScanWorks Optical Character Recognition, with an HP 735 File Server, perform Database and queue management at 11 Key Edit Workstations. To support image storage and printing requirements, the sites also have two HP Optical Disk Library Units and two laser printers.

La Hacienda incorporates client/server technology throughout its architecture. It demonstrates the scalability of a client/server architecture and provides sophisticated work flow management that looks for available processors to load balance much of the background processing.

The client/server architecture is very cost-effective for this type of system. It is quite clear that processors are becoming faster and cheaper at a rapid rate. Client/server architecture takes advantage of this trend.

Scalability comes with client/server architectures. This meant Hacienda was able to increase throughput by networking together subsystems of a convenient size. There are great savings in being able to do this. For example, the one-image-a-second scanner was about one-third the price of its two-images-a-second competitor. Because the remote sites did not require the higher throughput scanner, they were able to save the price differential seven times. The work flow management software enables Hacienda to take advantage of cheap processing power in an inexpensive manner.

Program Management Information System (PMIS)/Supplement Payment System (SPS)

The self-sufficiency Project is a seven-year research demonstration. The program's purpose is to test the effectiveness of an earnings supplement for qualified participants. The program focuses on the single-parent Social Assistance recipient who agrees to take a job and leave public assistance. The program offers a supplement to each qualified individual for a limited three-year period. It is employment-driven because only those who work full-time will be eligible. It is also generous enough to make work financially preferable to public assistance. The project operates out of offices in New Brunswick and British Columbia, with a payroll office in Halifax, Nova Scotia.

An interesting aspect of this project is the business engineering aspect that the client/server architectures provide. With the PMIS/SPS system, the creation of the business process took place in conjunction with the creation of the development system. There were no models from which to draw requirements for the solution. In some cases, the formulation of system requirements may have shaped the business processes and procedures.

Development of the PMIS/SPS applications took place with the product, Ellipse. These applications operate over a Microsoft LAN Manager Token Ring network with an OS/2 1.3 server running Microsoft SQL Server 4.2a, and Microsoft Windows 3.1 clients. An OS/2 2.0 client in each office provides a Microsoft Mail gateway and nightly database reconciliation. The application integrates commercial products from Microsoft, Pioneer Software, and Hilgraeve on the client desktop. These products provide the business functions of participant correspondence, data for external agencies, electronic mail, and remote system management.

The client/server architecture provides the infrastructure for sharing and integrating information between applications while giving the client the ease of use of a graphical user interface. In addition, the architecture provides the scalability and expandability that enables the deployment of the solution in other provinces—if the need arises.

In the second phase, a development environment was set up to assist in building future applications more effectively. Future applications are to be built on the workstation and then migrated up to the mainframe into production.

Case Studies and Project Examples

For readers who want to review the preceding specific projects in more detail, and in particular learn more about the specific technologies applied to solving the business problems presented, the following material and more specific examples will represent an opportunity to learn how client/server computing is having a major impact on today's business environment.

Major Pipeline Company Nominations, Scheduling, and Allocations (NSA) System

Some Southern Californians would be in the dark if it weren't for this major pipeline company. The company is a wholly owned subsidiary of a $13.5 billion energy company—the nation's largest provider of natural gas. Early in the spring of 1991, the pipeline company's executives found themselves examining a changing marketplace, redefining their business goals, and determining how to support their business focus. But they had a problem; their computer systems were not flexible enough to meet the pipeline company's changing needs.

"The nature of the pipeline business has changed in the past five years. In an environment of open access transportation, you have to find a new way to differentiate your company in the marketplace. Our customers never see a molecule of gas. They see the invoice and experience the service," explained the president of the pipeline company.

After focusing on needed business and operational changes, the company took a critical step; it began to define what it would take to become a world-class servicer of natural gas shippers. The employees knew they needed to improve pipeline processes by optimizing gas volume and monitoring throughput to prevent imbalances. They wanted to change their invoicing process and simplify the functions they planned to focus on in the future. The next step was to review their computer systems.

At a time when the company needed improvement in quality and service, it needed new levels of flexibility, functionality, and accounting in its systems. The existing systems ran on a number of IBM and DEC platforms—with some redundancies and delay between critical activities and information availability. (By the time measurement of gas volumes had been processed through the systems, the information was two days old. In addition, information related to the scheduling of gas transportation was on the VAX; uploading to the mainframe made the cycle for related activities at least overnight.)

Review of the systems also brought to light the fact that technology had come a long way since these systems were developed in 1987. For example, in the existing computer systems, the gas measurement process caused prior-period accounting adjustments to be the rule rather than the exception. Measuring movement of gas along a pipeline involves the difference between the pressure on one side of a compressor or meter and the other. For each delivery and receipt point along the pipeline, there are two meters—that of the operator who is delivering gas to the pipeline (or receiving gas) and the company's meter. With two measurements, there is often a reconciliation to deal with.

With the new systems, the company wanted to invoice what it scheduled to transport rather than wait for actual measurements of what was transported. By rethinking and reengineering the way its business is done, the company changed business processes so that the invoicing of gas scheduled to be transported along the pipeline is done the next day. Although there is some balancing to be done at a later point if "scheduled" doesn't become "actual," in the main, monies due are collected weeks earlier, and the whole process is "cleaner."

After examining the options available, the company chose a client/ server, graphical user interface (GUI) approach. When asked why, the president replied, "The culture in our company says that change is good and being on the leading edge is important. The company was taking an innovative approach to their business. The client/server/GUI approach for the new systems seemed to mirror what was happening on the business side of things, and the resulting systems would be the right size for our company."

The company required systems that could grow and migrate to new technologies as they were introduced. Some of the other requirements were:

- Use of the existing systems as building blocks for the new systems
- Prototyping so that the users would accept the new systems as they were being developed
- Use of development tools that would ensure development of flexible, portable systems
- A significant reduction in ongoing operating and maintenance costs

The new systems needed to provide a new customer interface, simplify allocations (the operational core of the company's business), and eliminate duplicate data, duplicate functionality, and duplicate work effort in the process. The company also finalized the decision to invoice for gas transportation on the day the gas flowed, based on scheduled rather than actual (measured) volume at this point.

As with most mission-critical systems, client/server systems developed to run on the company's local area network (LAN) operate in a multivendor environment. The production LAN itself is IBM Token Ring. The file server, a Compaq SystemPro 486/33, runs NetWare Version 3.11, communicating with the other servers and the workstations on the LAN using the IPX/SPX protocol. It uses the TCP/IP Runtime System Token Ring option, which allows communications with the corporate IBM mainframe and DEC VAX.

The database server is a Sun Sparcstation running Sun OS (UNIX). Sybase SQL Server for UNIX Version 4.8 is the relational database management system. Because the company did not want to be confronted with an upgrade decision in the near future, the user workstations are, in most cases, 486-based Compaq PCs. The workstation environment is MS-DOS Version 5.0 and Windows Version 3.0. Sybase Net-Lib for Windows, and Sybase DB-Lib for DOS/Windows.

The applications were developed using Powersoft's PowerBuilder Version 1.0 and BSG Consulting, Inc.'s Windows-based development toolset and architecture, BluePrint. A runtime version of PowerBuilder and Novell LAN Workplace for DOS round out the development and operational PC environment. All printers are Hewlett-Packard LaserJet IIIs. Under this environment, the following applications were completed:

- *Transportation Contract System (TCS):* to process natural gas transport service requests and contracts.
- *Nominations, Scheduling, and Allocations (NSA):* to process customer nominations for gas transportation, schedule gas within the pipeline, and do the accounting based on the scheduled delivery of the gas. (Nominations tell a company how much gas to expect receipt or delivery of at specific points along the pipeline.)
- *EDI portion of Customer Interface (CI):* to enable customers to submit their own nomination requests.

The president says the transition to the new systems was the smoothest he's ever seen. Around noon on conversion day he asked what had happened to the new systems. The response was, "We've been using them all morning."

Approximately 30 people, primarily in core business areas, use the new systems now, with the potential for about 300 users when additional integrated applications are completed.

California Unemployment Insurance Appeals Board Automation Project

Unemployment Insurance and Disability Insurance applicants who are denied benefits by the California Employment Development Department (EDD) have a right to appeal their cases to the California Unemployment Insurance Appeals Board (CUIAB). In certain circumstances, employers may also appeal EDD decisions. CUIAB holds hearings, adjudicates the appeals, and provides decisions. Appellants have a second level of appeal within CUIAB when they do not agree with the initial decision. The board has 11 field offices throughout the state, a Chief Administrative Law Judge Office, and an Appellate Office in Sacramento. Because of difficult economic times, the EDD case volume increased approximately 80 percent during 1991. Offices strained to maintain service levels.

The automation project is reengineering an existing eight-year-old ICL distributed processing system, developing a new generation of business applications on a new hardware/software platform to improve the board's ability to deliver its mandate. The $2.3 million project is based on a client/server architecture and includes application development, 130 Intel 386-based Digital Equipment Corporation workstations, 13 Novell V3.11 LANs with WAN connectivity servers, operating system and packaged software, and five years of hardware and software support. Figure A.10 depicts a high-level view of the platform.

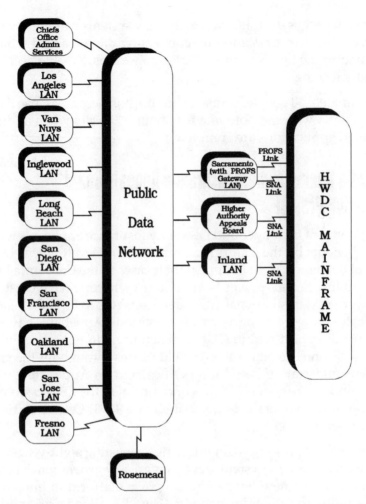

Figure A.10. *The components of the California Unemployment Insurance Appeals Board's automation project.*

United States Postal Service Comprehensive Tracking and Tracing System

The Comprehensive Tracking and Tracing (CTT) application tracks priority mail from receipt through delivery.

The handheld scanners are 80x86-based processors developed by Symbol Technologies of California. The processors run MS-DOS and three layers of software: IPL, communications, and application. All three layers were custom-developed for the CTT system. When a postal employee finishes scanning several pieces of mail, the scanner (client component) is returned to a cradle. The cradle serves to keep the batteries recharged and provides the communications facility to the host environment (server component). The scanner automatically dials a predetermined number to initiate data transmission after a fixed time. If the scanner is not in the cradle at that time, it will beep to notify the operator to return it to the cradle. If the scanner is unable to connect to the primary phone number after several attempts, it tries an alternate phone number.

When the scanner does connect, it establishes its connection to the IBM Information Network (IIN). The scanner identifies itself to the IIN during login. Then a session is established with the CTT host in Houston, Texas. In general, the scanners can access the IIN through local phone numbers from anywhere in the United States. IIN access is also available in several foreign countries. IIN provides the largest value-added network in the world.

When the scanner connects to the host (an IBM ES/9000 model 500) in Houston, it establishes a conversational session in a CICS region dedicated to capturing scanner data. At the communications level, the scanner communicates via the Extended Line Mode Protocol. An application-level protocol has also been established. The design criterion was that if a session is lost for any reason (such as a local phone line failure), the data captured in the scanner must not be lost; the scanner must automatically retransmit until the host acknowledges successful receipt. This verification is accomplished by a handshaking protocol in which the scanner and the host acknowledge to each other exactly where they are in the process after each major step in the transmission. Any failure to acknowledge correctly causes the scanner not to delete the captured data, and retransmission occurs until a positive acknowledgment is received.

One of the first steps that occurs in the scanner/host data exchange is determining what version of software the scanner is running and what version of the ZIP code edit file the scanner is running. If either of the versions is not current, the host either downloads new software immediately or requests the scanner to call back at a specific scheduled time to receive the new version of software. The scanner operator is unaware of this processing, because it occurs when the scanner is in its docking station.

Once the data is captured on the mainframe, it is put into transient data queues (TDQs) within CICS. In addition, all data received from the batch transmissions is also put into TDQs within CICS. This allows all DB2 insert activity to be scheduled within CICS and avoids contention between CICS and batch.

From this point, separate processes read the various TDQs and post data to the various partitions of the DB2 database. The database is partitioned to allow multiple concurrent tasks to be inserted to the database without fear of contention.

The database environment is unique in that more than 90 percent of the online activity on the database is insert activity. With overnight mail service, there is a large volume of mail event data captured, but chances are very low that someone will call to inquire about a package if it is delivered on time. So the better the delivery service becomes, the larger the ratio of insert activity to inquiry will become. In this environment, performance is geared toward sustaining extremely large volumes of data insertion.

The other factor that adds to the complexity of the operation is the requirement to provide 7-day-a-week, 24-hour-per-day operation.

The system is not yet in full production, but it is processing approximately 3.5 to 4 million events/acceptance records per week (more than 1 million via scanners). The current transaction rate is relatively consistent at 20 transactions per second. Stress testing has shown a capacity for 400 transactions per second.

Los Angeles Fire Department Fire Command and Control System

The Fire Command and Control System (FCCS) is a customized computer-aided dispatch (CAD) application. The main computing for the dispatching occurs on the workstations on the Token Ring. The system uses 70 IBM PS/2 workstations with Token Ring networking, 400 Motorola Digital Terminals (MDTs), and the Fireworks CAD software package from Lynx Graphics. Various interfaces from the Token Ring to an E911 SL-1/Positron, a Metro-media public pager system, a Centracom II radio system, an ADT 4504 display clock, a Veritrac 60-track voice recorder system, a digitized voice system, the city's IBM 3090 mainframe, and 114 separate fire station locations are controlled by a set of IBM PS/2 Model 95 workstations.

In addition to an MDT, each fire station is also equipped with an ETAK Travel Pilot (TP) that can display the exact location of an incident on a screen of the streets in the city. The TP also calculates and transmits the exact longitude and latitude of the vehicle back to the dispatch center via the MDT. This data allows the CAD to contain exact locations of all vehicles to facilitate assignments to new incidents.

Use of automated dispatching and electronic messaging between the dispatch center and field units will reduce dispatching time between the receipt of the call and unit dispatch from 76 seconds to less than 30 seconds. The system is designed to handle 300 incidents per hour with a maximum number of 1 million calls for service resulting in 500,000 incidents each year.

When an E911 or seven-digit call for service is received by the city's E911 operators, Fire Department incidents are transferred to the FCCS system via a Pac Bell SL1 device. The dispatch workstations are configured as call taker, radio controller, or supervisor positions. An incoming call is routed to an available dispatch call taker who verifies the address and determines the appropriate incident type. The application is written using IBM's standard graphical user interface (GUI) using C and Presentation Manager. This environment provides the functionality and performance necessary for this application.

The following is an example of one of the many features of the FCCS system that use the GUI and high-resolution graphics. If multiple callers dial E911 to report a fire, different call takers may receive these calls at different times. If the callers report nearby addresses, the system prompts the call taker that another incident exists in the vicinity. The call taker can point the mouse device at the appropriate command and retrieve a high-resolution graphical map of the city that displays all nearby incidents. In this way, if nearby incidents are reported on different streets, a call taker unfamiliar with the streets in the area can display a map and determine whether the current call is the same as an existing incident. This facility can help dispatchers prevent an unnecessary redundancy of firefighters and equipment.

In parallel to this activity, a mainframe query is generated to search mainframe files for information (noncritical data) that may be associated with the address. This data is returned to the user and is indicated by the appearance of a check box on one of the windows active on the PC workstation. If the user wants to review this information, he or she simply selects the check box and the data is displayed in another window (keeping the primary window available).

Once a call taker determines that fire units should be dispatched, he or she clicks the "dispatch" pushbutton, and the system determines the best units to dispatch. The system generates a digital or synthesized announcement, such as, "Engine 13 respond to a trash fire at 1234 Maple Street." This message is sent through the communications network directly to the appropriate fire station. A control box automatically opens the door of the fire station and turns on the light in the bay. When the firefighters get into the vehicle, the details of the emergency dispatch are already displayed on the screen of their MDT and the Travel Pilot is pointing to the location of the incident.

Once a unit is dispatched, the responsibility for the incident is transferred to the radio controller responsible for the part of the city where the fire is located. If the MDT operator in the vehicle fails to push the "en route" button on the terminal within two minutes, the unit number on the radio controller's unit status screen begins to blink and a warning sound is generated. At this point the radio controller can use the voice radio to contact the unit and determine whether it is already proceeding to the incident. Once the unit arrives at the incident, the MDT operator selects the "on-screen" button. This is the basic dispatch functionality provided by the FCCS system.

FCCS consists of two major technology platforms: the mainframe component was developed in COBOL using DB2, and the PC component was developed in C using Presentation Manager services under OS/2.

The following software tools are used for programming and development on the workstations:

- Presentation Manager Software Development Toolkit (SDK) and CodeView Debugger for workstation screen development
- ARTIC Developer's Kit and ARTICDEB for RTIC card programming
- Berkeley Speech Technology and the Natural Microsystems ME/2 Development Environment for synthesized and digital voice

For mainframe development, an internally developed Systemhouse systems development environment (SDE) was used to organize and manage various utilities and processes necessary for program and database development. The Automate-Plus CASE tool was used exclusively for database normalization. The Query Management Facility (QMF) was the primary tool used for DB2 development.

To facilitate the programming effort involved with the many interfaces, custom-written utilities and simulators were developed. To enable individual program modules to be unit-tested, internally developed tools and drivers simulate various interfaces, such as incoming E911 emergency calls, outgoing MDT dispatch messages, and incoming and outgoing fire station messages. These tools and utilities, developed by the senior technical architects, simplify the programming effort for the rest of the development team.

Because of the complexity of the multiple technology platforms, many kinds of communications devices are required to support this application. Because all of the workstations have a complete copy of all program software and resident dispatch data, to ensure fault tolerance, a network messaging protocol was developed to control communications between all the workstations on the Token Rings. Communications between the workstations (the client component) on the Token Ring and the IBM mainframe (the server component for inquiry data) occur through an Advanced Program-to-Program Communication (APPC) facility between CICS and OS/2. The data radio subsystem is supported by standard base station and radio equipment provided by MDI. This includes modems, antennas, radios, and controllers. Specially developed C programs control real-time interface cards (RTIC) in the interface computers that connect the external interfaces to the system.

The primary machine for the FCCS is an IBM PS/2 Model 70 (A21) with 8M of D-RAM and 120M of fixed disk storage. The primary dispatch workstation Token Ring (DWTR) contains 50 of these workstations. The external communications Token Ring (ECTR) contains six IBM PS/2 Model 95s with 16M of D-RAM and 640M on SCSI fixed disks. Each of the 400 fire department emergency vehicles contains an MDI KDT480C terminal and ETAK Travel Pilot. The 114 LAFD fire stations contain an IBM PS/2 Model 50SX with 4M of D-RAM and 70M of disk storage. The Token Ring workstations use a custom-developed Lynx database file management structure. This file structure has been custom-developed to provide the fastest possible access time for time-critical emergency dispatching. The primary operating system on the workstation Token Ring is IBM OS/2 Version 1.3.

FCCS II consists of one primary Token Ring and two supporting Token Rings. The primary Token Ring, referred to as the DWTR, is used to pass current dispatch data among participants on the ring. The participants are dispatchers, radio controllers, and supervisors. The second Token Ring, the ECTR, is primarily used to pass data to and from the main-frame and the MDTs as well as to accept and receive data from other interfaces. The third Token Ring serves as a backup dispatch Token Ring. It is located remote from the central site and is kept up to date with rel-evant dispatch data. This backup site, complete with its own MDT backup, will be used only if the main site is knocked out of service for an extended period of time. Communications between the DWTR and ECTR are via two pairs of interface machines (PS/2s). They are in pairs to provide fault tolerance; one interface machine can take over all tasks that the pair run should one of them go out of service. The pairs of in-terface machines are kept in synchronization via the ECTR.

An historical database is maintained on the city's IBM 3090 mainframe in 35 DB2 relational tables. Inquiry and limited updates are provided via city mainframe terminals. The connection between the Token Ring and the mainframe is via an IBM 3745-410 communications controller. Incoming messages from the Token Ring are placed on CICS's transient data queues (TDQ) for processing on the host. The communications between the Token Ring and the fire stations are provided via a time division mux (TDM) and a digital access cross connect (DAC) switch. Actual communications are transmitted via the city's digital microwave radio system. The city's mainframe runs under MVS/XA with CICS.

Los Angeles County Automated Case Tracking System (ACTS)

The Automated Case Tracking System (ACTS) is being designed and developed to provide automated support for the Los Angeles County Superior Court. This support provides an environment that standard-izes and streamlines the workflow. This system eliminates the redun-dant manual effort and duplication of data entry, and reduces paper flow. This support also enhances the accuracy, consistency, and timeli-ness of management information reports. ACTS provides the court staff, litigants and other interested parties with quick access to case informa-tion.

ACTS is designed to assist the court in fulfilling its role in the justice process by providing enhanced capabilities for

- Court calendaring
- Case decisions—recording court rulings/orders and producing the court's minutes
- Case dispositions—producing documentation for state and local agencies
- Appeals monitoring
- Exhibits management
- Bail management
- Case records creation, maintenance, and inquiry
- Management reports and statistics

Previously, all of these functions were performed manually or with minimal automation support.

As a component of the County Justice Information System (CJIS), ACTS is designed to both transmit and receive data from other CJIS components, including the following:

- Adult probation system
- County-wide warrant system
- Municipal court information system
- Defense management system
- Justice data system
- Jury management system
- Professional attorney court expenditure

These systems support the probation department, the Sheriff's department, the municipal courts, the public defenders' office, the superior courts, and the district attorney's office.

The vehicle for the transmission and reception of information from other CJIS components is the Proactive Information Exchange (PIX) system. PIX sends preestablished groups of data, known as *datagrams,* between systems. The PIX "contract" between the sending and receiving systems identifies the event in the sending system's processing life cycle that will trigger the passing of data via PIX. PIX uses predefined rules to translate data from the sending system to the structure required by the receiving system. PIX also performs certain edits and selects data that suits the requirements of the receiving system. The PIX datagram initiates, in the receiving system, a predefined transaction much like an existing online transaction. PIX uses LU6.2 to ensure end-to-end message integrity.

The ACTS application uses client/server technology to satisfy two basic requirements: the need to have up-to-date case data available to a large number of users (ACTS and CJIS) and the need to record rulings made in the courtroom very quickly.

To satisfy the first requirement, the master copy of the ACTS database (DB2) is stored centrally on the mainframe. This master copy is accessible for adding, updating, deleting, and inquiring by all authorized users.

To satisfy the second requirement, a copy of the specific cases needed for courtroom processing is downloaded to a workstation database server (using the IBM Database Manager product). This workstation database server provides restricted access for adding, updating, deleting, or inquiring. Only the workstations authorized to process a specific case are allowed access to it. Once the workstation user completes processing a case, all updated data is uploaded to the master copy of the ACTS database.

To maintain data integrity, programs that add, update, and delete data are sensitive to date and time stamps.

To ensure that data is transmitted to and from the workstation efficiently, an additional layer of application software has been developed to support four specific needs:

- Distribution of the daily court calendar from the master database (mainframe) to the courtroom (individual workstations)
- Processing of requests from the courtroom for information regarding cases not currently on the calendar
- Communication of orders made in the courtroom to the rest of ACTS and CJIS
- Communication of significant administrative events that may impact decisions made in the courtroom

All four needs are satisfied using the same underlying software solution. The daily calendar is produced in an overnight batch job that, for each case on the calendar the following day, inserts a transaction that begins to send the electronic case data to the appropriate workstation destination. The program that sends the case data to the workstation reads the master database (DB2), converts the data into delimited-string format, and sends it to a program on the workstation database server that inserts the incoming data into the corresponding Database Manager database.

Similarly, the other needs are met by having a program (either mainframe or workstation, depending on the direction of data flow) insert a specific transaction, along with the necessary data that initiates the desired activity. The receiving program responds to the transaction by reading and returning data or adding, updating, or deleting data depending on the request. Other than the distribution of the daily calendar, these transactions are initiated and processed online.

ACTS consists of two major technology platforms. The mainframe component was developed using TELON, under MVS, using DB2. The PC component was developed using Easel under OS/2, using DBM. Both components used the Excelerator CASE tool during the analysis and design phases.

The ACTS mainframe architecture integrates the capabilities of TELON, DB2, and ISPF, using both procedural and nonprocedural coding methods. The mixture of procedural and nonprocedural techniques, employing the advantages of several software disciplines, creates an environment that permits full development and fast prototyping of screen applications. With this development environment, the concept of "source code" encompasses more than just a series of language source statements in a COBOL library; it includes an interlocking configuration of both specifications and instructions that, taken together, generate application programs.

The mainframe ACTS systems development environment (SDE) standardizes development. It extends the capabilities of TELON and provides the programmer with documentation and automated methods to code the following features:

■ Application security in which users may have no, full, or varying degrees of access to screen programs, based on the user's assigned profile.

■ Screen navigation consistent with the guidelines of IBM's System Application Architecture/common user access (SAA/CUA).

■ Help and prompt screens that place the current screen on hold and provide assistance to the user.

- All informational, warning, and error messages coming from a single list of message skeletons, identified by message number and containing up to five substitution variables.

- An error screen that provides diagnostic information to the user whenever an unforeseen error (such as a database shutdown) occurs.

- An audit facility available to record changes to the database for selected transactions, errors, or statistics. Batch processes allow viewing the audit records by record type sequence and by chronological sequence.

- ISPF dialogs that generate source code for screen navigation, security, menus, PF keys, message skeletons, and cursor positioning.

- ISPF dialogs that generate JCL to perform various TELON functions.

- ISPF dialogs that generate JCL to perform compilations and assemblies.

- ISPF dialogs that execute SQL and generate JCL to perform database administration functions.

- The Automated Cross Reference that stores documentation information gleaned from program source code into DB2 tables. It reports, via ISPF dialogues, information such as what paragraphs, subroutines, tables, fields, error messages, and copy members a program uses. Conversely, it also reports what programs are used by each of these items. It brings the flexibility of DB2 relational database technology to the process of documentation.

The workstation ACTS SDE also standardizes development. Easel provides a tool for quick and efficient production of OS/2-based graphical user interface (GUI) systems. Included in its base components are a high-level language, a design tool for building SAA/CUA compliant screens, SQL, DDE, 3270, and APPC support, as well as business graphics. The Easel Prototype Development Facility (EPDF) extends Easel into a powerful prototype and development tool.

EPDF includes

- Integrated multiuser networked environment support.

- Extensions to the Easel CUA/Layout tool specific to the enduser product. These extensions include standardization options and prototype levels.
- Extensive navigation techniques to move through Easel dialog regions and dialog boxes. These extensions include window navigation, activity navigation (groups of windows), subactivity navigation, and spawned activity.
- Automated help and prompt information implemented via OS/2 windows.
- Messaging facilities with symbolic substitution.
- Automated verification rules (screen level).
- Cross reference, online help, and associated development tools.
- A driven program that provides consistency, flexibility, and performance.

The ACTS Easel Prototype Development Facility (AEPDF) provides specific application extensions to EPDF. These extensions include the ability to classify activities by case type (to allow specialized window performance characteristics) and the support needed to produce minute orders via an interface to WordPerfect.

Application peer-to-peer communication (APPC) is used to communicate between the mainframe and the system's workstations. APPC provides the ability for programs running on two independent conversations (LUs) (in any IBM SAA SNA platform) to communicate directly with each other. EPDF provides an architecture to support this coding.

EPDF provides two additional transactions in each platform. Each transaction represents a "to" and "from" element: the "to" transaction element on the sending LU and the "from" transaction element on the receiving LU from an APPC conversation.

EPDF uses CICS ISC to provide APPC support on the mainframe, and it uses OS/2 CM to provide APPC support on the workstation. An "outbound" and "inbound" queue mechanism is needed to store messages. For CICS the outbound and inbound queues are CICS transient data queues providing recoverability. The "from" and "to" CICS transactions are triggered by the TDQ to provide an alternative to polling.

For OS/2, the inbound and outbound queues are implemented as OS/2 datasets or OS/2 DBM tables providing recoverability. The "to" and "from" transactions use system functions to poll the queues on a regular basis.

APPC allows for the initiation of the partner transaction when a conversation is initiated, and it is also used for the constant running of the conversation. In most cases, one CICS region will be communicating with many (probably hundreds, if not thousands) of workstations. A single CICS region supporting all workstations is impractical. It is also impractical to use more than one CICS transaction. The overhead involved in initiating the partner transaction and starting the APPC session and conversation each time information must be passed is minimal. Because ACTS has a low percentage of connectivity activity, initiating a partner provides a more efficient solution than having a constantly running conversation.

Performing the connectivity as a background task frees the application transaction from connectivity concerns. This provides a more performance-oriented, straightforward solution for the application software. All connectivity concerns are addressed by the "to" and "from" transactions supplied by EPDF. This type of solution allows application processing to proceed despite system failures that inhibit connectivity. The impact of this solution is that updates do not occur simultaneously in both platforms. Because there will be a minimal delay (approximately five seconds, depending on the network and network traffic), data may be temporarily out of sync because of system outages.

Figure A.11 depicts the communications at a particular site. In a multistory building there is a wiring hub installed on each floor. Each wiring hub is "backboned" with an Ethernet strand. The Token Ring on each floor is bridged to the backbone Ethernet strand.

Installing these wiring hubs now enables the courts to upgrade backbone speeds and underlying protocols later by removing the Ethernet backbone cards and replacing them with FDDI Token Ring cards.

Figure A.11 also depicts 3270 terminals attached to a card that is emulating an IBM 3274 cluster controller. These cards have a standard 50-pin telephone company connection to a standard M66 punch-down block. The 3270 terminals use a coaxial cable to twisted-pair conversion Balun to interface to the 3274 emulation card.

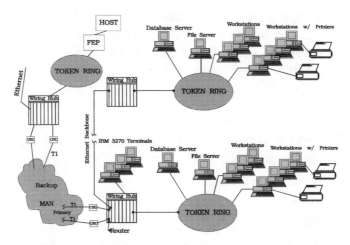

Figure A.11. *A typical building's integrated LAN.*

Note that Figure A.11 includes two T1-speed CSU/DSUs (digital modems). Because a municipal area network (MAN) is already in place, an intelligent T1 node (provided by vendors such as NET, NewBridge, Timeplex, and so on) has been chosen, along with a CSU/DSU that plugs into the T1 node chassis. The CSUs provide a link for a building's Ethernet backbone to the host site's Ethernet backbone via a TCP/IP router. There are two CSUs to provide a redundant path to the host.

At the host site there is a similarly equipped wiring hub with a short Ethernet strand and router. The 16-Mbps Token Ring is bridged to the Ethernet strand. All program software and application data reside on an IBM 3090 mainframe located at the county Internal Services Department's (ISD) installation. The IBM 3090 mainframe uses the MVS/XA operating system. The mainframe system uses DB2 as its file management system.

Los Angeles County Department of Public Social Services GAIN Employment Activity Reporting System

The GAIN Employment Activity Reporting System (GEARS) was designed and developed to support the Greater Avenue for Independence (GAIN) welfare program. The GAIN program, established in 1988, assists welfare recipients in finding employment by providing education and training services. During the education and training process, GAIN provides supportive services in the area of transportation, child care, and ancillary expense payments. GEARS supports 250 GAIN case managers who are responsible for an active caseload of 30,000 participants and a total caseload of 220,000 participants. GEARS provides the following capabilities:

- Appraisal
- Assessment
- Component assignment
- Supportive service payments
- Noncompliance tracking
- Employment tracking
- Automatic notice generation

Eligible AFDC participants are identified by the Los Angeles County Integrated Benefits Payments System (IBPS) and are transferred to GEARS via a tape interface. The participants are assigned to a GAIN case manager, an initial appointment is automatically scheduled, and the appropriate notices are generated. Any participant who does not keep the appointment is automatically placed into noncompliance and a noncompliance appointment is scheduled. Repeated noncompliance results in reduction or termination of AFDC Welfare benefits.

Each participant then begins an appraisal and assessment process to determine the individual's educational level and the type of job training needed to obtain gainful employment. The participant enters into a contract with the county to enter an education or job training component. While a participant is undergoing training, GAIN will provide funds to pay for the cost of transportation, child care, and ancillary expenses, such as books and equipment. GEARS tracks and reports on all aspects of a participant's progress through the GAIN program. GEARS has the ability to automatically generate all letters and notices required by the program. These notices may be generated in seven foreign languages according to the spoken language of the participant.

GEARS was developed using the following products from Software A.G. of North America, Inc.:

- ADABAS
- PREDICT
- Natural
- CON-NECT

GEARS uses a standard system development environment (SDE), which provides the following features:

- Application security users may have no, full, or varying degrees of access to screens and fields, based on the user's assigned profile.
- Screen navigation, to provide the allowed paths through the system.
- Standard model programs to facilitate the development process.

The use of the SDE ensured a consistent architecture across the entire GEARS system.

CON-NECT is an office automation tool with a wide variety of features, including calendaring, meeting scheduling, electronic mail, and reminders. GEARS used both the calendaring and reminding features of the product. Each user is assigned a cabinet, the CON-NECT term for an office file. At logon time the cabinet is shown and appointments and reminders are displayed. The user is able to go directly from the cabinet to the GEARS application.

The GEARS network has two digital circuits and six analog circuits. The analog circuits generally support PCs running 3270 Emulation. These PCs are managed by the NetView control desk the same way as 3174 cluster controllers and 327x terminals. Figure A.12 illustrates the network management components.

In a client/server network, it is important that fundamental network management processes are in place. A network management architecture is the single most important entity in a network. GEARS is a conventional SNA host/slave network that uses many of the networking concepts required in a client/server network.

One concept that is common is that of *redundancy*. The GEARS architecture called for two telco data circuits to be dropped into each larger address. These circuits were ordered from the local exchange carrier as "diversified pathing." Diversified telco circuits ensure that the two circuits are not multiplexed together on the same telephone company facilities. This technique reduces the risk of both circuits being "down" at the same time. Remotely bridged LANs can also use diversification to ensure there is an alternate route back to the host.

Another concept that is common is that of *load balancing*. The GEARS architecture called for two large digital multidrop digital circuits

(56Kbps). Analysis showed that an oversized multidrop circuit will handle individual bursts of data (print streams) quickly while providing service to a larger number of users. Load balancing is an important mandatory feature in a network supporting client/server processing. In a bridged Token Ring LAN that is matrixed, each dynamic APPC (SQL call) session will find the path of least resistance.

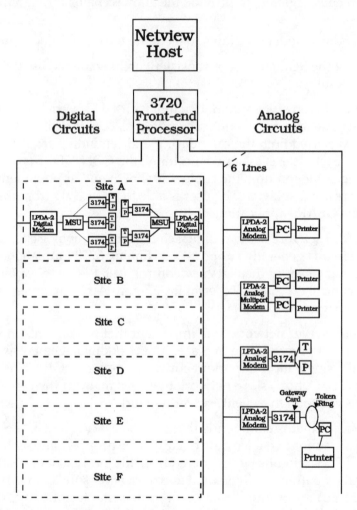

Figure A.12. GEARS network management components.

Network management, or proactive management, is another common concept. To proactively manage you need to know where your devices are and what they are connected to. You need to be able to run a nondisruptive loop-back test to sessions running at the workstations. NetView is the central concentration point in this network. Each controller, terminal and printer ID, and modem is monitored and alerts are generated at the network control console. The architecture is designed so that problems can be proactively avoided. For example, in the GEARS network, if a terminal is not on the network, while others on the same eight-port internal multiplexor are operational it is reasonable to assume the terminal is turned off. If all eight attached devices are off the network it is reasonable to assume there is a problem. The network control staff will run loop-back tests through the controller to confirm that the problem is isolated to that particular mux, possibly will phone the users of those terminals to confirm the eight devices are not shut off, then, if necessary, will dispatch a field service representative.

Proactive management is important at the session level and at the hardware level. The GEARS network employs modems and digital modems that support NetView's LPDA-2 (Line Problem Determination Aid Version 2).

These modems sense the telco line quality and report that line quality to the host-based NetView. LPDA-2 also supports loop-back testing directly from the NetView console.

In an online environment it is important to isolate a problem quickly without waiting for a phone call from the end-user. For example, with a solid network support architecture in place you can confirm that a circuit is working and that it is the controller that has the problem. In most instances the problem will be detected and a technician dispatched before the users call to complain.

A Major California Telephone Company's Service Order Load and Retrieval (SOLAR) System

The objective of this development project was to provide a user-friendly, online order system that would simplify telephone service order processing and provide accurate and timely order information without having to rewrite the existing systems that support this effort. The major benefits of the system are an overall improvement in the quality of service to customers and a reduction in the number of order processing personnel.

The Service Order Load And Retrieval system handles the data-entry requirements of the Order Processing Centers (OPC), Business Service Order Centers (BSOC), and Customer Service Order Centers (CSOC). It automates service order issuance, routing, rate calculations, and file maintenance, and it also provides interfaces to the following systems:

- Customer Billing and Information System (CBIS)
- Online Master Account Record (OMAR)
- Telephone Number Selection (TNS)
- Automatic Distribution System (ADSII)
- Special Service Order Administration System (SSOAS)
- Mechanized Directory (MD)
- Street Address and Community (SAC)

All of the systems for which interfaces are provided are IMS DC/DB systems except for SSOAS which is a Tandem-based system.

SOLAR is comprised of the following functional areas:

- Enter and Maintain Orders
- Work Orders
- Close Orders
- Inquire on Orders

The order entry and maintenance function provides a set of data entry and maintenance screens that will be used for order creation, service selection, and customer and billing information input and maintenance.

The work order function provides the selection and assignment screens that are required to select, route, display and print orders.

The close order function consists of the processes that mark orders complete and a batch process that reformats orders and passes them to the Mechanized Directory system.

The order inquiry function provides an inquiry on SOLAR orders in the Advance Service Order System (ASOS) format, an order itemization inquiry, an audit history inquiry, and an order investigation inquiry.

SOLAR functions will be used by the following personnel and departments:

- Customer representatives
- Assignment department
- Dispatch department
- Mechanized Assignment and Record Keeping department (MARK)
- Testboard department
- Quality Checking department

The customer representatives use SOLAR to enter the order, and to capture the required information while speaking to the customer on the telephone.

The assignment department uses SOLAR to view the order to determine what facilities are required and then assign to the appropriate facilities required to complete the order.

The dispatch department uses SOLAR to obtain the necessary information to complete the dispatching of the order.

SOLAR was designed to front-end existing IMS based systems. Programmer access to the SOLAR system is via DB/2 and user access is via the SOLAR front-end. SOLAR manages the communications between the DB/2 view and the existing IMS application databases.

The technology base is TELON/DB2 Systems Development Environment (SDE). The basic infrastructure is depicted in Figure A.13, and includes:

- Screen standards
- Program navigation
- Application security
- Standard function key processing
- Menu generation
- Online help
- Standard error messaging
- Generalized code table field editing, look up, and maintenance

Both the application requirements and the development environment were modified to simplify development and to standardize functionality. The resulting system has reduced the training time for order takers from six months to six weeks and significantly reduced the staff turnover in this position.

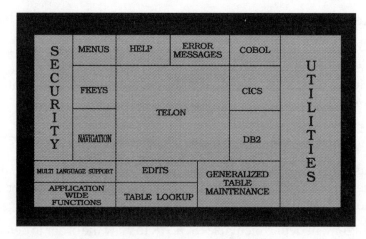

Figure A.13. SOLAR application infrastructure.

All development was done on an IBM 3090 under the MVS/XA operating system. The project made extensive use of TPNS for performance and regression testing.

Winnipeg Fire and Ambulance Departments' Fire and Ambulance Command and Control System (FACCS)

The Fire and Ambulance Command and Control System (FACCS) is a customized computer-assisted dispatch system (CAD). The dispatch functions are provided by software resident on the workstations on the Token Ring. Although there is one physical Token Ring, there are two logical rings. The fire department workstations pick up only fire department messages and the ambulance department workstations pick up only ambulance department messages as they pass on the Token Ring. The system uses seven IBM PS/2 workstations with Token Ring networking and a CAD software package from Lynx Graphics. There are external interfaces to the E911 system, fire and ambulance stations, the WWVB clock synchronization, the Winnipeg City Police system, the two city utilities, the ambulance department administration center, and the radio system.

Incoming calls may be from the E911 system or from a telephone call. The call is routed to a call taker who verifies the address, determines the incident type, and whether or not units should be dispatched. If units are to be dispatched, the system generates a unit proposal to be accepted or modified by the dispatcher. The system alerts the dispatcher if the location has special requirements (such as a high-rise building or hazardous materials on site). Under certain circumstances the system will generate an automatic transfer between departments; for example, a transfer to the fire department if information about an ambulance department call indicates that the patient is not breathing. A transfer between departments or to the Police Department may also be manually requested by clicking a mouse pointer on a transfer pushbutton.

Dispatch instructions are sent to the fire or ambulance station over a leased line. Dispatch instructions are printed at the station and the gong is rung. The dispatched units indicate their progress by pushing buttons on a radio unit ("enroute," "at scene," "clearing scene," and so on).

The messages generated on the Token Ring are sent to a backup machine for each department and to an administration machine for each department (all PS/2s running OS/2 Version 1.3). Reporting information is extracted from the messages and stored on an Oracle database for the fire department and a DBM database for the ambulance department. These databases are used for statistical and management reporting. The ambulance department database is also used for generating invoices to be paid by the user of the service or transmitted to Blue Cross for payment.

The primary machine for the FACCS system is an IBM PS/2 Model 70 with 8M of D-RAM and 120M of fixed disk storage. The primary dispatch workstation Token Ring contains seven of these workstations.

All of the programming and development on the workstations is done using the C programming language. Screens were built using Presentation Manager. The Token Ring workstations use a custom developed database file management structure, Lynx Database Manager (LDM). LDM was developed to provide the fastest possible access time for the time-critical function of emergency dispatching. The primary operating system on the workstation Token Ring is IBM OS/2 Version 1.3.

Custom written utilities and simulators were developed to facilitate the programming effort. These internally developed tools and drivers simulate various interfaces, such as incoming E911 emergency calls or incoming and outgoing fire and ambulance station messages, to enable individual program modules to be unit tested. The real-time interface cards in the interface machines (PS/2 Model 80 with 8M of D-RAM and 320M of fixed disk), which provide external communications, are controlled through special C programs.

Also attached to the primary dispatch Token Ring is the fire department local area network. It is bridged to this ring by a PS/2 Model 80 with 600M of fixed disk and 12M of D-RAM running Oracle Server software. The ambulance department LAN is bridged to the FACCS primary ring through a leased line on one of the interface machines. The 27 fire stations and nine ambulance stations are equipped with 386 systems with 1M of memory and without a hard drive. These systems are print servers and also control the gong relay within the station.

Esso Chemical Canada (ECC) System for Customer Appreciation and Marketing Potential (SCAMP)

The system provides ECC with the capability to develop and implement customer agreements, to process order transformation up to and including invoicing, and to perform price management. The application also provides the ability to maintain data on products and services, customers, suppliers, and competitors. The system will handle the creation and monitoring of shipments and freight liabilities, forecasting, and process feedback information. The application includes interfaces to suppliers, other corporate systems, and customers.

The development environment uses client/server technology with Oracle as the database. The development network consists of 14 SUN SLC workstations each with a 207M disk drive connected to two SUN SparcStation 2 servers using a Cabletron MMAC concentrator with the 10BaseT wiring standard. There are two IBM PS/2 Model 70 386 workstations on the network as well as one IBM PS/2 Model P70. Printing is performed by a Hewlett-Packard LaserJet IIISI printer (17ppm). The network can also support 22 VT220 terminals, one terminal serially connected to each SLC, plus eight terminals on a terminal server.

The development software consists of Oracle's RDBMS, Oracle CASE tools, Oracle communication products, Oracle 4GL application tools, SQ Solutions, Inc. report writer (SQR), and WordPerfect 5.0 for word processing. Support of the production environment is provided through dialup connection over a normal telephone link.

In the production environment, a SUN 4/470 Server will be attached to Esso's corporate network using DECNet. This will be available to all PCs, Macs, VT100s, and printers on the network.

Syncrude Canada Limited Slope Inclinometer Data Management System (SLOPE)

The Syncrude open pit mine produces an average of 150,000 bank cubic meters (BCM) of oilsand per day from an area approximately 5 kilometers long by 9 kilometers wide. The mine is divided into four independent production systems, each consisting of a large dragline, a bucketwheel reclaimer, and a series of conveyors. Each dragline uses a 60 cubic meter bucket to excavate the oilsand from the mine and deposit it in a series of windrows near the edge of the pit. The bucketwheel reclaimer then loads the ore onto the conveyer system which moves it to the production area.

During mining, the draglines sit at the crest of a 40- to 50-degree slope that is 40 to 50 meters high. The weight of such a large piece of machinery operating so close to the slope face has the potential to cause instabilities in the ground, which may result in the loss of a dragline. In order to understand and monitor the movements of the ground below the draglines, a series of vertical boreholes with grooved PVC pipe cemented into them are located in the operating bench (the area near the edge of the pit). Probes are then lowered into these boreholes (called Slope Inclinometers or SIs) and the angle of incline is measured. Subsequent readings are taken, and any change in angle is used to measure the nature and velocity of ground movement at various depths. If, during mining, the movement indicated by the SI increases, steps will be taken to ensure the safety of the dragline.

The movement of the SIs is measured via electronic signals that are transmitted from the probe and captured by special recorders that translate the data into digital form. These readings are monitored in the field using special software provided by Pulsearch, a firm specializing in this technology. Stand-alone laptop computers are used to record, store, and monitor this data in the field. At the end of each shift, a diskette containing all the readings from that shift is transported to the geotechnical office, where it is entered into the SLOPE system. The data is then available to the geotechnical engineering group via the Token Ring network.

This data is heavily used for analysis of current and historical movement patterns that, when combined with geological information, allows the engineers to reliably predict the likelihood of any major ground movements in the area of the current mining operations. It also allows the definition of an effective, but not overly cautious, safety margin for dragline operations, which helps to increase productivity and reduce dragline downtime.

The system provides access to the corporation's IBM mainframe database in order to both archive data to, and access data from, an historical DB2 database.

The SLOPE system uses a client/server architecture based on the Microsoft/Sybase SQL Server and intelligent workstations equipped with an object-oriented graphical user interface (GUI) that conforms to IBM's Common User Access (CUA) guidelines.

The mouse-driven system relies heavily on the use of icons, graphs, scrollable online reports, and high-speed printers and plotters to assist in the rapid and on-demand analysis of movement data.

The SLOPE workstations are IBM PS/2 Model 55SXs and Model 65SXs with 8M of D-RAM. They operate under OS/2 Extended Edition (EE) Version 1.2.

The LAN and Database server is an IBM PS/2 Model 80 with 16M of D-RAM, also running OS/2 EE Version 1.2. A Microsoft/Sybase SQL Server is used as the database server.

Upload and download facilities are provided to the corporate IBM 3090 mainframe and a DB2 database is used to archive data that is no longer required on the LAN on a regular basis. This historical data can subsequently be retrieved and returned to the LAN database as required.

Easel 2 was used as the primary development environment on the workstations. Some C programs were written to provide specialized graphics capabilities. The Excelerator CASE tool was used in analysis and design, while development took place using a prototyping approach.

A Life Assurance Company "Model Office"

The parent company of this large North American company maintains a base of approximately 650,000 customers. The system developers used rapid prototyping techniques to develop functional building blocks for the business application and gain approval from the users in servicing, billing, fulfillment (order processing and telemarketing), finance, marketing, and claim adjudication. Once the model office was working and accepted in prototype, it was transferred to the full-scale environment. In production operation it is more efficient to run the applications locally in the workstations than from the database server. This keeps LAN traffic to a minimum. The database server is then accessed only when necessary to retrieve or update data. Applications such as word processing, spreadsheets, and so on have their software and data files resident on the workstation hard drive. This gives the user maximum response and keeps the LAN available for database and communication services.

The basic technical environment consists of a series of networked applications running Hypercard and Oracle tied to a VAX 6220 running Oracle as a database server. Additionally, there is a download capability for existing client data from an Amdahl 5880. The Macintosh was chosen as a workstation because of its extreme amenability to rapid prototyping using Hypercard and Oracle SQL*Forms as a development environment. Oracle was chosen as the DBMS because of its multi-platform operating capability and its ability to interface smoothly within the Hypercard environment. Silverun was used as the upper CASE tool. It provides a data dictionary, as well as data- and process-modeling capabilities.

The workstations selected were geared to provide the customer support representatives with the most flexibility and power on their desks to help them do their jobs effectively and efficiently.

The model office was designed for "roll-out" capability into the production environment. The architecture is directly scalable so that the home office can be implemented without having to redesign or reimplement any software or hardware components. It was initially envisioned that the operating environment would be a workstation approach. This would allow for linear and incremental growth in terms of power and price. However, this evolved into a central file server design when it was decided that the database in this particular application would not distribute well and central control and data management became significant issues. Therefore, a file server approach was developed in which workstations could be added and the file server increased in power as necessary to meet increased load requirements without impacting the production environment. Appletalk is the LAN protocol. Physically, the network topology is a daisy chain. Optimally, the server is in the middle of the chain with the most active workstations as close as possible to the printers on one end. The communication gateway is the Netway 1000AE from Tri-Data which provides up to 16 3270 sessions plus file transfer capability to the host. This uses a 9600 baud conditioned line over sync modems and is connected to the LAN. The gateway allows a 3270 session to be displayed on the workstation in real time and allows other model office transactions to be performed concurrently.

The expected growth path of the system is first to add application functionality, secondly to add additional customers, and, as the system becomes saturated, migrate to a VAX-based Ethernet LAN. By implementing an SQL database architecture, migration to another server should not impact the interface with the users and will insulate the workstation-based software from the new server.

Blue Cross of Atlantic

In January, 1991, Blue Cross of Atlantic began making the transition from maintaining and developing their business applications on an IBM 3090 M200 mainframe (at a very high cost in CPU cycles) to maintaining and developing them on IBM PS/2 workstations in an OS/2 client/server networked environment (using models 50, 55, and 70s). This process was accomplished using a two-phase approach over a course of eight months.

In the first phase, a workbench environment was set up to assist in migrating OS/VS COBOL programs from the mainframe down to workstations for maintenance activities. After maintenance was completed, the programs were re-migrated back to the mainframe into production.

In the second phase, a development environment was set up to assist in building future applications more effectively. Future applications are to be built on the workstation and then migrated up to the mainframe into production.

These goals were achieved, and the following objectives were met:

- Mainframe CPU cycles associated with development were reduced.
- The transfer and management of objects between the host and workstation were streamlined to ensure there was as little manual intervention as practically possible.
- Maximum dollar savings were achieved within three to six months. 70 percent of the typical programmer's host costs were eliminated. There was a ramp up period in which programmers consumed host cycles in downloading of objects until the base was built at the workstation.

- Maximum programmer productivity gains were achieved within three to six months, improving productivity by 25 percent. Initially, the programmers experienced a learning curve slowdown with the tool set because of their propensity to "over-test."

- A productive environment for the analysis, design, development, and installation and maintenance of COBOL-based software applications at Blue Cross was provided. This environment provided a stable platform and included a set of procedures and standards for each of the phases in a typical systems integration life cycle.

More specifically, productivity gains were realized in the following ways:

- There was a reduction of time spent on each unit of work; in other words, the combination of transfer time, data preparation time, debug time, and compile time.

- There was a reduction in overall development time spent on rework, because of a higher quality initial product.

- There was a reduction in overall maintenance time spent on rework, due mainly to the advanced debugging facility of Microfocus COBOL and the flexibility of manipulating the emulated DB2 and CICS in the maintenance environment.

- The introduction of CASE tools for analysis, design, and development helped simplify the process of revising and enhancing the applications being developed.

- The centralized storage of analysis, design, and development information and objects helped to reduce the redundancy that can occur when producing a system in all phases. This storage also improved the accuracy and speed with which information was communicated throughout the team.

Several strategies were adopted in order to ensure that the objectives of the project were met:

- The hardware was configured to provide the capacity, reliability, availability, serviceability, and performance for the analyst/designer/developer to consistently do quality work productively.

- The system software was chosen to take advantage of the hardware components, providing the organization with the most durable platform for the 1990s.
- The standards and standard procedures were used to supplement and extend the environment to provide the analyst/designer/developer/end-user with a consistent look and feel.
- Training was given to ensure that current and future system development staff understood how to work within the two environments. This included methodology training as well as product training.

Blue Cross had already made a significant investment in software products that were currently being used in the mainframe environment to maintain and develop business applications. In order to avoid costs associated with training and education of new workstation products, they chose to continue with a platform and product base similar to the one used on the mainframe. A summary of the chosen mainframe/ workstation products is as follows:

Component	Mainframe Product	Workstation Equivalent
Hardware Environment	IBM 3090 M200	PS/2 Model 50, 55, and 70
Operating System	MVS/XA	OS/2
Object Control	PANVALET	PAN/LCM
Transaction Processor	CICS	CICSVS86
Data Environment	DB2, VSAM	XDB, simulated VSAM, Sequential
Analysis/Design CASE Tools	none	TELON/ TEAMWORK
Productivity Tools	TSO	OS/2
	ISPF	SPF/2
TELON/PWS		
IPE Macros		
JCL Utilities	IBM JCL	CMD and REXX
Screen Dev. Facility	SDF	CICSVS86 SDF

Component	Mainframe Product	Workstation Equivalent
Extract Aids	custom routines	Data extractions are done on the host
Testing Aids	various	MF COBOL
Debugging Aids	various	MF COBOL
Dumping Aids	IBM Utilities	MF COBOL
Languages	COBOL, COBOL2	COBOL,COBOL2

The workstation environment installed was composed of

- 3 servers
- 2 PS/2 Model 80—16M RAM, 320M hard drives
- 1 PS/2 Model 70—8M RAM, 120M hard drive
- 7 PS/2 Model 50Z
- 11 PS/2 Model 55SX
- 25 PS/2 Model 70
- A LAN

  OS/2 EE and IBM LAN Servers were installed and used over two backboned Token Rings.

  The line speed of the LAN was four megabits per second along unshielded twisted-pair cable. A type three media filter was used at each workstation to reduce line noise.

- Within the systems development department, there were approximately 39 maintenance and development programmers.

The LAN was linked to the mainframe via two IBM 3164 controllers using 3270 emulation software over a Token Ring network.

Before the implementation of the first phase of the project, the analysts, designers, and developers typically used the workstations for terminal emulation to the host and for word processing.

After the implementation of the first phase of the project, the maintenance programmers were using the workbench environment product set on the workstations for importing, changing, testing, and exporting objects back to the host into production. They were also using terminal emulation and word processing.

After the implementation of the second phase of the project, the analysts, designers, and development programmers were using the development environment product set on the workstations for analyzing, designing, database administration, programming, testing, and exporting objects to the host into production. They were also using terminal emulation and word processing.

An integral part of the development environment was the installation of the IPE. The IPE was written and enhanced over a period of 15 years by various technical architects. It was installed at Blue Cross to help development programmers decrease development time and increase quality and uniformity. The IPE extended the capabilities of TELON and provided the programmer automated methods to code the following features:

- Application security. Users may have no, full, or varying degrees of access to screen programs, based on the user's assigned profile.
- Screen navigation consistent with the guidelines of IBM's System Application Architecture/Common User Access (SAA/CUA).
- "Help" and "table" screens that place the current screen on hold and provide assistance to the user.
- All informational, warning, and error messages coming from a single list of message skeletons, identified by message number and containing up to five substitution variables.
- An error screen that provides diagnostic information to the user whenever an unforeseen error (such as a database shutdown) occurs.
- Code generation that works during TELON compiling to support the "help," "table," program function key, and menu creation functionality.
- OS/2 command files that generate source code for
    - screen navigation
    - security
    - message skeletons
    - cursor positioning

- OS/2 command files to perform various TELON functions.
- OS/2 command files to perform Micro Focus checks (compiles) and assemblies.
- OS/2 command files that execute SQL and perform database administration functions.
- Working TELON model programs that may be tailored as an application model.
- TELON model programs that may be tailored and used for security (signon, signoff, user maintenance), help (multipage display, load), generalized tables (tables list/return, maintenance, table copy member generation, table access), and ABEND handling.
- An environment that is fully supported by technical architecture documentation that extensively describes the features of the development environment and standardizes its usage.
- Standards and suggestions on areas such as
  - Application-level locking—locking out applications from data held by other applications.
  - Current key handling—communicating the current key from screen to screen.
- DB2, COBOL, and CICS considerations.

Sample Scenarios

The following paragraphs contain samples of how the two environments were used.

Maintenance Environment for the Blue Cross System

Application program maintenance using the new maintenance environment is depicted complete with scripts in Figure A.14.

When a maintenance programmer is assigned to make changes to a program, he or she must identify all components (submodule, copybooks, and BMS maps) needed in order to completely transfer the program and its associated routines from the host to the Maintenance Workbench environment. This enables a proper testing of changes made to the program at the workstation. This set of components is referred to as an "Object List."

The components are then downloaded from the Host to the network server using the Import and Checkout Objects option of the Object Processing custom software residing on the network server. This process uses the Object List as input. Each object in the list is checked out from the PANVALET library and downloaded to the corresponding PAN/LCM library on the server. The Object Processing module also checks out those objects that the programmer expects to change and move into his or her designated work area from the PAN/LCM library.

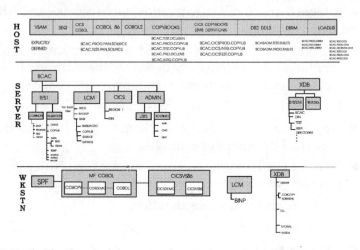

Figure A.14. *The Blue Cross maintenance environment.*

The maintenance programmer then makes the necessary changes to the programs in his or her designated work area using the MicroFocus tool set to edit, compile, test, and animate (debug).

When the changes have been completed, the Export Source Objects option of the Object Processing software is used in conjunction with PAN/LCM to check the objects back into the LAN server PAN/LCM library. It is also used to upload the new version of the objects to the Host PANVALET test environment. From there it is promoted into the production library.

Data for testing maintained programs is also obtained from the host data files. Data Extract custom software assists in preparing the appropriate test data files on the server. The process extracts data for testing from the host data files, imports the data to the server into temporary sequential files, generates the required data structure (for example, VSAM file or DB/2 table) on the server, and populates the data structures with the imported data.

Printing is performed on workstation- and mainframe-based printers using custom developed print routines. Large printouts are printed on the mainframe printer. Small printouts (for example, SPF documents) are printed using customized print routines to insert HP Laserjet printer codes directly into the SPF/2 document and to route the file to the network laser printer.

Backup & Recovery software is used to provide a partial or full recovery of the environment.

Blue Cross Development Environment

Application program development using the new development environment is depicted in Figure A.15.

During the analysis phase of a project, the analyst uses TELON/Teamwork to

- Create a context diagram for the system.
- Model the existing and proposed entity relationships.
- Create a logical data model for the application while populating the Teamwork Data Dictionary.
- Model screen layouts to assist in representing the data to the users, for verification of actual/proposed processes, and to assist in the preparation of an acceptance test plan (these screen layouts are prepared using TELON).
- Model existing and proposed processes and data flows in data flow diagrams, decomposing the processes down to a level where a general process specification could be derived.
- Create a logical database design, producing a first normal form layout.
- Using manual normalization processes, produce a third normal form database design.

PAN/LCM Archive is not used for versioning, because Teamwork controls versioning of its models and no external objects are created that can or need to be manipulated by LCM.

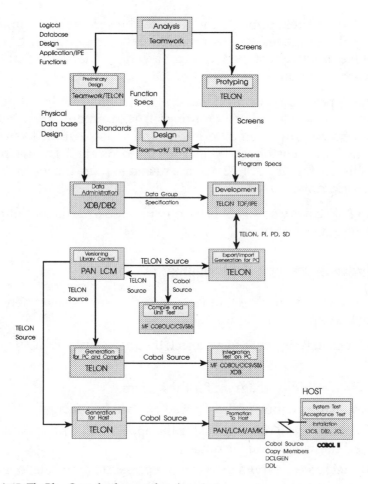

Figure A.15. *The Blue Cross developmental environment.*

The analyst may also consider using the prototyping facility of TELON/ PWS to refine the user requirements, data model, and process specifications.

During the design phase of a project, the designer uses the TELON/ Teamwork tool and the Teamwork Data Dictionary, and the SILC Design Methodology to

■ Conduct preliminary design activities, verifying that the analysis deliverables and architecture definition are complete, mapping the logical database design to the physical database being used, and defining standards and common functionality for use in detailed design. This includes the functions provided by the IPE.

■ Design the application, deriving program specifications from the process specifications, DFDs and Teamwork Data Dictionary, making sure the specifications are created in a format consistent with the format used in TELON code generation.

■ Create the system test plan, using information from the Data Dictionary and the prototype (if one exists) to define test scenarios.

During the development phase of a project, the programmer uses the TELON/PWS facility, the IPE, and custom maintenance environment routines to

■ Generate the COBOL II programs from the design specifications, incorporating the IPE macros where appropriate, and creating panels (or using any panels that may have been created by the analysts and designers).

■ Using customized maintenance environment functions, export the TELON source, generate the COBOL II program source for the PC into the developer's personal library with read-only access (it is not recommended to modify the source after generation), and automatically run a compile using the Microfocus Workbench and CICS emulator.

When a program is successfully unit-tested, the developer uses a custom function to check-in the TELON source to the LCM archive, which then checks-out the program specification and generates COBOL II source for the PC into the integration library (again with read-only access). An executable version of the program is then created for access in subsequent integration testing. Batch programs are integration-tested using .CMD files or REXX execs to simulate the job stream that will be used on the mainframe.

When the programs are successfully integration-tested, another custom function generates COBOL II source for the mainframe using the completed version of the TELON source in the LCM archive. Additional custom processes prepare the COBOL II source code for compilation on the mainframe, and then export it to the mainframe. The maintenance environment also provides functions to export any associated PARMLIB, COPYLIB, DCLGEN, or DDL member to the mainframe.

Any JCL required for batch testing must be derived manually (at this time) from the .CMD files or REXX execs used in the maintenance environment.

Data in the Help and Tables XDB tables are exported from XDB to the host and then loaded into the corresponding DB2 tables.

Data for system testing can be created on the mainframe or brought up from the maintenance environment. At this point, system testing is performed on the mainframe using the scenarios defined during the design phase. Any modifications required as a result of system testing must be done using the maintenance environment. This should not require bringing anything back from the mainframe. The modifications will be done directly in TELON/PWS, and then tested and moved back to the mainframe using the same functions that are available during normal development.

Printing, backup and recovery, and system management are managed using the same procedures used in the maintenance environment.

California Unemployment Insurance Appeals Board (CUIAB) Automation Project

The CUIAB application suite encompasses three primary subsystems, each serving the unique needs of part of the CUIAB operation within the context of a board-wide architecture and database structure. The three subsystems support the following office systems:

- Field operations
- Chief's office
- Appellate operations

Appeals filed in EDD offices are downloaded via the WAN to the local CUIAB office for processing. The office registers the case, calendars the hearing, sends notices to the involved parties, holds hearings, documents decisions, and informs the involved parties of those decisions. The application supports case tracking, inquiry, document generation, and management reporting. Office automation functionality (word processing, e-mail, and calendaring) is also included.

The telecommunications network provides for communications within and between all CUIAB offices and with the State of California Health and Welfare Data Center in Sacramento.

The CUIAB application was designed to use a client/server architecture. The system functions are logically shared between the workstations and the servers. The workstation handles the user interface including data entry, display, program navigation, and option selection. On request from the workstations, the servers provide print, file storage, LAN control, database access, software storage, and communications services.

There are two servers on each LAN. A file server supports the Novell LAN-related functions. All programs and flat files reside on the Novell NetWare Version 3.11 file server. This facilitates program-level maintenance, security, and backup. All database files reside on the Microsoft SQL Server database server. The database server handles all aspects of the relational database. In this way, such things as security, integrity, and the actual database searches are handled by the dedicated server.

Access to other LAN servers on the network is via Gateway Corporation's IPX Bridge/Router over a public data network (PDN). Both binary and ASCII files may be copied to or from any other CUIAB LAN. E-mail is sent to other LANs as required or on a scheduled basis.

Access to the HWDC mainframe is via Gateway's G/SNA 3270 program running on the workstation, in conjunction with Gateway's G/SNA product running on the three centralized servers (Higher Authority, Inland, and Sacramento). Multiple concurrent 3270 sessions and local 3270 host printers are supported. File transfers to the mainframe are supported in either direction via the TSO file transfer facility. Electronic mail (e-mail) is localized to each individual LAN but can access other LANs in addition to the PROFS and EMC2 mail users on HWDC. Microsoft Mail is the e-mail package. Scheduling is integrated with the e-mail package via Network Scheduler II. Both are Windows-based products.

The environment is based on Digital Equipment Corporation's personal computers configured in a client/server architecture. Local Area Network (LAN) and Wide Area Network (WAN) connectivity is based on Novell NetWare v3.11. Figure A.16 illustrates the overall network architecture.

The following sections contain a more detailed narrative on the workstation, LAN, and WAN layers of the architecture.

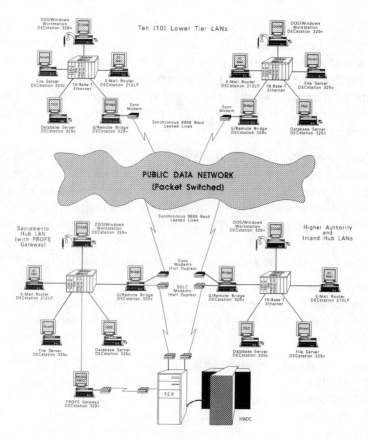

Figure A.16. WAN and host connectivity overview.

Workstation Hardware

The workstation hardware consists of Digital DECstation 320+ workstations. Each includes an Intel 386DX 20MHz CPU with 4M of D-RAM. The workstation is configured as a "hard diskless" LAN workstation, with a 3 1/2-inch floppy. It has much greater expansion capability than traditional diskless stations, because it is actually a full desktop PC without a hard disk. It can also operate as a stand-alone PC as configured.

A bar code reader is connected between the keyboard and the system unit. The application is designed so that the user may use the bar code reader's wand to scan the case number or other bar-coded data interchangeably with the keyboard. For example, when the application positions the cursor to the case number field, the user can either scan the case number bar code on the file folder, or type the case number at the keyboard.

Theft is discouraged by a device that attaches the workstation system unit, printer, and monitor securely to the desk.

Workstation Software

MS DOS and Microsoft Windows 3.x provide a consistent user interface that is common to all applications (except WordPerfect 5.1 and 3270, which currently run in fullscreen mode). This reduces training time and is more productive and accurate for both novice and expert users. The software running on the workstation is

- MS DOS 3.3
- Microsoft Windows 3.x
- Easel/Win (includes Microsoft SQL Server requester)
- Novell DOS Requestor
- Gateway 3270 emulation program
- CUIAB Application Programs for Windows
- WordPerfect 5.1 (LAN version)
- Microsoft Mail for Windows (LAN version)
- Network Scheduler II for Windows (LAN version)

DOS, MS Windows 3.x, and Easel/Win provide a consistent graphical user interface. Pull-down menus and pop-up message boxes simplify option selections and data entry. The interface complies with IBM's Common User Access (CUA) guidelines. The primary advantage of CUA is that all applications written under it have the same "look and feel," thereby reducing training and increasing user productivity. CUA is part of IBM's Systems Application Architecture (SAA). Windows 3.x, Easel, and Gateway's G/SNA products are all SAA-compliant.

Easel/Win is a productivity tool and Graphical User Interface (GUI) for developing windowed applications for personal computers. It currently runs under DOS, OS/2, and Windows 3.x. Easel/Win generates a state-of-the-art Macintosh-like user interface with pull-down menus, pop-up dialog boxes, selection boxes, and so on that seamlessly integrates the CUIAB application with other Windows applications. With Easel/Win, maintenance costs will be lower because it requires much less source code to develop an application compared to C or other 3GL languages.

The development team is using the Easel Workbench to develop the system.

Multitasking Environment

The multitasking environment allows multiple applications to be run concurrently. The windowed environment allows multiple overlapping windows that display the active jobs together on the same screen. The same interface is used by OS/2 PM. Both OS/2 and DOS workstations may coexist on the LAN at the same time. The CUIAB application has been designed to run identically on either DOS/Windows 3.x or OS/2 PM. The other application software packages selected have both DOS and OS/2 versions available, assuring a smooth migration when or if required.

The CUIAB application developers use the Easel Workbench development system under OS/2. OS/2 provides a more robust development environment than Windows. Since Easel/Win is upwardly source code compatible with Easel/2, the CUIAB application can be tested in both environments by simply recompiling for Windows. The CUIAB/EDD application is being designed and tested to run with both Easel/2 under OS/2 and Easel/Win under Windows 3.x.

Local Area Network

Each of the 13 primary locations has its own LAN based on Novell NetWare v3.11. As shown in Figure A.17, each LAN is a network of 8 to 30 workstations supported by a file server, a database server, a remote access gateway, an e-mail router, and a bridge to other networks.

The file server is based on Novell NetWare v3.11. It provides basic flat-file and printer sharing among the workstations. Advanced features may be provided in the future by software modules called Network Loadable Modules (NLM). Currently available NLMs, which will be installed at each LAN, include NetWare Remote Management Facility (RMF) and the tape backup NLM (ARCserve).

The database server is based on IBM's OS/2 standard edition running the Microsoft SQL Server database. It provides advanced database functions and security to the workstations.

The workstations and servers are physically cabled together as an Ethernet 10BaseT LAN running at 10Mbps. Each PC is connected in a star configuration via a central Ethernet concentrator using plenum-rated, unshielded twisted-pair wire.

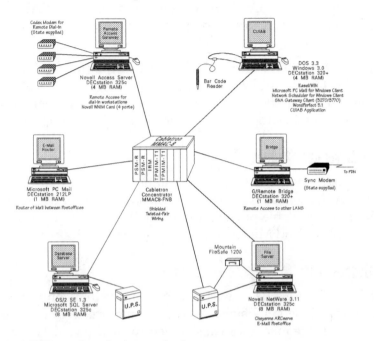

Figure A.17. *LAN overview—hardware and software.*

File Server Configuration

The file server is a Digital DECstation 325c system with 8M of 32-bit D-RAM, 320M of hard disk memory, and a 1.3 gigabyte external tape backup unit. The software consists of MS DOS 3.3, Novell NetWare Version 3.11, and Cheyenne ARCserve tape backup NLM.

Database Server

The Database Server software is Microsoft SQL Server, the Microsoft OS/2 licensed version of the Sybase database. It runs on a dedicated PC under the OS/2 1.3 Standard Edition operating system. Both DOS and OS/2 clients can access the server over the Novell NetWare Version 3.11 LAN.

This client/server architecture has proven to be the most effective method for database access. It offloads CPU processing from the workstation while maintaining a centralized approach to security, backup, and administration. The application will use Structured Query Language (SQL) to access the database. The database will support both DOS (MS Windows 3.x) and OS/2 clients concurrently. The CUIAB application has been designed to run identically on both DOS/Window and OS/2 PM.

Easel/Win (for DOS/Windows 3.x) and Easel/2 (for OS/2) directly support the TRANSACT-SQL interface to the Microsoft SQL Server. Operating on a separate dedicated processor, the SQL Server is designed for growth and will support this application and future applications.

Database Server Configuration

The database server is a Digital DECstation 325c system with 8M of 32-bit D-RAM, 320M of SCSI hard disk memory, 40M of IDE hard disk, and an uninterruptable power supply (UPS). The software consists of IBM OS/2 SE 1.3 and Microsoft SQL Server for OS/2.

Wiring Concentrator

Each of the 13 LANs has a wiring concentrator that connects all the workstations, file server, database server, remote access gateway, e-mail router, and bridge machines via shielded twisted-pair (STP) Ethernet 10BaseT cable.

Network Management

Cabletron provides an exceptional network management facility. One of the slots on the MMAC-8 contains the intelligent repeater Module (IRM) that has the dual function of a repeater and network management module. This hardware is used in conjunction with the Remote LANView/Windows package to gather and display network diagnostics and performance measurement on the LAN and transmit it on request to the remote EDD/CUIAB support groups in Sacramento and Inland. Faults can be isolated to the individual workstation and the workstation can be removed from and restored to the LAN remotely. This is a full-function network analyzer that also provides diagnostics, automatic fault isolation, monitoring, performance graphs, and control of not only a complete LAN segment, but also of individual ports and the Workstation's Network Interface Card (NIC). Based on Microsoft's Windows 3.x and Hewlett-Packard's OpenView, it provides a graphical view of the WAN. The support staff can click pictures and icons to focus on areas of interest.

Cabletron's 16-bit Desktop Network Interface (DNI) NIC cards are intelligent devices that fully support remote diagnostics via LANView/Windows. In addition, there are indicators on each card that display transmit, receive, collision, and link status. A user can glance at the back of the card to visually confirm whether the device is connected to the concentrator and whether data is being transferred. The DNI NIC cards, the MMAC-8, and LANView/Windows support the industry-standard Simple Network Management Protocol (SNMP). This allows any SNMP-compatible program, from any vendor, to interact with and support the management of the network.

Equipment and software level management is essential to successful remote management of LANs. The combination of the intelligent 16-bit DNI cards and LANView/Windows allows a remote network manager to interrogate and update a workstation's DNI to determine the type of PC, levels of system and application software installed, the user's name and location, and other vital configuration management data.

Uninterruptable Power Supply

Two Elgar IPS 1100 uninterruptable power supplies (UPS) will be installed on each LAN to protect both the file server and database server. This will provide a minimum of 20 to 30 minutes of standby power when the primary power fails. The servers are notified of a power failure via the serial port connection to the UPS. Novell NetWare Version 3.11 then notifies the workstations, and does an orderly shutdown of the system. The workstations will probably have failed already, because they are not on a UPS, but the orderly shutdown of the database and file servers will ensure that the databases and all other files will not be corrupted. Upon restoration of stable power, the servers will automatically power up, restart the applications, and be ready for user logons.

The uninterruptable power supplies protect the file server, the database server, the tape backup unit, and the LAN wiring concentrator.

Tape Backup Unit

A Mountain FileSafe 1200 1.2 gigabyte DAT tape backup unit is installed on the file server. It will back up all files on both the Novell file server and the OS/2 database server to a single tape cartridge. Unattended backup will allow the LAN administrator to insert the tape before going home at night, and the system will back up all data sets on both servers, automatically, overnight. EDD/CUIAB support staff also can start or monitor (or both) the tape backups remotely.

Printers

Each location has a combination of laser and dot matrix printers. The printers are attached to either the file server or any workstation. They may be shared by any user on the LAN/WAN.

The laser printers are HP LaserJet model IIID. Each IIID will be configured with 2M of memory, two letter-size trays, one legal-size tray, one bar code, and one more font cartridge. Two input trays of 200 sheets plus the 50-envelope power envelope feeder may be installed at the same time. The printer has two font slots, one of which will be occupied by the bar code font cartridge.

Microsoft SQL Server

The CUIAB application will use Structured Query Language (SQL) to access a Microsoft SQL Server relational database. Microsoft markets the OS/2 version of the Sybase relational database under license from Sybase Corporation. The software uses an enhanced version of SQL called Transact-SQL. Transact-SQL is designed to benefit both SQL beginners and those who have SQL experience. Through the use of stored procedures, Transact-SQL has enhanced standard SQL database access. Stored procedures can combine almost any SQL statement with control-of-flow language. This greatly enhances the power, efficiency, and flexibility of the SQL database language.

Easel provides an I/O interface designed for Microsoft SQL Server access. This makes it easier to code Easel programs that access the database.

The SQL Server controls referential integrity through the use of table creation parameters and system tables. The SQL Server automatically manages all requests to change the database and records each request on the system controlled transaction log. This transaction log is then used to control database backup and recovery. Through the use of the SET statement each query against the database can be monitored for performance. Utilization of SP Monitor can also monitor the performance of the SQL Server itself.

The database server will contain a separate hard disk drive for the database transaction log. This will enhance database performance as well as recoverability in the event of a problem.

Wide Area Network

The proposed WAN provides two major functions:

- Connectivity among the various CUIAB LANs
- Connectivity to the HWDC mainframe

The physical layer of the WAN consists of leased-line modems, voice-grade telephone lines, bridges, gateways, and the front-end processor at the California State Health and Welfare Data Center (HWDC). The software layer at the host consists of CICS, TSO, PROFS, EMC2/TAO, VTAM, and NCP. The PC software includes the gateway and protocol converters, bridge and routers, e-mail routers, and e-mail gateways. All of these products, working together, comprise the WAN.

The net effect of this configuration is total transparency across the wide area network. Any authorized user on any of the 130+ workstations can access any other LAN and can do anything that could normally be done if he or she were physically on the other LAN. Any authorized user can also access the HWDC mainframe.

SNA Access

Gateways provide SNA access from the three central LANs (Sacramento, Inland, and Higher Authority) to the HWDC host. The gateways are based on Gateway Communications Inc.'s G/SNA Gateway product. This product is a combination of hardware and software residing in a "gateway server." It communicates with the host over a leased voice-grade telephone line running at 9,600 bits per second. It uses an SDLC adapter in the Gateway server and a State-supplied synchronous modem (for example, Codex model 1130).

G/SNA Gateway supports 3270 emulation with file transfer capability. G/SNA Gateway acts as a 3274-51C cluster controller and as such is a PU type 2 device. As configured, each of the three gateways will support 128 concurrent host sessions, or 384 host sessions in total. This is well over the 20 host sessions per LAN requirement of the application. The workstation component acts as a 3278 or 3279 (CUT) device and can support up to 4 concurrent 3270 SNA sessions.

Gateway's 3270 emulator runs on the workstation in fullscreen mode. Although multiple 3270 sessions may be run concurrently, they cannot run in the background.

Bridge

For inter-LAN connectivity, a bridge connects each LAN to the Public Data Network (PDN), and deciphers the routing information to deliver a data packet to its destination.

The bridges will be connected to a PDN via synchronous voice-grade leased lines running at 9,600 bits per second over state-supplied Codex synchronous modems. The PDN acts as a multiplexor so that each LAN is in effect simultaneously connected to every other LAN.

A user on any LAN can log onto the server on any other LAN to transfer files. The user may, with proper authorization, also access the database or execute any job on the other LAN as if physically locally connected to the other LAN. However, performance will be poor in this mode. This function rarely will be used for production work and is available primarily for support. Performance is determined by the speed of the lines into the PDN and has been set by the state to be 9,600 bps. This speed is upgradable to 19.2Kbps. If two sites need to engage in a large amount of communication, a leased line service can be installed to upgrade the speed to 56Kbps or 1.2Mbps.

This WAN has been designed for light and infrequent data traffic, which is consistent with the autonomous functioning of the individual CUIAB sites. Performance will suffer if traffic grows due to new applications being installed. At that time, upgrades to the number of lines and/or line speeds and/or dedicated lines may be required. The hardware and software have been chosen to be scalable in this regard.

Bridge Device Configuration

There are 14 bridges, one for each LAN, and Rosemead. The bridges are based on the Digital DECstation 320+ PC. Each bridge consists of a DECstation 320+ with 1M of D-RAM, running MS DOS 3.3 and Gateway Communication's G/Remote bridge software.

SNA Gateway Configuration

There are three SNA gateways. Each consists of an adapter card and software and physically resides in the same machines as the bridges in Sacramento, Inland, and Higher Authority. In addition to the bridge equipment listed previously, the gateway function will be provided by the following hardware and software:

- Gateway Communication's G/SNA Gateway adapter card.
- Gateway Communication's G/SNA Gateway software for 128 LUs. This software includes the 3270 emulation program that will be installed on each workstation.

Remote User Access

Users on workstations directly connected to other LANs in the network can access all functions on a remote LAN by logging into that LAN as described in the WAN section.

As shown in Figure A.18, these requirements will be met via the use of Novell's NetWare Access Server software running on a dedicated remote access gateway on each of the 13 LANs. A Digital DECstation 325c 25 MHz/386 machine will act as the remote gateway on each LAN. As configured, it will support four concurrent dial-in users via a Novell WNIM+ four-port adapter card and four state-supplied 2400 baud modems. The access gateway is expandable to support up to 15 concurrent dial-in users.

The remote user will be able to access all files on the Novell file server and transfer files in either direction between the remote PC and the file server.

In addition, the remote user will be able to run any character-based program as if directly connected to the local LAN, including e-mail, scheduling, word processing, and spreadsheets.

The CUIAB application is being developed as a Windows application and the communications traffic generated by a GUI application is not practical on a remote PC via the access gateway.

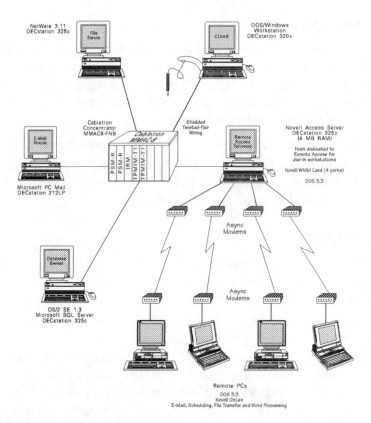

Figure A.18. Remote access overview—hardware and software.

Remote Access by Technical Support Staff

From any CUIAB LAN workstation, EDD/CUIAB technical support staff will be able to log on to any LAN for the purposes of system and application support. Novell's Remote Management Facility will be used. It provides the necessary capabilities to manage the LANs from any remote location.

Cabletron's LANView/Windows will be installed in Sacramento and Inland. It provides all of the necessary troubleshooting, preventative, and management capabilities. EDD staff in Sacramento and Inland can remotely monitor suspicious LANs or individual ports, shut down a port, and determine if a machine is connected or powered on. To assist in asset management, staff can remotely view or update user name, machine type, location, contacts, and software levels.

Host Access

Host access is supported via Gateway Communication Inc.'s G/SNA Gateway product.

An authorized user on any workstation on any LAN can start a 3270 emulation session on his or her PC and logon to TSO, CMS, CICS, EMC2/TAO, or PROFS on the host. This provides access to current and future applications on the HWDC mainframe. The 3270 emulation program runs as fullscreen applications on the workstations. The SNA gateways have been configured to support a maximum of 384 concurrent LUs (sessions) with the HWDC host (128 per gateway). Although all 130 workstations can start multiple 3270 emulation sessions, only 128 sessions per gateway can be active at any one time.

3270 file transfer is supported via IND$FILE. 3287 printer emulation allows the workstation's locally attached printer to act as a 3287 attached to a 3274 controller.

Electronic Mail and Scheduling

Each LAN will have Microsoft Mail for Windows installed to support the locally attached DOS/Windows workstations. Each LAN will also have the CUA character-based version of Microsoft Mail installed to support the remote (laptop) users.

Powercore Inc.'s Network Scheduler II for Windows is a full-function scheduling package that interfaces with Microsoft Mail. Each LAN will have both the character-based version (for remote users) and Windows version (for local users) installed.

E-mail is localized to each individual LAN. It provides a mailbox for each user that resides on the user's directory on the file server's hard disk. A post office resides on each LAN's file server. Because 80 percent of all mail typically is sent within the same work group, this results in faster service with no mainframe overhead and reduced communications costs. Access to other post offices can be done as required or on a scheduled basis.

Access to PROFS and therefore EMC2/TAO on HWDC is via a Microsoft Mail PROFS gateway on the Sacramento LAN. PROFS users can create a memo in the standard PROFS format and send it to any user on the network. It will automatically be converted to the Microsoft Mail format when presented to the CUIAB user, and vice versa. Files can be attached to the e-mail and sent back and forth between the two different e-mail systems. The PROFS's gateway hooks into the existing EDD connection between PROFS and EMC2/TAO on the HWDC mainframe. In this way, any PC user can send and receive mail from EMC2/TAO mail users and PROFS mail users.

Appendix
Apple/IBM Joint Venture

B

In late 1991, executives from Apple, IBM, and Motorola announced their intent to ensure the control of the desktop market with a new hardware standard for the desktop computer. Their motives were driven by the following factors:

- IBM believes that it invented the Personal Computer (PC) technology and that clone makers stole the technology without proper compensation for IBM's R&D and marketing expenses.

- Apple, which also believes that it invented the PC technology, feels that it cannot grow without penetrating in a major way the organizations that have standardized on IBM compatible PCs. Apple knows that it lost considerable momentum because of Motorola's delay in the 68040 delivery.

- Motorola is concerned that lack of clear direction on its part will allow the SPARC and MIPS chip sets to gain enough momentum to become de facto industry-wide standards.

Their much-heralded announcement centered around several key joint ventures.

- Development of the Power PC, a new generation of chip set and computer hardware.
- Development of a new object-oriented OS, codenamed PINK, for the Power PC via a new jointly-owned company named Taligent.
- Development of an extensive suite of new multimedia applications.

The next generation of entry-level Power PC machines will have the power of a current IBM RS6000. Pricing for desktop machines will start at $1,000 for entry-level systems and rise to only $3,000 for the most powerful configurations. All machines will be LAN-ready and operate both as remote and local workstations. Motorola's considerable expertise in the cellular communications arena will ensure that these machines come WAN-ready and able to use cellular communications. Motorola's marketing might add to that of IBM and Apple to create considerable market acceptance and demand.

With the announcement of their joint ventures, Apple, IBM, and Motorola are betting that microprocessor marketshare leader Intel will stumble. Most important is the trio's belief that Intel (maker of the 80x86 processor products) has the disadvantage of being stuck with an architecture defined prior to the 80386 chip set. Intel may, and should, decide to drop this downward compatibility in the Pentium and follow-on the next generation's chip set. Intel's reluctance to have its chip set second sourced and the relatively high cost of the 486 and other chip sets, and a clear statement of direction for 686 and beyond may allow Intel to maintain its strong lead on the desktop. Recent contracts that allow IBM to develop 80x86 chip sets and the Supreme Court's acceptance of Advanced Micro Device's right to second source has driven prices down on 386 chips and has pressured 486 prices.

With the work at Taligent, IBM and Apple want to define a new desktop software standard. Apple has—through its license relationship with Microsoft—the user and application interface that everyone wants and IBM has the basic software everyone uses and needs for future compatibility. Software development productivity—especially through end-user access—is becoming the overriding consideration for organizations that make platform technology buying decisions.

The combination of the three companies—IBM, Apple, and Metaphor—brings together the necessary expertise including personnel from IBM's software company, Metaphor, to build a new object-oriented operating system platform with embedded support for UNIX, OX/2, Windows 3.x, DOS, and MAC OS without the need to maintain a compatible hardware platform. This software will be made available to any and all developers at very competitive prices in an attempt to create the new desktop standard. Compatibility with Microsoft's next generation 32-bit Windows (Chicago) or Windows NT will not be provided except as these products are compatible with existing Windows 3x.

IBM and Apple believe Taligent can gain a substantial share of the OS market, because they are assuming that the need to maintain architectural and binary compatibility with old DOS-based applications constitutes a ball and chain to Microsoft's future OSs. If this compatibility is provided through emulation in future Microsoft product lines, serious performance problems may occur. Unless the new platform is better than the IBM/Apple platform, there will be no motivation for users to support it. If support is provided at the native level, all new applications will suffer from the performance limitations inherent in the old architecture.

In the new IBM/Apple model, all PCs will provide the necessary multitasking and multiuser capabilities required for applications, database, and communication servers. All internetworking will be peer-to-peer. The distinction between client and server will blur as the desktop adds server functionality. Truly distributed processing will be the norm.

Organizations that want to be ready to take advantage of this technology when it becomes available within the next four years should use tools that absolutely isolate the developer from the underlying OS and hardware. This requires discipline in the establishment of standards and use of development tools. Products such as Windows 4GL, Easel, PowerBuilder, and, to a lesser extent, Oracle provide the appropriate isolation of developer from platform. If Microsoft's Chicago or NT platform is successful, these tool vendors will provide support for that environment.

For Fortune 1,000 users, the Apple/IBM alliance could offer some important benefits: easier integration in from Mac to IBM-based networks; IBM's AIX fans get popular personal productivity applications; and a

RISC-based, follow-on product is sure from Apple. Within the next few years, the barrage of new technologies, such as those begun by the IBM, Apple, and Motorola alliance will hit the market. These technologies promise to radically change your relationship with your customer, product features and service delivery, and the structure of manufacturing, sales, service, and distribution.

Electronic Document Management Standards

This book has repeatedly referred to the need to define standards as part of all system development environments (SDEs). The purpose of these standards is to identify distribution, collection, and indexing standards and functional capabilities necessary to support electronic management of this information at the lowest cost. Suggested standards are included here both as an example of the type of standards an organization should define when it wants to achieve the benefits of an SDE, and as a specific reference for organizations looking to use electronic document management.

Each of the defined standards is a requirement that selected products must be able to support. Not every application uses all the features defined nor does every product purchased contain all of the features. Selected products must have the capability to support all the relevant standards and features defined as mandatory.

A few fundamental standards are required of all systems to provide the basic platform for the sharing of electronic images:

■ Image indexing must be done using an ANSI standard SQL DBMS that can reside remote from the image storage location. The index must be accessible and manipulatable through user-friendly, standard application development languages subject to the appropriate security considerations.

■ Image presentation must be supported in a standard windowing environment.

■ Image distribution must support the CCITT Group III or IV fax standard.

■ Image indexing and entry must be supported through a communications protocol providing end-to-end message integrity, such as LU6.2, OSI, or TCP/IP peer-to-peer equivalent standards.

■ *Imaging:* Imaging is the process of converting information into a bitmapped digital format. In this format, information is represented and manipulated through its shape, not its internal ASCII or IBM's EBCDIC representation. Thus, numbers in an image cannot be added without additional conversion (*a la* OCR), but they can be moved, printed, and displayed.

■ *Image Entry:* Images may be entered in the imaging system from scanners, other computers, fax machines, fetal monitors, x-ray devices, fingerprint devices, digital cameras, and so on.

■ *Workflow-Image Queuing:* The workflow-management function must include the capability to receive an image and hold it for later processing.

■ *Workflow-Image Priorities:* The workflow-management function must include the capability to prioritize images in the queue. Higher-priority images must be presented first when the next image is selected.

■ *Workflow-Image Distribution:* The workflow-management function must include the capability to distribute images to named destinations (for example, users, processes, and so on). Ideally, a scripting language will be provided that allows dynamic determination of distribution destinations.

■ *Archiving:* Archiving is the process of moving images from the storage location and providing immediate access to a separate location where storage is less costly. Access may be slower and human intervention may be required to handle the archive medium to retrieve the image. An image is considered deleted when it is removed from the index; therefore, an archived document must remain in the index with appropriate information to locate its archived location.

■ *Image Indexing:* The system must provide the capability to index images on user-specified search arguments. Index searches must return a "not found" message or the image-management system required "key" to recover the image. Support must be provided for this index to be stored remotely from the image storage location. Index searches must be supported by ANSI 1 standard SQL requests. This index may be in addition to the index used by the local system for local searches or it may be the same. The indexing system must ensure that no image may be added or deleted from the permanent store without updating the index.

■ *Image Migration:* The system should not preclude the use of a hierarchy of storage devices, such as optical disks, magnetic disks, or disk caches.

■ *Production-Class DBMS:* A production-class DBMS is expected to ensure data integrity under all circumstances. Provisions must be included to ensure that once a user receives confirmation that an image is added, it can always be recovered. The image DBMS must provide at a minimum the following capabilities for index and image maintenance and access:

  ■ Automatic error detection and recovery

  ■ Dynamic backout of in-progress updates after process failure

  ■ Roll back from/roll forward to last backup

  ■ Maintenance of accurate and duplicate audit records on a separate physical medium

  ■ Support for mirrored (duplicate) images

  ■ Locking mechanisms to guarantee data integrity

  ■ Deadlock detection and prevention

  ■ Multithreaded processing

  ■ Multiuser concurrent processing

■ *Image Folder:* The system must have the capability to combine multiple images into a singly accessible entity (folder). It must be possible to access all the images in a folder as an image or one or more of the entries as an image.

- *Printing HPCL:* Images must be printable to Hewlett-Packard-compatible laser (HPCL) printers using the standard HP Series II or better laser printer. Only printer memory should restrict the size and resolution of the printed image.
- *Printing PostScript-Compatible:* Images must be printable to PostScript-compatible printers using only the standard PostScript language.

The following information is from specific electronic document standards published for vendors in Los Angeles County and many other counties in California, and will serve as a useful example of the type of detail which should be spelled out in a standards specification. The standards that are coded (code P) must be adhered to for all image related products procured by agencies of Los Angeles County. The standards coded (code E) are necessary in all products that are used in systems required to support document interchange in Los Angeles County.

Image Entry

PE: Minimum resolution is 200 pel (at 1 bit per pixel).
P: Must provide automatic indexing at entry from bar codes, OCR, and operator entry.

Fax Services

PE: Minimum resolution is 200 pel (at 1 bit per pixel).
P: Must provide automatic indexing at entry from bar codes, OCR, and operator entry.
PE: Must support image input via group III or IV fax (recognizing group III destination).
PE: Must support output via group III or IV fax (recognizing group III destination).

Image Workflow

P: Must support image queuing, priorities, and distribution.
P: Must support the migration of images from an optical storage location to a higher-speed medium (such as magnetic storage or D-RAM cache).
P: Must support an image archive capability.

Image Folder Management

PE: Must support the combination of images into a single folder.

PE: Must enable access to a single image in a folder.

Image Storage

P: Must support the storage of images on optical storage devices.

P: Must provide backup/recovery/restart capabilities consistent with a production class DBMS.

Image Compression/Decompression

P: Must provide software that is 100-percent compatible to hardware used for decompression.

Image Indexing

The indexing of interest is based on the image content description (such as client number, client name, or case number).

E: Must use an ANSI SQL-compliant DBMS for indexing.

E: Must support index storage remote from image storage that is capable of being maintained through a peer-to-peer processing protocol equivalent to LU6.2.

PE: Must support image existence determination without the need to retrieve the image.

PE: Must support application program reads from the index.

PE: Must support application program additions to the index.

PE: Must provide backup/recovery capabilities consistent with a production-class DBMS.

Image Presentation

P: Must support one of the following windowing environments in a "well-behaved manner": Windows 3.x, OS/2 Presentation Manager, OSF/Motif, OPEN LOOK, Nextstep, or MAC OS; this includes the capabilities to open multiple windows in an overlapped manner, to scroll windows independently, to move windows, to close windows without terminating the application, and to multitask to the extent of allowing a local, host, and image application to be active in separate windows simultaneously.

P: Must support resolutions that adapt to the display device.

P: Must support, at least, the following monitor resolutions with a maximum dot size of 32 mm for color images:

- 70-dpi VGA for viewing less than one hour per day
- 100-dpi Super VGA for viewing less than three hours per day
- 150-dpi high resolution for viewing greater than three hours per day

Image Integration

P: Must support a well-defined application program interface (API) to enter, access, distribute, and index images.

Image Annotation and Modification

P: Must support the ability to annotate an image without physically modifying the image.

PE: Must support the Standard Generalized Markup Language (SGML) standards for image modification (only if image modification is allowed).

Image Printing

P: Must support printing at least one of the following printing standards: HP-compatible Laser (HPCL) or PostScript-compatible.

Image Distribution

PE: Must interface with one of the following e-mail standards: directly to IBM PROFS or via an X.400 gateway.

PE: Must be able to distribute images in one of the following formats, at the option of the sender: CCITT group III or IV fax bitmapped.

Image Communication

PE: Must operate in the following LAN topologies: Ethernet, Token Ring, or FDDI.

PE: Must operate in the following WAN environments: SNA/SDLC, TCP/IP, or OSI.

Image Security

PE: Must provide C2-level security against update of the index or stored images.

This security standard is defined by the National Computer Security Center (NCSC) Trusted Computer System Evaluation Criteria (TCSEC).

A complete definition is available from NCSC; however, in general, the standard implies the availability of

- Granular discretionary access controls.
- Increased accountability, including configurable identification and authentication mechanisms, user auditing enabling administrative checks for potential and actual security violations, and a trusted communications path to be used when secure communications between a local user and the system are required.
- Secure system administration, including the ability to define and verify the secure system status.

References

P: Must have a referential site with the products installed or be able to provide demonstration of the product's capability to meet all standards at a site designated by Los Angeles County.

Index

Add to Your Sams Library Today with the Best Books for Programming, Operating Systems, and New Technologies

The easiest way to order is to pick up the phone and call

1-800-428-5331

between 9:00 a.m. and 5:00 p.m. EST.
For faster service please have your credit card available.

ISBN	Quantity	Description of Item	Unit Cost	Total Cost
0-672-22804-1		Reorganizing MIS: The Evolution of Business Computing in the '90s	$34.95	
0-672-30153-9		Downsizing Information Systems	$39.95	
0-672-30382-5		Understanding Local Area Networks	$26.95	
0-672-30173-3		Enterprise Wide Networking	$39.95	
0-672-30180-6		Insider's Guide to Networking	$29.95	
0-672-30119-9		International Telecommunications	$39.95	
0-672-30005-2		Understanding Data Communications	$24.95	
0-672-30293-4		TOP SECRET: Data Encryption Techniques (book/disk)	$24.95	
0-672-22790-8		Data Communications, Networks and Systems, Second Edition	$49.95	
0-672-30467-8		Sybase Developer's Guide (book/disk)	$40.00	
0-672-30209-8		Netware Unleashed (book/disk)	$45.00	
0-672-30191-1		DB2 Developer's Guide	$59.95	
0-672-22794-0		ORACLE 7 Developer's Guide	$39.95	
❏ 3 ½" Disk		Shipping and Handling: See information below.		
❏ 5 ¼" Disk		TOTAL		

Shipping and Handling: $4.00 for the first book, and $1.75 for each additional book. Floppy disk: add $1.75 for shipping and handling. If you need to have it NOW, we can ship product to you in 24 hours for an additional charge of approximately $18.00, and you will receive your item overnight or in two days. Overseas shipping and handling adds $2.00 per book and $8.00 for up to three disks. Prices subject to change. Call for availability and pricing information on latest editions.

201 W. 103rd Street, Indianapolis, Indiana 46290

1-800-428-5331 — Orders   1-800-835-3202 — FAX   1-800-858-7674 — Customer Service

Book ISBN 0-672-30473-2

GO AHEAD. PLUG YOURSELF INTO
PRENTICE HALL COMPUTER PUBLISHING.
Introducing the PHCP Forum on CompuServe®

Yes, it's true. Now, you can have CompuServe access to the same professional, friendly folks who have made computers easier for years. On the PHCP Forum, you'll find additional information on the topics covered by every PHCP imprint—including Que, Sams Publishing, New Riders Publishing, Alpha Books, Brady Books, Hayden Books, and Adobe Press. In addition, you'll be able to receive technical support and disk updates for the software produced by Que Software and Paramount Interactive, a division of the Paramount Technology Group. It's a great way to supplement the best information in the business.

WHAT CAN YOU DO ON THE PHCP FORUM?

Play an important role in the publishing process—and make our books better while you make your work easier:

- Leave messages and ask questions about PHCP books and software—you're guaranteed a response within 24 hours

- Download helpful tips and software to help you get the most out of your computer

- Contact authors of your favorite PHCP books through electronic mail

- Present your own book ideas

- Keep up to date on all the latest books available from each of PHCP's exciting imprints

JOIN NOW AND GET A FREE COMPUSERVE STARTER KIT!

To receive your free CompuServe Introductory Membership, call toll-free, **1-800-848-8199** and ask for representative **#597**. The Starter Kit Includes:

- Personal ID number and password

- $15 credit on the system

- Subscription to CompuServe Magazine

HERE'S HOW TO PLUG INTO PHCP:

Once on the CompuServe System, type any of these phrases to access the PHCP Forum:

GO PHCP
GO QUEBOOKS
GO SAMS
GO NEWRIDERS
GO ALPHA

GO BRADY
GO HAYDEN
GO QUESOFT
GO PARAMOUNTINTER

Once you're on the CompuServe Information Service, be sure to take advantage of all of CompuServe's resources. CompuServe is home to more than 1,700 products and services—plus it has over 1.5 million members worldwide. You'll find valuable online reference materials, travel and investor services, electronic mail, weather updates, leisure-time games and hassle-free shopping (no jam-packed parking lots or crowded stores).

Seek out the hundreds of other forums that populate CompuServe. Covering diverse topics such as pet care, rock music, cooking, and political issues, you're sure to find others with the sames concerns as you—and expand your knowledge at the same time.